Astral Projection

Other Brad Steiger books
by Para Research

True Ghost Stories
Kahuna Magic

ASTRAL PROJECTION

Para Research, Inc.
Rockport
Massachusetts

International Standard Book Number: 0-914918-36-2

Typeset in 10 pt. Paladium on a Compugraphic Editwriter 7500
Typesetting by Elizabeth Bauman
Edited by Shaun Levesque

Printed by R.R. Donnelley & Sons Co.
on 55-pound Surtone II

Published by Para Research, Inc.
Whistlestop Mall
Rockport, Massachusetts 01966

Manufactured in the United States of America

First Printing, March 1982, 5,000 copies

Contents

1

Mind Travelling through Time and Space

One night Sara Norris arose sleepily from her bed, reluctant to leave the hollow of warmth beside her husband. It was 3 A.M. Time to feed the baby.

She walked into the kitchen and turned up the gas flame beneath the old pan she used to warm the baby's bottle. While Sara waited for the water to heat, she looked out over the moonlit farmyard and listened to the night noises.

She had felt exhausted when she went to bed that evening. She had carried the heavy load of her pregnancy through an exceptionally hot summer. The delivery had been long and difficult, but Sara had left her hospital bed to come back to the farm at harvest time, and she was never able to get caught up on her sleep. There was extra cooking for the hired hands; the meals were often late; and they could not afford a woman to help with the housework.

Then, while her husband slept, she had to get up during the night to see to the baby.

What she wouldn't have given to be able to sleep one night through. Just one night's sleep without interruption.

The bottle was ready. She tested it on her arm, then walked into the baby's room and slid the nipple between his lips before he had time to cry.

Sara did not want to waken her husband or their two other children sleeping in the next room. Nor did she wish to hear a piercing scream shatter the kind of blissful somnambulism in which she moved.

Returning to bed, Sara was startled to see her own sleeping form lying next to her husband. Hair in disarray, mouth slightly open, one forearm resting across her brow—the form was unmistakably that of her own body.

But how could she be in two places at once?

There was a tingle of fear . . . a strange tugging sensation . . . then Sara jerked awake with a jolt.

A dream.

A bizarre dream.

But the baby had his bottle and lay contentedly working the rubber nipple. Had Sara's soul, her essential stuff, her basic essence, separated itself from her sleeping body so that the bone-tired physical shell could rest undisturbed while her spiritual self saw to the baby?

A prison inmate decided to blunt the ragged edge of his loneliness by taking an afternoon nap.

"I had one wild trip," he writes. "You see, I am very much in love with this lady, and she with me. But we are apart for two reasons. One, I am here; two, she is married and lives in Idaho.

"But this one day I went to sleep and dreamed that I was there. I saw that she lived in an upstairs apartment, and I could see that it was raining very hard. It was so real that I kept trying to talk to her, but she just went about her business doing housework.

"Then I was outside and saw her girl coming home from school in the rain on her bike. I saw the girl fall off her bike and hurt herself. I tried to help the girl, but I could not. This is when I woke up.

"Later I got a letter from my lady written on the day I had my dream. She told me that her little girl fell off her bike and that she took her to the doctor. So I wrote back and asked her what was the weather like the day she fell. She wrote back and said it was raining, *plus* she wanted to know how I knew she lived in an upstairs apartment. I had never been to Idaho in my life."

Jewell Hooker says when she was seven years old, she died of pneumonia. Early in April, 1923, in her farm home in Missouri, two doctors removed a rib and part of a lung in their efforts to rid her of the infection. They slipped a door off its hinges to serve as an operating table.

Jewell's father had died only three years before, and the child's mother prayed that she would not have her daughter taken from her as well. But Jewell heard one of the doctors say, "No use now; she is gone."

Then the girl found herself walking across a footbridge into a beautiful place she thought must be heaven. At the end of the footbridge stood her father with an angel. "Go back, Julie May," he said in a gentle voice, "your mother needs you."

Mrs. Hooker writes that she protested that she wanted to stay there with him in that beautiful place.

"Childlike, I turned to the angel and said, 'I want to see Jesus.' She smiled and said, 'Not this time. You have a lot to do yet and your mother is waiting.' My father urged, 'Go back now. You can come later. We all will be together later on.' "

The child seemed to walk back to the room in the farm house where the doctors stood over her mother, holding the child's body in her arms and sobbing over and over, "Thank you, God!" When she was older, Jewell learned that she had been dead for fifteen minutes.

The three cases just cited appear to be sound examples of what parapsychologists term *out-of-body experience* (OBE); instances in which the spirit, the mind, the very essence of a man or woman is projected outside the body to locations across a room, across the country or into another plane of existence, able to return with conscious memory of the experience. Spontaneously, at the moment of accident, sorrow or death, certain individuals have transcended the boundaries of time and space. Others, during acute illness and suffering, have testified to having travelled on other planes, perhaps in other dimensions, of reality.

There exist the testimonies of thousands of witnesses who claim to have seen the spirit-like image of a friend or relative appear before them, while the living, physical counterpart of the apparition is known to reside thousands of miles away. Numerous individuals claim to have had these experiences during sleep, and maintain that they witnessed certain activities during strange "dreams," activities which were later verified. Some even argue that they received or conveyed messages of great personal importance during out-of-body experiences.

I have long nurtured an interest in what is commonly known as "astral projection," perhaps more properly termed "out-of-body experience." Whatever term we choose, we are generally referring to those instances in which the very essence of a man or woman is somehow freed from the physical confines of the body to soar over the city, across the transcendent boundaries of other dimensions, or perhaps merely to cross the room and bob about under the ceiling.

Most people who bother to think about such experiences at all usually associate such dissociation of body and soul with the moment of physical death. But the special element in an out-of-body experience is the fact that the soul is able to return to the physical body with conscious memories of the ethereal excursion. Indeed, this essential factor makes the whole transcendental act an experience, rather than a conclusion.

For those who steadfastly deny the existence of the soul, no amount of empirical evidence will convince them that men and women claiming out-of-body projection during acute pain, sorrow, illness or fatigue are not hallucinating. To those who do accept the concept of the soul, but are convinced that the essential spirit and the flesh cannot separate until the moment of physical death, research in the area of out-of-body experience tends to border on the blasphemous. For those who do accept the possibility of out-of-body experience, but are quite certain that it is but a facet of psychic phenomena, such as "travelling clairvoyance," the claims of those adept at freeing their souls from the physical shell tend to rest on the "wrong" side of the amorphous, but stoutly maintained, line of demarcation that separates *occultism* from *psychical research.*

There seem to be at least seven types of spontaneous, or involuntary, out-of-body experiences:

1. Projections that occur while the subject sleeps.
2. Projections that occur while the subject is undergoing surgery, childbirth, tooth extraction, etc.
3. Projections that occur at the time of an accident, when the subject suffers a violent physical jolt which seems, literally, to catapult the spirit from the body.
4. Projections that occur during intense physical pain.
5. Projections that occur during acute illness.
6. Projections that occur during pseudo-death, wherein the subject is revived and returned to life through heart massage or other medical means.
7. Projections that occur at the moment of physical death when the deceased subject appears to someone with whom he or she has had a close emotional link.

In addition to these spontaneous, involuntary experiences, there are voluntary and conscious projections. During these experiences, the subject deliberately endeavors to free the essential self from the physical body.

The late Dr. J.B. Rhine, world-famous parapsychologist and head of the Foundation for Research on the Nature of Man, was said to have records of some ten thousand OBE cases from people all over the world. How many undeclared experiences exist may never be known, but OBE is neither as uncommon nor as strange as one might suppose. In the great number of letters I receive from readers of my books and articles, OBEs are reported as frequently as are instances of precognition or telepathy. Such experiences are also commonly reported to me during my personal appearances and lectures.

In the late 1960s Dr. Eugene E. Bernard, professor of psychology at North Carolina State University, conducted research on OBE and admitted that he believed in the reality of the phenomenon. In fact, Dr. Bernard claimed that he personally had experienced OBE on three different occasions.

Dr. Bernard told Thomas Leach of the *Chicago American Magazine* that, from his study to date, he would estimate that one out of every one hundred persons has experienced out-of-body projection. "It doesn't seem to be confined to any one sex, age range or economic scale," the psychologist said.

Dr. Bernard compared the phenomenon to "...lying on a sofa, getting up, and seeing your body still lying on the couch." According to Dr. Bernard and other researchers, the mind may remain in the same room or be projected thousands of miles away. The separation of spirit and body may last from a few seconds to a few hours.

In an interview with Rob Wood of the Associated Press, Dr. Bernard said that he uncovered one case in which an individual had an out-of-body experience while sitting at his desk. The subject's mind was projected to a city that the subject had never visited. Upon the reunion of the subject's mind and body, the astral traveller was able to describe in detail a street, an office building and the persons he had seen at work within the building. Dr. Bernard said he personally investigated and found the street, the building and the people.

As with nearly all other psychic phenomena, the psychologist learned that OBE most often occurs "...during time of stress; during natural childbirth; during minor surgery, and at times of extreme fear."

Among those who had undergone OBE, Dr. Bernard found a certain number who had developed the ability to make their minds leave their bodies at will. Dr. Bernard hoped to test the talents of some of these individuals under laboratory conditions. For his clinical study, Dr. Bernard planned to take the temperature of the subject while he was in projection trance (the body temperature is said to drop during OBE), and he also wished to make use of an electroencephalograph to measure brainwave patterns. The subject would be asked to project his mind into a closed vault to read a list of words and recite it later when the OBE had ended.

"It is improbable that so many people who are apparently psychologically healthy are having hallucinations," Dr. Bernard commented to journalist Leach. "There is still much we don't know about the mind and its abilities. I don't know how long it will take, but I believe the astral projection theory can be proved and controlled."

If the existence of out-of-body experience could be established to the satisfaction of the scientific community, textbooks of the physical sciences would have to be rewritten. The implications of such academic acceptance of OBE are staggering and would reach into every area of human endeavor. Religion, philosophy, psychology and medicine as well as physics would come in for some vital revisions.

Psychical researcher Frederic W.H. Myers called astral projection the most extraordinary achievement of the human will. "What can lie further outside any known capacity than the power to cause a semblance of oneself to appear at a distance?" Myers asks. "What can be more a central action—more manifestly the outcome of whatsoever is deepest and most unitary in man's whole being? Of all vital phenomena, I say, this is the most significant; this self-projection is the one definite act which it seems as though a man might perform equally well before and after bodily death."

In 1952 Dr. Hornel Hart submitted a questionnaire to 155 students at Duke University. Dr. Hart asked this question: "Have you ever actually seen your physical body from a viewpoint completely outside that body, like standing beside the bed and looking at yourself lying in bed, or floating in the air near your body?"

Thirty percent of the students answered yes to this question. After extensive studies of several other student groups, Dr. Hart concuded that at least 20 percent of college-level young people believe that they have experienced some sort of astral projection or out-of-body experience.

Dr. Hart's research led him to conclude that ". . . a world exists which is invisible to our physical senses and which yet is a realm of objective experience and of social contacts between conscious personalities."

Although such a view had become unpopular among contemporary psychologists and social behaviorists, Dr. Hart postulated the brain to be an instrument by which the consciousness expresses itself, rather than a generator whch produces consciousness. Dr. Hart ventured the opinion that the "essential core" of personal consciousness "can observe and act at long distances away from the brain."

Dr. Hart's conclusions were enthusiastic about the staggering prospects of scientifically-proved OBE: "Suppose it could be proved in even one conclusive case that a full-fledged personality observed and functioned fully at long distances away from the physical brain which it normally used; or suppose that, in even one conclusive case, it could be shown that such an apparition functioned in the described way after or while the brain which it normally used was physiologically dead, then the central biological denial of survival would break down."

In the opinion of the majority of the scientific establishment, no "one conclusive case" has yet been produced by the parapsychologists. Absolute proof to satisfy every skeptic may never be provided in this area which deals with "whatsoever is deepest and most unitary in man's whole being." But we do not lack empirical proof and personal testimony of this "most extraordinary achievement of the human will." I have compiled this casebook of out-of-body experiences so that the reader may, to borrow an admonition from Sir Francis Bacon, "read not to contradict and confute, nor to accept and take for granted, but to weigh and consider." At the same time I will include a number of meditations, mental exercises and spiritual techniques which I have found extremely successful in encouraging controlled OBEs for every sincere seeker.

2

The Spiritual Body of Man

"Also when they shall be afraid of that which is high, and fears shall be in the way, and the almond tree shall flourish and the grasshopper shall be a burden, and desire shall fail; because man goeth to his long home, and the mourners go about the streets. Or ever the silver cord be loosed, or the golden bowl be broken, or the pitcher be broken at the fountain, or the wheel be broken at the cistern. Then shall the dust return to the earth as it was: and the spirit shall return unto God who gave it."

Ecclesiastes, XII: 5–7

The Biblical reference quoted above is often given as scriptural testimony of the reality of our spiritual bodies and our ability to separate spirit from flesh and travel apart from all physical considerations. Many of the mind travellers do indeed see themselves as "golden bowls," or globular spheres of some sort, and just as many see a "silver cord" of great elasticity which connects the astral, or spirit, body to the physical body. Although the astral body may sometimes assume a form that duplicates the physical body, generally both the occultists, who have been speaking about astral bodies for centuries, and those who have had a one-time spontaneous OBE, describe the astral body as being more or less eggshaped with an orange glow—the "golden bowl."

Numerous occultists, clairvoyants and people gifted with extrasensory talents claim to be able to see an aura of psychic emanations surrounding the human body. Some maintain that it is the etheric power of the astral body that transmits this glowing aura. Others contend that the aura can be used as an indicator to reflect disordered vibrations (disease) in the physical body.

Most people dismissed psychic auras as esoteric mumbo-jumbo until 1908, when Dr. Walter J. Kilner offered the first scientific proof of these emanations. While performing some electrical experiments, Dr. Kilner, a physician at St. Thomas' Hospital in London, happened to use a viewing filter which had been stained with dicyanin dye. Through the filter he saw hazy, glowing outlines surrounding the bodies of the people in the laboratory.

Intrigued by his ability to sight auras, Dr. Kilner extended his accidental discovery to include two screens of glass cells filled with an alcoholic solution of dicyanin. He was then able to see auras so plainly that he devoted twelve years to their study. In 1920 Dr. Kilner published *The Human Atmosphere* in which he stated his conviction that the examination of the aura would some day be of great importance in the diagnosis of human disease.

What Dr. Kilner saw was a radiation, or glow, which extended from six to eight inches around the human form. The physician noted that the aura's size and shape was determined by such variables as the person's state of health, mood and mental alertness. He also conducted experiments demonstrating that the auras might be influenced by electricity and drugs. Dr. Kilner found his viewing glass to expedite greatly the observation of the aura, but he expressed the belief that 95 percent of all people with normal eyesight could learn to see the radiation under favorable circumstances.

It appears that modern science has usurped a portion of the occultists' domain. For centuries occult philosophers spoke of the aura. Then, in the twentieth century, a scientist decreed that such radiation did exist and could be used in the diagnosis of disease.

The June 1964 issue of *Fate* included some pertinent comments concerning the human aura by Rolf Schaffranke of the Saturn V moon rocket program in Huntsville, Alabama.

Schaffranke said that aura research and analysis has become "a new branch of modern science—a branch of growing importance in Europe." Photographic film made sensitive to infrared rays, Schaffranke reminded his readers, can capture the images of objects that are invisible to the human eye. Such film has been used to good advantage in recent years by psychical researchers. Schaffranke theorized that if a human could ever develop the ability to adjust the frequency-sensitivity of his or her eyes to ultraviolet or x-ray wavelengths, he or she would discover a most amazing other world.

"It has become the fashion in modern times, even among parapsychologists, to scoff at the human aura, to deny its existence and to equate it with the imaginative creations of the occultists," Schaffranke wrote. It was his firm contention that physics and parapyschology need to get together on the matter of the human aura. "More and more scientific investigations are revealing significant findings in this field. Scientists of international stature have been interested and have left the occultists far behind."

Numerous mediums and clairvoyants have described the aura and have interpreted the significance of the various colors and shadings of the radiation. Eileen Garrett, an internationally-known medium, recorded her impressions of the psychic aura, which she said "surrounds" each person or thing. Mrs. Garrett described the aura as a "misty, multicolored envelope" which surrounds all living objects and varies according to the mood or the changing conditions of one's life.

Psychic sensitive Phoebe Payne co-authored the book *The Psychic Sense* with her husband, Dr. Lawrence Bendit, a London psychiatrist. In it she too told of her ability to see the misty radiation that envelops all living things in a colorful, swirling aura. To the Bendits, the aura acts as a "...bridge between our world of dense matter and another world of consciousness."

Practical-minded readers will no doubt ask *how*, if OBE is possible, does the astral self leave the physical body? But most who experience out-of-body travel have no concept of the mechanics involved—it just happens. Some experts have outlined carefully-constructed sets of directions by which persons of the proper sensitivity can achieve astral projection. Others feel they have perfected a particular method which will work for almost anyone. The most cautious of those who claim conscious OBE say only that they have discovered a *modus operandi* that works for them.

I reserve further discussion of the methodology of astral projection for later chapters. But for the reader who insists on an answer to "how" at this point, I shall point to Dr. Alexander Cannon, British scholar and world traveller, who never hesitated to give a direct answer to a direct question.

In *The Power of Karma*, Dr. Cannon tells us that the astral body leaves the physical body "...through the aura known as the glabella (between the eyes), which is the strongly positive physical pole, and re-enters through the nape of the neck or the strong negative physical pole of the body, both inter-linked with the astral-etheric poles. This bears out the claim made by mediums that an 'entity' enters by the nape of the neck (actually a little to the left side, because if the etheric body were truly centralized, the 'entity' could not enter)."

Dr. Cannon believes in the existence of three bodies, the physical, astral and etheric, and holds that they are, respectively, the vehicles of the physical life, the soul and the spirit.

"Astral travelling is a fact," Dr. Cannon writes, "whether people like to believe it or not, and is controlled by two types of vibrations. One is the very rapid vibration known as telepathy, and the other is a fairly slow vibration known as clairvoyance: The former works best in a blue light, and the latter works best in an orange-red vibration. I have demonstrated the truth of this very clearly the last few months to several scientific friends. . ."

Dr. Cannon, the indefatigable explorer of the unknown, stated that in sleep and in trance the astral body may become partially or completely liberated from the fleshy envelope of the physical body, except, he observed, for the "extremely tenuous filaments [the 'silver cord'] by which contact is preserved with the body."

Dr. Cannon spent much time in the Orient, and says the Eastern school of initiation teaches the *chela* (student) how to withdraw his astral body under the direction of a master. The Oriental student submits himself to a rigorous and prolonged period of training before he is deemed ready to begin conscious out-of-body projection. He must demonstrate his ability to control his mind, his desires and his passions.

"He [the student] knows that a strong power of will is essential for the exercise of the faculties with which he explores the unseen," Dr. Cannon comments. "Knowledge is power, and the knowledge of the East has been acquired by centuries of effort and experiment. In the West, we are begining to be aware of the existence of an astral body. . .we have also made some discoveries as to the aura and the etheric body, which are confirmed by clairvoyance. We may look forward to a general recognition soon of those facts with which Eastern teachers have been so long conversant."

Although Dr. Cannon writes from what is generally an occultist's point of view, it is interesting to observe and worthwhile to note that a good many so-called ordinary people who have experienced spontaneous OBEs have reported leaving the body through the glabella, or through the sagittal suture on the crown of the head where the two parietal bones join. I am also intrigued by Dr. Cannon's mention of guides and masters who stand by to aid the neophyte in his or her out-of-body projection. So many individuals who have experienced astral projection mention either the unseen presence of a guide or a master, or visual manifestations of white-robed "teachers," that the assisting spirit motif seems to be almost a phenomenon within a phenomenon.

In his book *You Do Take It With You*, R. De Witt Miller emphatically states his belief in the "second body." Miller insists that the second body is necessary to explain a host of psychic phenomenona, and that the contemporary conception of the state of matter allows one to consider an astral body as not at all improbable.

"The desk top before me means perfectly *solid* to my fingers," Miller writes. "Yet present-day physics has demonstrated that the desk top is composed of atoms which in turn are composed of nuclei and electrons. Even the nuclei are now considered as composed of many distinct types of particles . . . the desk before me is *solid* only in the sense that it *seems solid* to the sensory organs with which my fingertips are equipped. Actually, the *solid* desk top is largely made up of what, for lack of a better word, is usually called 'empty space.' "

Miller goes on to theorize that, just as there is no reason why that empty space should not be occupied by another form of matter or conventional matter at a different rate of vibration, there is no reason why man's physical body could not be "interpenetrated" with a second body composed of a different form of matter or existing in a different range of vibration. "The desk top," Miller observes, "would not be solid to such a body, but objects in the world to which that body belongs would be."

Writing just before the atom became a serious addition to modern physics, Sylvan Muldoon, a professional in astral projection, tried to explain his concept of the astral body by telling his reader to take an ordinary glass tumbler and fill it to the brim with round lead bullets. When this was accomplished, Muldoon pointed out, it was still quite possible to pour in a good amount of buckshot, which would filter into the intervening spaces without really making the glass any more full. After the buckshot, a person could pour in a large quantity of sand; and finally, water could be added before the glass might truly be said to be "full."

"What all this amounts to is really this," Muldoon explained. "That between all particles of matter there is still room for still smaller particles, which fill the spaces between them. So far as we can see, this is true of everything down to the atoms themselves."

If Mr. Muldoon had written this a few years later, he would have had Mr. Miller's advantage of knowing that even the atoms themselves are full of "holes."

Can we say, then, that the "holes" in our physical body may be filled with the stuff of a much more subtle body? Or is it only our pernicious human nature that tries to find a specific location for everything in our experience? Heaven is spoken of as being "up" and hell is supposed to be "down." Also, in the vernacular, we still use the medieval concept of the heart as the center of emotion. So perhaps we need to accept the possibility of an astral self and examine the testimonies of those who have actually experienced out-of-body travel.

3

Projection at the Time
of Accident

"The automobile was right on top of me before I had a chance to step back on the curb," wrote Mr. R.E. of St. Louis. "For a split second that seemed like an eternity everything seemed frozen in time. It was in that same eternal moment before impact that the true, conscious part of me seemed to jump out of my body.

"I seemed to soar high above the street, and I could see the automobile about to hit me and I could see my physical body standing away from the curb. I had a stunned look at my face and a lady watching from the curb seemed about ready to go into hysterics. I knew that car was going to hit me, but it seemed as though my real consciousness couldn't care less.

"Then I saw my body go sailing through the air like someone had just drop-kicked a football. I didn't feel any pain from my physical body, and I seemed to have a strange feeling of indifference at the dummy I saw flying in the air. I had no sense of consciousness connected with the body that had just been struck by the speeding automobile. I was the dispassionate observer.

"I saw a crowd gather around the crumpled body. I wanted to leave the scene, to soar free in space, but something held me to the pitiful scene below me. There was a wail of sirens as a police car and an ambulance arrived at almost the same time.

"One of the doctors knelt beside my body and filled a syringe from a small bottle. He shot something into my arm, and it seemed to act like some kind of magnet pulling me back into my body...it was like I was one of those balls on a rubber string that had been thrown as far as the string would stretch and was now being pulled back.

"The next thing I knew, I was blinking my eyes. Everything was blurred. Most of all I remember the terrible pain. I wished that I was back floating above my body, away from the hurt."

Those readers who have made a study of the literature of psychic phenomena are well aware that such experiences provide a great stimulus, or catalyst, for spontaneous psychic function.

Dr. Joseph Rush has observed that crisis situations in which the normal, rational sensory-motor system is inadequate or frustrated or blocked present "...a favorable field in which the [psychic] functions take over or come into expression."

Dr. Gardner Murphy of the Menninger Clinic agrees that severe illness, personal crisis, "...disrupting, alerting situations that we have to be ready for, capable of assimulating, warding off, or that call for defense or the ability to incorporate" can encourage psychic experiences.

With the exception of the adepts who have attained a great deal of facility at slipping in and out of the body at will, the vast majority of those who have out-of-body projections experience them in crisis situations. Like other facets of psi phenomena, OBE seems to function best when there is a need for men and women to utilize the hidden powers of their minds. The need to exercise such abilities may exist whenever we find ourselves in a situation where our normal sensory channels no longer serve as an effective means of communication.

Dr. Jan Ehrenwald is another researcher who has noted that telepathy and other psi phenomena seem to function most effectively when the conscious mind is groggy with sleep, benumbed by pain, fever, physical exhaustion or befogged by trance or hypnosis.

A man I shall call K.L. figured in a case of out-of-body experience in which the astral self served to communicate a telepathic plea for help to a close friend.

K.L. was alone in a 14-foot trench, welding some new water pipes for a soon-to-open housing development in a large New England city. It is quite unlikely that K.L. had ever given the slightest thought to any sort of ESP ability, either in others or himself; and if anyone had told him about the possibility that one might travel in the mind independent of the body, K.L. would have laughed aloud. He had a wife and six children to support. He worked on a city maintenance crew from 7:30 A.M. to 4:00 P.M. and had a second job as a garage attendant from 7:30 P.M. until midnight. He would not seem to have had time to devote to metaphysics.

Then late one afternoon in the spring of 1955, K.L. was given a most dramatic, albeit painful, demonstration that human beings have within themselves remarkable resources which lie ready to serve them in crisis situations.

By 3:30 P.M. the power-shovel crew had laid the last pipe in place for the day. At 4:00 P.M. the crew knocked off work for the day, but K.L. did not have to report for work at the garage that night, so he decided to pick up some overtime by finishing the welding on the seam between the last two pipes in the trench.

He had finished his work on the inside seam and was about to begin on the outside of the joint when tons of earth, clay and stone fell on him. K.L. had had absolutely no warning noise of any kind. The trench had caved in as silently as if it had intended to trap him. K.L. was knocked down in a kneeling position against the big pipe. His nose was crunched up against the plate of the welding mask.

For a few moments K.L. was conscious of searing pain as his right shoulder was pressed against the hot weld he had been making on the pipes. In agony, he tried desperately to squirm away from the burning pipe, but the press of the cave-in held his shoulder against the red-hot weld.

He tried to twist his face free of the welding mask, then realized that it had saved his life. Without the pocket which the mask had made around his face, the loose dirt would have covered his nose and mouth and he would have suffocated.

The welder lay still, taking stock of his situation. He had been covered by a landslide in a trench in a new housing district. His crew had gone home. No construction workers or carpenters were working on this side of the district, but chances were strong that some of them might have occasion to walk by the trench and see the cave-in.

But how would they see him? The terrible thought dug into his consciousness and began to slice away at the thin mental barrier that had saved him from panic.

Then he realized that his right hand was sticking up through the dirt! Somehow, when the force of the cave-in had struck him, his right shoulder had been pressed forward against the hot weld and his right arm had been straightened back and above his body, allowing his hand to remain above the surface like a lonely five-fingered flag. His hand could be his salvation.

Time quickly became a concept devoid of all meaning. He had been there days, weeks, months. How long? Perhaps five minutes.

Already it was becoming very difficult to breathe. He had been fortunate in that he had been forced up against the pipe, thereby creating large air pockets near him.

But the blood from his broken nose kept dripping into his throat, and he feared that he would soon strangle on it. Would no one ever come by?

He thought of his wife, his children, and he was startled by the vividness of his thoughts. It seemed as if each member of his family had suddenly entered into the trench to be with him in his anguish.

"The more I thought about my family," K.L. remembered, "The more I wanted to be with them. Each breath I was taking was beginning to feel like hot lead forced down my nostrils. The next thing I knew, I seemed to be floating above the trench. I figure now the thing is that I fainted, but then I thought I had died.

"I could see my hand kind of dropping down over a bit of my wrist sticking above the dirt. I didn't really seem to care about what had happened to me. I didn't feel sad.

"Then I thought of my family, and just like that I was there in the kitchen. My wife was peeling potatoes for the evening meal. My oldest girl was helping her.

"I walked through the house and saw each one of the kids. Some were watching television. Others were doing homework. I wanted to hug them one last time. I wanted them to see me. That's when I felt sad. That's when I knew I didn't want to die. I knew that it didn't hurt to die, but I just didn't want to leave the wife and kids.

"I seemed to float back into the kitchen, and I got up right next to my wife's shoulder, and I tried to scream in her ear that I needed help. She just couldn't hear me.

"I reached out to touch her, and whether it was coincidence or what, she jerked around with a surprised look on her face. But I couldn't get through to her.

"Then I thought of B.J., my best friend and another welder. I no sooner pictured him in my mind than I was beside him.

"I could see his wristwatch, because he had his shirt sleeves rolled up. It was 4:45 P.M., which meant that I had been in the caved-in trench about fifteen minutes. B.J. works for a commerical firm, not the city, and he would be working until five o'clock, or after, depending on the job.

"Welding work becomes automatic after a while, so B.J. was welding away, not really thinking about much of anything. I could actually know what he was thinking, and it was all jumbled up like a dream. I suppose he was kind of daydreaming, and maybe that's how I was able to get through to him.

"I tapped him on the shoulder, and he shut off the torch and lifted up his face mask. I thought just as hard as I could: 'I need your help.'

"B.J.'s eyes opened wide like he had seen a ghost. And I guess he had. He said my name just once in kind of a hoarse voice. O.A., who was working with him, asked him who he saw, and B.J. said he thought he had seen me standing in front of him.

"O.A. said he must be seeing things, and I thought, 'Oh, God, dear God, please help B.J. to come to me.'

"The next thing I knew, I felt some hands pulling at me, and I could hear a lot of excited voices and above them all I could hear was B.J. telling everyone to be gentle and take it easy.

"At first I was still confused. I didn't know if I was still above floating around like some ghost, or if I was really back in my body. I felt scared right away, because I thought that maybe my mind was just playing tricks with me and that now I really *was* dead. Then a wonderful kind of peace came over me, and when I woke up again, I was in the hospital and all my family was standing around me."

K.L. was impressed by the authenticity of his experience. He had never been concerned with psi phenomena before, nor had he ever read any literature that dealt with psychic experiences. Now he is convinced that human minds and bodies are more than physical things.

His friend B.J. was quite vocal concerning his own experience. When he looked up from his welding, he first thought his eyes had not yet adjusted to the light, after the bright glare of the welding torch. Although welders wear a tinted face plate in their helmets, they are still susceptible to an after-image. As he became convinced that his eyes were not playing tricks on him, he was certain that he could distinguish a misty outline of his friend K.L. standing before him. He also had a strong sense of danger and was motivated to leave his work and drive to the housing development where he knew K.L. had been working with his crew. Although B.J. knew that his friend should have ceased working nearly an hour before, he was convinced that K.L. was still there and needed his help.

B.J. has had a number of experiences he considers to be paranormal. He believes in the immortality of the soul and is convinced that man's spirit, or essence, survives physical death. B.J. had had a prior experience similar to that of perceiving the "living ghost" of K.L. when his sister appeared to him at the moment of her physical death in the form of a crisis apparition, a spirit that appears at time of crisis. It appears, then, that B.J. served as precisely the proper receiver for K.L.'s telepathic projection, and K.L. was indeed fortunate to have a friend who was so readily able to "tune in."

The Reverend L.J. Bertrand, a Huguenot minister, declared that he had found personal proof of what he had been preaching all his life when he experienced an astral projection while on a mountain-climbing holiday in the Alps.

He had gone on ahead of the rest of his party and had sat down to await their survival. The students who had accompanied him on the holiday were not in as good condition as their youthful confidence had suggested, and they lagged behind in company with a local guide. Reverend Bertrand wished they would hurry because they were bringing his lunch with them.

While he sat and waited, he found himself drifting into the "sleep of the snows." He felt his body gradually becoming immovable and he realized with a start that he had sat still too long and was freezing to death.

There was a sudden moment of agony, which the clergyman interpreted as the act of physical death. Then Reverend Bertrand found himself bobbing above his physical body like a balloon on a silver string. He thought of his students, and at once his consciousness was with them, watching them make wrong turns, observing their amateurish climbing methods. He felt a strong irritation when he observed the guide retreat behind a rock to eat the lunch he was supposed to have brought up the mountain for Reverend Bertrand.

The clergyman thought next of his wife, who was to join him in Lucerne three days later. He was surprised to see her arriving ahead of schedule in a carriage with four others. As he was watching his wife go through the details of checking in at the hotel, his students and the guide came upon his frozen body.

At once the guide began to rub Reverend Bertrand's body with snow in an attempt to revive him. But the essence of the clergyman, high above the scene, bobbing about on a silver cord, felt great reluctance to return to the frozen shell which had housed it for so many years. The choice did not seem to be his however and moments later he became conscious of the exclamation of relief from his guide and the cheers of his students.

Reverend Bertrand rose stiffly to his feet, shuddered with the chill, wiped a bit of snow from his sleeve, then set about berating his students for not having followed his instructions and for not having taken the correct turns. He left the young men astonished and frightened, then turned his attention to the guide and scolded him for having nibbled at his lunch. The superstitious guide was ready to flee down the mountainside from the man "who sees everything."

Later, Bertrand's wife was to experience the same astonishment when her husband described the carriage in which she had arrived and the other four members of her travelling party. The clergyman himself had no easy analysis of the experience, but he remained convinced that he had been granted a most impressive demonstration of the soul's capacity to survive physical death.

On August 23, 1944, an armored-car officer received a similar demonstration that provided him with his personal proof of survival. The car in which the officer had been riding was transporting explosives. When it suffered a direct hit from a German antitank gun, the car split apart like a tin can.

The officer was thrown about twenty-five feet away from the car and over a five-foot hedge. According to the officer (*Journal* of the Society for Psychical Research, Vol. 34): "I was conscious of being two persons—one lying on the ground in a field where I had fallen from the blast, my clothes on fire, waving my limbs about wildly, at the same time uttering moans and gibbering with fear. The other 'me' was floating up in the air, about 20 feet from the ground, from which position I could see not only my other self on the ground, but also the hedge, the road, and the car, which was surrounded by smoke and burning fiercely."

The officer remembered having told himself that there was no value in thrashing about and babbling. With an effort of will, his "floating consciousness" impressed upon his body that it should roll over and over to put the flames out.

Then, as if it were a puppet being directed from above, his physical body rolled over until it fell into a ditch under the hedge where there was a puddle of water. The flames went out. It was then that the officer again became one person.

"Of course the aerial viewpoint can be explained up to a point as a 'photograph' taken subconsciously as I was passing the hedge as a result of the blast," the officer theorized. "This, however, does not explain the fact that I saw 'myself' quite clearly on the ground and for what seemed a long time, though it could not have been more than a minute or so."

Ernest Hemingway, who for many years seemed both to epitomize and to glorify the man at war, had an out-of-body experience of his own while serving in the trenches near Fossalta. It was about midnight on July 8, 1918, that a mortar shell exploded near the nineteen-year-old Hemingway, badly wounding him in the legs.

Hemingway later told Guy Hickok, a European correspondent for the Brooklyn *Daily Eagle*, that he had experienced death at that moment. He had felt his soul coming out of his body "...like you'd pull a silk handkerchief out of a pocket by one corner. It flew around and then came back and went in again and I wasn't dead any more."

No personal experience is ever lost on a writer. Whatever happens to him, good, bad, trivial or other-worldly, may someday be used in his work. Hemingway utilized his out-of-body travel in *A Farewell to Arms* when he had his fictional hero, Frederick Henry, undergo a similar experience.

The novel's protagonist is also positioned in the Italian trenches when "...a blast-furnace door is swung open, and a roar that started white and went red and on and on in rushing wind." Henry feels his essence rush out of him and soar with the wind. He believes himself to be dead and realized that there is an existence beyond physical death. Then, "...instead of going on, I felt myself slide back. I breathed and I was back."

In a 1952 edition of *Fate* magazine, Paul M. Vest told of the time that he was swimming in the ocean and found to his awful fear that the current was too strong for him. He became alarmed, shouted for help, but the wind was blowing against him and he was really too far out for his voice to carry to shore under the best of conditions. He fought with all his strength to best the powerful undertow, but then a large wave pounded him under the water.

In that instant he was suddenly no longer in his drowning body. "As swift as a flash my consciousness, or self, had withdrawn to a distance ten or twelve feet above and was looking down at my body floundering in the sea."

Vest's body had not entirely lost consciousness. It beat its arms spasmodically and kicked and fought for breath. The "I" consciousness remained above, serene, calm, almost disinterested in the fate of the physical body. The "I" consciousness "knew with absolute certainty that [it] was timeless, ageless and eternal. Thus it watched the drowning body dispassionately as you might watch an old coat being discarded...."

With the same disinterest, the "I" consciousness observed swimmers rescuing the unconscious physical body and bringing it to shore. Only when the body began to respond to artificial respiration did the "I" begin to be drawn back to the physical shell by "an irrestible force." The essential self seemed almost reluctant to have to put on the cumbersome apparatus of a body once again.

"Since that day," Paul Vest wrote, "I no longer think of my body as 'I' any more than I would think of one of my garments as 'I.' "

According to the February 1967 edition of *Fate* magazine, it was two o'clock in the morning on July 17, 1957, when Patricia Mann opened her eyes to glimpse a shadowy form that resembled her mother.

"Come, I need your help," the apparition said to her.

Her mother lived ten miles away from her, but Patricia was convinced that the form was truly hers. She picked up the telephone, dialed her mother's number. She could only get a busy signal. A call to the telephone company produced the information that the line was "out of order."

Patricia Mann knew somehow that she could not wait until morning. She dressed hurriedly, drove to her mother's house.

When she arrived, she found all the lights on, and she could hear the television set blaring full blast. She pounded on the door, called her mother's name, but received no response. At last she found an unlocked window and crawled through. She found her mother lying in a pool of blood, clutching the telephone receiver in her hand. Patricia called an ambulance.

After her mother's forehead had been stitched up in the hospital's emergency room, she told Patricia what had happened:

"She had fallen and from the gushing blood she knew that she had sustained a deep cut. She was trying to phone me when she blacked out, but she remembered calling my name. She also knew that it had been about 2:00 A.M. when she fell."

4

Leaving the Body during Intense Pain

Mary W. had always had an aversion to drugs, and so—in spite of her physician's instructions to flash the nurse if the numbing effects of the "hypo" started to wear off—she refused to call for the blissful relief of another hypodermic injection.

In a letter to me, Mary W. wrote: Just at the point where I was about to reach for the bulb by my pillow and flash for the nurse, I had an odd sensation, like my feet, my legs, my body, were being rolled up like a giant toothpaste tube. Then my *real* self seemed to be all rolled up in a corner of my skull. There was a really intense spasm of pain, and then I seemed to shoot up into a corner of the room.

"I thought I'd died. For a fleeting moment I felt upset and angered at the injustice of dying as the result of such a minor operation. I morosely attributed my 'death' to the inadequacies of the hospital staff and the incompetence of my doctor. Then a warm wave of peace seemed to wash over me, and I thought how foolish it was to care about a continued existence in that painfully throbbing shell that lay stretched out on the hospital bed.

"I was appalled at my appearance. My cheeks seemed drawn, and my eye sockets looked hollow. My eyes were closed and I studied myself for a bit, because I had never been able to imagine what I would look like with my eyes closed. I looked terrible.

"Just then a nurse came into the room. She must have just come on duty, because I had not seen her before. I at once had an impression of a very conscientious and responsible woman who, though efficient, went about her work with compassion.

"She took one look at my body, and I perceived a flash of anxiety and concern. She called for orderlies, interns and other nurses. They all started working over my body, and I thought, 'Oh, no, you don't! I don't want to return to my body. I like it fine up here in a corner of the room!'

"But I began to feel guilty after wave after wave of anxiety began to buffet me from the group of medical personnel who were desperately trying to bring me back to life. Then one of them gave my body an injection, and I began to feel drawn back toward my body.

"It seemed as though there was an opening on the top of my skull. I rolled myself back up and aimed myself like a bullet for that hole.

"Everyone smiled when I opened my eyes, but I knew that I had only come back to pain."

One of the most extraordinary of the classic cases of projection while undergoing severe pain is that of Ed Morrell, the convict who was able to leave his physical body while sadistic prison guards subjected it to heinous tortures. Morrell's experiences contained certain information which was later substantiated by numerous individuals of unassailable reputation. The governor of the state of Arizona, George W.P. Hunt, verified the truth of Morrell's projections, and author Jack London based his book *The Star Rover* on Morrell's incredible experiences.

Ed Morrell had resisted the petty abuses and minor tortures of the prison guards, and the brutal men decided to subject him to the "bloody strait jacket" in an effort to break his will. In a variation of a primitive torture device, the guards had hit upon the idea of binding a prisoner into two tightly laced straitjackets, then pouring water over the two outfits and allowing them to shrink. The sensation would be comparable to being slowly squeezed to death by a boa constrictor.

His cell was a dark, windowless, underground dungeon completely sealed off from the outside world, yet each time the guards trussed Morrell up in the canvas jackets, his mind soared free of the pain-wracked body and the grim prison cell.

For half an hour Morrell would lie in agony as the jackets tightened. His eyes would burn with intense pain, and the cords in his neck would tighten to the bursting point as the breath was forced from his body. For a brief time, Morrell would seem to be smothering, then a strangely peaceful sensation would suffuse his body and the pain would cease.

Then it was that Ed Morrell became aware of a detachment of his mind from his physical torture. Time and space took on new meanings as the prison walls seemed to dissolve into nothingness. The essential self of Ed Morrell was free to wander outside the physical limits of bound body, prison walls, geographical distance and man-made time. In that state of absolute freedom, Morrell's astral body was able to witness events which he later discovered actually had happened at the time.

Once he observed the violent tragedy of a shipwreck. Another time he saw the young woman who later became his wife. During one projection he confronted the governor of the state and predicted the exact date and hour of his release. On numerous occasions he witnessed the activity of people whom he later came to know. It was as if Ed Morrell possessed a second body which could soar free of the tortures whenever the pain became too intense.

Morrell's tormentors became frustrated in their attempts to break his spirit. Baffled, they would find Ed Morrell sleeping soundly. Only a whitish foam that flecked his lips gave evidence that Morrell was not at peaceful rest.

Determined to crack his will, the guards kept Morrell in the shrinking jackets for days. Once he was kept in the pressing canvas for five days before the guards roughly rolled his bruised body out of the jackets and onto the bare stones of the cell floor.

Once Morrell was left alone, his astral travelling consciousness returned to him, and he again became aware of his surroundings. He would drag himself weakly to the water bucket, drink deeply, crawl over to his pile of straw and lapse into strength-restoring sleep.

During days of peace when his jailors were not tormenting him, Ed Morrell tried unsuccessfully to project his mind out of the grim underground cell. It seemed as though he had to experience what Jack London later termed the "little death" before his mental body could escape the physical barriers of time and space.

It is one of my personal hypotheses that "psi" abilities operate most efficaciously when there is a psychological need for them to come into being. Such a need might exist under severe emotional stress, physical disability, illness or any time when the normal channels of sensory communication are blocked.

Ed Morrell was introduced to the mystery of out-of-body experience when he was in the depths of despair and agony, but he, unlike certain adepts, was unable to exercise the phenomenon at will. Yet for Ed Morrell, this remarkable "psi" ability enabled him to endure four years of imprisonment and torture.

On May 27, 1962, two sisters experienced an externalization of a living phantom when one sister was undergoing intense pain during childbirth. (*Fate*, December 1967)

According to author Mercedes Colon, Victoria and Isabel Carenas have always been extremeley close. As children they maintained telepathic communication with one another by a method they referred to as "the game."

Victoria and Isabel were separated for the first time when Isabel and her husband Carlos moved from New York City to Cleveland, Ohio where Carlos had been transferred by his company. Isabel was expecting her first child at the time of the move, and Victoria made plans to travel to Cleveland when her sister went to the hospital.

One night in May 1962, Victoria sat alone with her small terrier in her apartment. It was several weeks until she expected to be called to Cleveland. Suddenly she felt as though a heavy blanket of depression had been dropped upon her. She became nervous and edgy. She looked around for her dog and saw it tense and alert, ears standing straight up.

The terrier made a movement as if it were about to rise on its hind legs, as it usually did when greeting someone familiar. Then, at the last moment, the dog seemed to change its mind, scurried into the bedroom and slid under the bed.

There, before Victoria's disbelieving eyes, was "...a vaporous human figure in a white garment, framed by an aura of pallid light.... Although the features were nebulous there was something intensely familiar about the apparition."

Victoria fainted, but when she regained consciousness, she felt strangely relaxed. The terrier lay beside her, its muzzle on her breast. Victoria had managed a sitting position when the telephone on the night table rang.

It was Carlos, and in a voice that quavered with emotion and fatigue, he told her that the baby had been born three weeks earlier than expected. Both mother and baby boy were out of danger, but there had been some very anxious moments.

"Isabel has been calling for you," Carlos told Victoria. "For hours she has been calling for you."

It seems that the "game" the sisters had played in their youth prepared them for such an experience, for the channels for such communication had long since been opened. Later, Isabel said that all day she had been thinking of her sister and that when she thought she was to die, she was seized by an overpowering desire to see Victoria one last time. She began, mentally, to call to Victoria, utilizing the same method they had once employed in the "game."

As she was slipping into unconsciousness as a result of the ether being administered to her, she ". . . suddenly found herself in the apartment in New York. She remembered seeing the little dog in the hall and then seeing her sister in the moment before everything went black."

H.E. of Idaho wrote me of an out-of-body experience she had as a girl. She awakened one evening with a terrible case of indigestion as a result of having eaten too much unripe fruit. She described the pain as "absolutely unbearable." Her mother immediately diagnosed the symptoms as being indicative of appendicitis and called the doctor.

As H.E. lay thrashing about in agony, her thoughts dwelt upon the possibility of somehow being able to escape the pain that had seemed to fill every corner of her being. How wonderful it would be to be able to leave her pain-wracked body, she said mentally. A spasm of pain doubled her over and the move seemed to shoot "the thinking part of me up to the ceiling."

H.E. writes: "I could actually see Mom fussing about, and I could see me tossing about on the bed, whimpering and crying. But I, the *real* me, couldn't feel a thing. The pain remained down below with my body and the bed. Then I started feeling kind of ashamed about the way my body was behaving like such a baby. I really should go back, I decided.

"Just like that, I was back inside my body and howling in pain. If it hurt to be in my body, it didn't take me long to decide where I wanted to be. I doubled over again and moaned like I did before (although I don't really know if this had anything to do with it or not), and I was back up floating on the ceiling.

"I wondered when the doctor was going to come, and I was suddenly inside the doctor's car as he stopped at the stoplight.

" 'Why the hell do they keep these darn things going all night?' he was mumbling. 'Why don't they just keep them blinking on yellow?'

"I rode along with the doctor for a while, then I thought about Mom and about my body. This time when I shot back to my room, my body was lying very still and Mom was crying. I looked terrible. My face was gray and my mouth was hanging open.

" 'My God,' I thought, 'I'm dead. I died that last time. So this is what it is all about. Men talk about death and fear death, but there is really nothing to it. You just sort of 'pop' out of your body.'

"By this time Dad was standing beside Mom. He was sober-faced and feeling my pulse. He told Mom that I was not dead, but why in thunder didn't the doctor get there.

"I thought again of the doctor, and I could see him pulling up in front of the house. I followed him up the walk and was able to see him ring the bell and see my father running down the steps to answer the door all at the same time.

"I still thought that I was dead, regardless of what Dad had said about my pulse. At first I felt sad. I thought about the prom coming up, and I wondered if R.J. would be sorry that I had died. I wondered if he would cry. I thought about how my girl friends would be upset, and I wondered if Grandma would be able to withstand the shock. Maybe she would be joining me soon. Then I thought about R.J. again, and I seemed to know that if I wanted to, I could be right in his room. That made me feel like a peeping-Tom, though, so I didn't do it.

"Below me Mom started crying, and Dad put his arm around her to comfort her. The doctor frowned and got a syringe out of his bag. I could see his thoughts or know what he was thinking, and he was saying to himself that a good jolt of this should bring her around!

"I've always hated to get shots from the doctor, and even though I knew I wouldn't feel it, I didn't want him sticking that big needle into my arm. It was like I took a running jump for my body, and I actually heard a thump like someone hitting a mattress hard with his open hand. I guess that my arms and legs straightened out, and I halfway sat up. I startled the doctor, as well as Mom and Dad.

"The doctor gave me a shot anyway, though; only this time it was for the pain. No one seemed to believe me when I told them about my experience, but the doctor did give me a funny look when I told him what he had said at the stoplight."

On Christmas morning, 1957, Mrs. Oleta A. Martin was straightening up the house for her children, who had arrived with their families for a holiday dinner. Then, suddenly, a pain near her heart made breathing so difficult that she could not call for help. Her youngest daughter saw her agony and ran upstairs to awaken the late-sleeping family.

Her husband moved her to a sofa. The entire family stood by, helplessly watching the woman in her excruciating pain. Someone went to call for a doctor.

Mrs. Martin's eyes closed, and she thought she was dying. She seemed to be floating away, and she lost all sensation of pain and all consciousness of her surroundings. When she stopped floating, she found herself at the edge of a wide chasm, "so dark beneath [her] that [she] could not see the bottom." She experienced great fear, then calm, when a bright, "spiritual" light appeared on the other side of the abyss.

She could make out the general form of a being in the midst of the light, but the illumination was so brilliant that she could see no part of him from his shoulders up. To the entity's left stood a dozen or so other beings in long, white garments. They seemed to be telling Mrs. Martin not to be afraid, that she could cross the chasm without danger and that they would be waiting for her on the other side.

Mrs. Martin was eager to join them, but the awareness was heavy upon her that once she crossed that wide chasm she might never return. She thought of how greatly her daughter needed her.

"The pressure on my chest returned. I gasped for breath and again became conscious of the world around me. I opened my eyes to see my family's tears change to surprise as they saw that I smiled weakly."

Her assembled family cried "Mother!" and moved toward her as one, but the family doctor held them back with a warning that she had just had a close call and must not become excited. Mrs. Martin later improved her heart condition with rest, medication and a change of diet, but she writes: "...when the time does come I shall be less afraid to die because of that memorable experience at the brink of death." (*Fate* June, 1969)

5

Out-of-Body Experiences during Illness

On February 26, 1937, Sir Auckland Geddes, a medical doctor and professor of anatomy, read a paper to the Royal Medical Society of Edinburgh in which he related the experience of a colleague, who requested anonymity but at the same time wished to make his out-of-body experience known to fellow members of the healing sciences.

The anonymous doctor said he had stood at the gates of death and had been conscious while out of his body. After medical treatment had restored him to a normal condition, the doctor immediately dictated his remarkable experience to a stenographer.

The doctor had been stricken by acute gastro-enteritis shortly after midnight, and by ten o'clock the next morning found himself too weak even to ring for assistance. Although he was very ill and suffered violent intestinal pains, his thinking processes were in no way effected and he set about reviewing his financial position.

It was at this point that he realized that "...my consciousness was separating from another conciousness, which was also 'me.'"

The doctor called these dual states of consciousness, "A" and "B." The ego, or essential self, aligned itself with the "A" state of consciousness. The "B" personality remained with the physical body.

As his condition worsened, the doctor noted that the "B" consciousness began to disintegrate, while the "A" personality became more completely himself and removed itself entirely from the physical body, which he could see lying in bed.

As he slowly became adjusted to the sensation, the doctor realized that not only could he see his body on the bed, but he could see things in the entire house and garden—and even in London, Scotland or wherever he directed his attention.

He sensed the presence of a "mentor" who explained to him that he was "...free in a time dimension of space, wherein *now* was equivalent to *here* in the ordinary three-dimensional space of everyday life."

The doctor next realized that, in his out-of-body state, he was able to see things in four or more dimensional places, as well as the ordinary three-dimensional space of everyday life.

Sir Auckland Geddes quoted his colleague as saying that there were no words to describe adequately what he saw. He understood from his "mentor" that "...all our brains are just end-organs projecting as it were from the three-dimensional universe into the psychic stream, and flowing with it into the fourth and fifth dimensions."

Around each living brain the doctor was able to perceive a "condensation of the psychic stream" which formed a kind of cloud.

His "mentor" explained to him that the fourth dimension existed in everything that existed in the three-dimensional space and everything in the third dimension existed in the fourth and fifth dimensions. *Now* in the fourth-dimensional universe was equal to *here* in the three-dimensional universe. A fourth-dimensional being was "...*everywhere* in the *now*...just as one is *everywhere* in the *here* in a three-dimensional view of things."

The doctor came to the realization that he, in his present state of existence, was a blue-colored "cloud" of psychic condensation. Many mysteries were being revealed to his "A" consciousness, when he saw a servant enter his bedroom and respond with shock to the condition of the "B" body which lay in bed. He saw the servant rush to the telephone and call the doctor and, at the same time, he saw his doctor answer the telephone and leave his patients.

When the doctor arrived, the "A" consciousness was able to hear the doctor think, "He is nearly gone." He was able to hear his colleague speak to him, but he was unable to respond because he was no longer in the "B" consciousness and the physical body.

The "A" consciousness became angry when he saw the physician take a syringe and rapidly inject his body with camphor. His heart began to beat more rapidly, and he began to feel himself drawn back to the body lying in disarray on the bed.

"I was intensely annoyed," the doctor dictated afterward, "because I was so interested and was just beginning to understand where I was and what I was seeing. I came back into my body, really angry at being pulled back; and once back, all the clarity of vision of anything and everything disappeared, and I was just possessed of a glimmer of consciousness which was suffused with pain."

The doctor firmly stated that his out-of-body experience had shown no tendency to "fade like a dream would fade...nor to grow or to rationalize itself." He was convinced of the reality of his experience and of its momentous significance to the life of every man.

"What are we to make of it?" Sir Auckland asked his colleagues when he completed his reading the paper. "Of one thing only we can be quite sure—it was not fake. Without that certainty I should not have brought it to your notice."

Sir Auckland told his fellows that his colleague's experience had helped him to define the idea of a psychic continuum and had brought "...telepathy, clairvoyance, spiritualism, and indeed all the parapsychic manifestations into the domain of the picturable."

In *Memories, Dreams, Reflections*, the eminent psychoanalyst C.G. Jung describes an out-of-body experience of his own which took place after he had broken a foot and suffered a heart attack.

"It seemed to me that I was high up in space," Jung wrote. "Far below I saw the globe of earth, bathed in a gloriously blue light....Below my feet lay Ceylon, and in the distance ahead of me the subcontinent of India. My field of vision did not include the whole earth, but its global shape was plainly distinguishable and its outlines shone with a silvery gleam through that wonderful blue light."

The psychoanalyst described the reddish-yellow desert of Arabia, the Red Sea, a bit of the Mediterranean.

"The sight of the earth from this height was the most glorious thing I had ever seen," Jung wrote. He estimated that his consciousness would have had to have been at least a thousand miles up to have perceived such a panarama of the globe.

Jung was most emphatic in stressing his belief that the experiences he had during his illness were not the products of imagination or a fevered brain.

"The visions and experiences were utterly real," he wrote. "There was nothing subjective about them; they all had a quality of absolute objectivity."

In a classic case of projection during illness, J.S. Thompson called at the photographic studio of James Dickinson in Newcastle, England, on

January 3, 1891, and asked for the set of prints which he had ordered.

Dickinson apologized to Thompson and told him that the prints had not yet been processed.

"Ah, that's too bad," Thompson said in a tone of deep disappointment. Indeed his countenance became so morose that the photographer assured him that he would have the prints the first thing the next morning.

"That's no good," Thompson sighed. "I have little time left, and I did so want to see those photographs."

Commenting sadly that he would be unable to return later for the finished prints, Thompson walked out of the studio, leaving Dickinson and a number of patrons with the distinct impression that they had just seen a most disconsolate man.

Later, the photographer and the clients in the studio would be repeatedly interrogated by investigators for the British Society for Psychical Research. Although the witnesses swore that J.S. Thompson had called on Dickinson and requested his prints and the photographer had noted the time of his visit in the studio record book. Thompson had been at home in bed that day and had been under the constant observation of a trained nurse.

Mortally ill and mumbling in delirium, Thompson spoke continuously of obtaining his prints. Just a few hours after he was seen in the studio of James Dickinson, Thompson died.

A correspondent from New Jersey writes to tell me that he acquired the knack of slipping in and out of the body during a bout of childhood disease.

"It seemed as though I had one darned thing after another—chicken pox, measles, mumps. I missed two months of school, and I had to try to keep up with the rest of my class by doing my homework from my bed. I started getting behind and I became frustrated. I was so tired of lying there in bed that more than anything else in the world, I wanted to be back in school.

"I remember the first time I had an out-of-body experience, I just lay there one morning and concentrated on going to school. I mean, in my head I went through all the motions of getting dressed, eating breakfast and walking to school. I didn't neglect a thing. I completely re-created a typical morning's preparation and journey to the school building.

"Then a kind of cloud seemed to pass before my eyes. I heard a funny sort of popping noise, and I was there in school. It was spelling class, and one of my buddies was having a tough time spelling 'geography,' and I kept wanting to tell him to remember 'George Elias' old grandfather rode a pig home yesterday.'

"It was all so clear. I could see all the guys. Miss K. was tugging on the tip of her chin like she always did when she was impatient, and I could see a couple of the fellows passing notes. Miss K. saw them, too, and made them stand in separate corners of the room for the rest of the class period.

"That night when one of my friends called, I told about the incident, and he wanted to know how I had found out. Of course I didn't tell him, but I actually used this method to enable me to keep up with my classmates in school."

Major Sir Carne Rasch apparently used a similar method to enable him to attend a certain session of the British House of Commons a few days before the Easter parliamentary recess in 1908. Rasch intended to support the government in an ensuing debate, and he realized full well how important it was for every government supporter to attend each session to indicate a show of strength for the government debaters.

Then, just before a most important debate to be conducted by his friend, Sir Gilbert Parker, Rasch was struck by a severe attack of influenza and was confined to bed. Even so, Major Sir Carne Rasch found a way to support his allies.

Although he was actually tossing feverishly in his bed under a doctor's care, Rasch was seen by several members that evening sitting on the bench he regularly occupied. Sir Gilbert himself noted that his friend was seated at his usual place when he was at the very peak of his debate, and he stated afterward how reassured he had been to see Major Sir Carne Rasch in attendance.

As Mrs. R.M. lay violently ill from ptomaine poisoning, she was conscious of something she described as resembling a "wispy puff of cotton" floating away from her physical body.

"When it floated to the middle of the hospital room," Mrs. R.M. writes, "it seemed to unravel itself into another version of me. This new body seemed to contain the 'real me'—if you know what I mean. I could stand there and look down on my old body lying there in the bed. Lord, I looked a sight. There was a tube running out of my mouth and nose, and a couple of nurses were fussing over me.

"I suppose I thought I was dead at first, but I could see me lying on the bed, and I was still breathing, so I didn't really know what was going on. I moved on out in the corridor, and I saw my husband sitting slumped in a chair smoking a cigarette. His hands were shaking and he looked nervous and concerned.

"I seemed to slip right through a wall and into a room where two doctors were talking about me. They were wondering whether or not they should contact the health commissioner and have him close down that restaurant where we had eaten.

"I wondered where my daughter was, and the next instant I was standing beside her in a gift shop. She was looking at some get-well cards.

"She took one down off the rack, and it was one of those humorous contemporary cards. She read it, and I could 'hear' her reading the verse. She decided it would be disrespectful, and she bought a nice, flowery card instead.

"Then I heard the doctors talking to a nurse about giving me just a few more cc's, and I felt myself being pulled away from my daughter's side. Just like that, I was back in my physical body, and I felt terribly sick.

"When my daughter came in with the card, I told her that I could have used a good laugh, and I repeated the verse she had read in the humorous card. She looked real pale, and her eyes got big and wide, but I wouldn't tell her and my husband about what had happened until the doctors and nurses left the room."

When T.H.P. was twelve years old, he suffered a severe attack of bronchial asthma. Before his parents could summon a doctor, the lad felt himself slipping into unconsciousness.

"All at once I felt peaceful and completely relaxed. The *real* part of me just seemed to float above that poor wheezing body on the bed, and it didn't seem to bother me at all that the physical me couldn't breathe. I have never experienced such a wonderful sense of freedom.

"I can vividly remember seeing the doctor come puffing into my room. 'Oh no,' the real me thought, 'now he will make me breathe again, and I'll have to go back to that clumsy, imperfect body.'

"The doctor shot a powerful jolt of adrenalin into my lifeless body, but I tried my best to resist being pulled back into that lump of clay that was so susceptible to disease and physical ailments. Then I saw Mom and Dad and they were both crying. I didn't want to hurt them, so I stopped struggling and let myself be sucked back into my body.

"I opened my eyes, took a deep breath, and was at once conscious of terrible pain in my chest and back. I value my life here on this physical plane, but I know that to die is to enter a free, spiritual state, and I do not fear death."

When fifty-three-year-old Mrs. Muriel May was a girl of ten, she lay seriously ill with diphtheria. She was so ill that, she learned later, her parents and her physician had resigned themselves to her imminent death.

One night she was lying in her bed looking at the ceiling when she suddenly found herself floating up through the darkness until she "saw some light and...a beautiful garden."

In the garden filled with lovely flowers, she could hear soft music and laughter and was suddenly watching dozens of happy, shouting children at play. When little Muriel tried to join in their play and be seated with them at the drawing table, two gentle women appeared on either side of her. "We are not ready for you yet," one of them said to her.

The two women led Muriel back the way she had come and then the girl felt herself "falling through darkness...down and down."

"I know it was not a dream," Mrs. May says today. "I know that I stepped over the threshold of life and death and that I saw what the after-life holds for us." (*National Enquirer*, January 26, 1969)

Colleen Pechinski was surprised and shaken when her father, Mel Lightner, suffered a stroke in February, 1966. He was taken to the hospital, but the doctor offered little hope for his recovery. Mr. Lightner was, after all, seventy-eight years old.

Mrs. Pechinski knew that any arrangements that would have to be made in the event of her father's death would fall on her shoulders. She was also cognizant of her father's wishes that upon his death both his body and the body of his wife, who had died eleven years earlier, be returned to their hometown of Barron, Wisconsin. The fulfillment of such a last request would be expensive, and since Mr. Lightner had had no insurance, the older children were against such a move.

One night after she had visited her father in the hospital, Mrs. Pechinski awakened at three in the morning to see a man standing at her bedroom door. She jumped out of bed, followed him to the kitchen. He seemed to disappear, and she dismissed it all as a nightmare.

The man also appeared on the next night, and Mrs. Pechinski knew that she was not dreaming because she had been wide awake when the apparition appeared for another fleeting moment.

When the apparition appeared on the third night, Mrs. Pechinski was shocked to see it take the form of her father "...clad in his hospital gown, thin and pale" with a searching, restless look on his face.

The next morning she summoned her brothers and sisters and told them of her nocturnal visitations. She argued that such a manifestation was their father's way of emphasizing his desire that his request to be buried in Barron be respected. When Mr. Lightner died on March 17th, he was interred beside his wife in the Wisconsin town he loved so well. (*Fate*, July 1967)

6

Projection during Surgery

Reports of projection while under anesthesia during surgery are common and often judged to be hallucinatory. But to researchers who have experience in the matter, the high incidence of out-of-body projection during surgery does not seem unusual. They point out that, since the astral self is the vehicle of consciousness and can withdraw from the body whenever it becomes unconscious, and since the application of anesthesia produces such a deep state of unconsciousness, the "essential self" might be encouraged to slip out of the body.

Out-of-body experience occurs during natural sleep, self-induced trance, fainting, coma or unconsciousness brought about by physical or mental trauma. In the deep unconsciousness of anesthesia, the astral self may literally be forced out of the body by a state of unconsciousness so much more complete than that of natural sleep or trance.

A close friend reported to me that she felt herself spinning rapidly upward from the operating table "like a propeller without an airplane." She had a fleeting glance at the doctors and nurses working over her, then she burst into the bright sky of mid-morning.

"I can't remember anything else," she complained wistfully. "But I know the experience was real, and I know that there was so very much more to it. If only I could remember."

Psychical researcher Hereward Carrington suggested that such is the disadvantage of the levels of unconsciousness brought about by pathological states. Although anesthesia produces a depth of unconsciousness that projects the subject farther from his or her body and allows a more striking experience than a projection during natural sleep or self-induced trance, the anesthetic also drugs the percipient so that he or she is often unable to recall much of the experience after returning to animate the physical body.

A correspondent from the Midwest told me of her experience while under the surgeon's knife.

"My doctor hadn't been honest with me; I knew that. I knew that I was much sicker than he had told me I was. Two young interns sprinkled the powdered ether onto the mask while I lay on a wheeled table in the hall outside the operating room. They were talking about what they were going to do on their double-date that night. I thought about how wonderful it was to be young and to be able to plan for the future. I felt that I had come to the end of my life.

"Then I started to spin around and around. I heard a kind of crackling noise, like stiff paper being crunched up into a ball. Then I seemed to be bobbing like a balloon on a string. This is the best comparison I can make: I was a shining balloon attached to my body by a silver string. I could see my body below me and the two interns still chattering about their plans for the evening.

"My doctor came down the hall in a green smock. He took a last puff on a cigarette, then put it in an ashtray filled with white sand. He took one look at me and got very angry.

"He swore at the two young interns and scolded them as if they were small boys. He shouted down the hall, and nurses came running. My body was quickly wheeled into the operating room.

"Oh, no, I thought. Something has gone terribly wrong. I thought of my husband and my two children and I felt sad—not for me, but for them. I guessed that I was dying, and I didn't really want to watch what was going on in the operating room.

"I didn't feel any more sickness or pain, but I just felt kind of indifferent.

"Then I heard bells tolling, as they do after funerals. Yes, I thought, I must be dead. But suddenly a deep voice said: 'Not yet!' And I felt myself being pulled upward and upward, like a bullet being shot into the sky.

"The next thing I knew, I was no longer a shining balloon kind of thing, but I was 'me' again. Before me were several figures in bright, shining gowns. They just seemed to glow with an inner radiance. To me, they were what angels were supposed to look like, only they didn't have wings.

" 'You can stay here for a while,' one of them told me in a gentle voice, 'but you will have to go back.'

"When I look back on the experience now, I seem to remember seeing green fields and trees and brooks and streams. How beautiful Heaven is, I thought.

"Then, at almost precisely the same time, I thought that if this was Heaven, I would be able to see my parents. In a twinkling, Mom and Dad were standing beside me, and we were all weeping tears of joy at our reunion. Neither of them looked old as they had when they died, but both of them appeared to be as I remembered them from my childhood.

"It seemed as though I visited with them for hours, perhaps even days. Then one of the 'angels' in a white robe came for me and said that it was time for me to return.

"No sooner had he told me this than I was bobbing near the ceiling of a hospital room. I was shocked to hear Father S. below me giving the last rites to my body. My husband was crying, and I had an impression of my younger sister outside in the hall with my children. A nurse stood at the left side of the bed, her fingers on my pulse.

" 'It is not yet your time,' the same deep voice said. I heard that same crackling noise, and I saw the color of blood all around me. I realized at last that I was back in my body, and I moaned with the pain of my illness and the recent operation.

"When I opened my eyes, my husband and Father S. were smiling, and the nurse had just reentered the room with our family doctor.

" 'I've been to Heaven,' I told them.

"Father S. chuckled and said I had them all worried that I might very well be knocking at St. Peter's gate. Our doctor said that he had given me only a matter of a few minutes to either pass the crisis or die. Father S. had been called to administer the last rites, because my chances to live seemed almost nonexistent.

"I believe my experience was genuine, and I told my sister later that I had seen Mom and Dad in Heaven."

Another correspondent told me of an out-of-body experience that occurred while he was having a tooth extracted.

The dentist had just administered a syringe of pain-killing anesthetic when ". . . I started to feel dizzy. The doc had told me it was some new stuff, and I was about to complain that it was too strong for me when I found myself back in my bookshop. I had been worried about leaving P.V. in charge, and sure enough, there she was chatting with one of her girl friends while a customer, Mr. J.L., stood by the cash register, impatiently drumming his fingers on the countertop.

"Finally I saw him slap a five-dollar bill on the counter and call out sharply. 'You can give me my change some day when you are less preoccupied with lunch-hour gossip!' Then he slammed the door, and it was like the force of that door slamming shut shot me out of a cannon and landed me in a garden in what I'll swear was Japan! I just kind of strolled about lazily for a while until I felt like someone was poking me. There was a rapid blurring of images, and I opened my eyes to see my doctor grinning above me and boasting that his dentistry was so painless, that his patients could even take naps in the chair.

"When I got back to the bookshop, I asked P.V. how things had gone in my absence. She assured me that everything had been fine and that I shouldn't worry about leaving her in charge. I told her how pleased I was, then suggested that she stop by Mr. J.L.'s on her way home and give him his change.

"P.V. blushed and got flustered and wanted to know how I had found out about that. I shrugged and tried to act mysterious. She was puzzled for a few days, especially when Mr. J.L. assured her that he had not seen me that afternoon and had not complained of her lack of professional service. I'm afraid the incident didn't cure her of chatting with her girl friends during their lunch hours, but the experience certainly convinced me that there is a great deal more to man and his mind than the physical side of life."

Dr. Franz Hartmann came to a similar conclusion in 1884 when he visited a dentist in Colombo, Ceylon. Writing of the incident in the *Occult Review* in 1908, Dr. Hartmann states that he had hardly begun to inhale the chloroform when he found himself standing behind the armchair in which his body was reclining.

He was able to see himself and to feel exactly as he did when in a waking state. He saw everything around him and was able to hear what was being said in the dentist's office, but when he tried to touch various objects, he saw his fingers pass through them.

With this out-of-body experience serving as a primer, Dr. Hartmann was successful in separating his essential self from his physical body on numerous occasions.

"The facts convince me," Dr. Hartmann wrote, "that man has an astral body capable of existing independently of his physical body. For one who has had personal experience of this, the *a priori* denials of those who have had no personal evidence to bring forward seem so specious that one cannot admit them."

Carlotta Van Buren knew she would have a difficult delivery. The doctors had debated whether or not to take the child through caesarean section, but decided to wrestle with the breeched baby in the delivery room.

Carlotta, however, would be given only a mild pain-killer. They could not anesthetize her, because she, the mother, would have to help.

"Then the worst happened," she wrote me.

"My doctor was out of town when the labor pains began. He had planned to be back in time, but my baby wouldn't wait. And the pediatrician with whom he had discussed my case in the event that something should prevent his being there was in the midst of a difficult surgery and absolutely could not be disturbed. I am afraid the doctor summoned to assist me was not the best example of the devoted practitioner. He seemed hardly interested in the difficulty of my delivery or in alleviating any of my pain.

"When the dilation had neared completion, the birth agony was nearly driving me out of my mind. And maybe that was just what happened. I felt a strange whirling sensation, like I was a propeller on an airplane. I seemed to go faster and faster and then...pop! I was floating over the bed in the labor room looking down on my body and the nurse who sought to ease my pain.

"I was shocked to see how contorted my facial features were. At first I thought that I must have died, but then the body on the bed thrashed wildly and let out a terrible cry of pain. I was baffled. That was me down on the bed writhing in what was obviously awful agony, but it was also me up near the ceiling watching the scene below and feeling absolutely no pain at all.

"I saw the nurse measure my dilation. 'You're ready, honey!' she said. 'Now where's that doctor?'

"She left the room and I followed her. I watched her find the doctor, and I saw him scowl as if he hated to be interrupted in his conversation with one of the interns just to deliver my baby.

"Almost at once after viewing that distasteful scowl, I was back in the bed in the labor room, moaning with the terrible pain. I wished I could go back up near the ceiling again where there was no hurt.

"I did flip out of my body again during the delivery. I saw my face so pale and glistening with sweat...then the baby came and I saw that everything was all right. For the first time in what seemed like hours, I thought of my poor husband sitting in the waiting room. Just like that, I was hovering over him, watching him play a nervous game of solitaire.

"While I was watching him and wanting to tell him about the baby, I was conscious of a tugging, a pulling, and I seemed to be being dragged into some kind of tunnel with a light at the end. The next thing I knew, I had opened my eyes and a nurse was bending over me. 'Hey,' she smiled, 'where were you? Did you leave us for a while there?' I guess that I really had in a way that she couldn't imagine."

In July 1966 Mrs. Marian Walker of Plymouth, England underwent two operations. As she was coming to the morning after her second visit to the operating room, she remembers lying in bed listening to her heart, "pounding like a dynamo."

Then she felt herself slipping away. She was no longer in bed but standing at the doorway to a vast gray hall. Seated in the middle of the hall was a darkened figure dressed in long, flowing silvery robes. At first she was frightened, but then Mrs. Walker felt that if she could reach the figure she would be safe.

However, each time she tried to move forward she could feel something holding her back. She wanted to cry in despair because she desired so very much to reach the figure.

Then she felt the presence of a friend, who had died a few years before, standing near her. As soon as she saw her friend, she felt warm and comforted.

"I looked back at the figure and no longer felt this great yearning to reach it. Now I could see it was a man, and that he was smiling. I turned away. My friend had gone. I felt myself floating back, warmly and quietly. Then I knew I was going to get better."

A hospital spokesman stated that they had nearly lost Mrs. Walker because of the loss of blood and the strain on her system. Mrs. Walker herself feels that she now knows what death means. She is convinced that if she had reached the dark figure in the hall she would have been dead. When her spirit friend came along, however, she knew that she must return to her body.

"The strange thing is," Mrs. Walker said, "I wanted to stay there and not return. I know now that death is nothing to fear." (*National Enquirer*, February, 1969)

7

Astral Travel during Sleep

To primitive cultures a dream was an actual experience enacted by the soul as it wandered about during sleep. Today, we still do not know a great deal about the true mysteries of sleep and dreams but electroencephalograph records of brainwaves and the study of rapid-eye-movement patterns have convinced psychologists and dream scientists that the action of a dream (for *most* people) takes place within the individual dream machinery and is confined within the labyrinth of the brain. However, precognitive dreams that view the future, clairvoyant dreams that witness scenes of faraway places and telepathic dreams which convey information from one mind to another remain as mysteries which must be thoughtfully studied and tested.

Philosophically, you can argue that when you glimpse the Taj Mahal in a dream, you are in reality having an out-of-body experience and actually seeing the beautiful white monument. But unless you can in some way substantiate such travels of the mind, the experience remains a dream to all but the most credulous. For some who have accomplished OBE, their belief is meaningful and subjective proof that their experience was indeed genuine. Others are able to substantiate their projection with objective proof or testimony of witnesses.

R.R. of Alaska runs a butcher shop and maintains his living quarters above his place of business. One afternoon he suffered an onslaught of influenza and decided to take a couple of aspirins and go to bed for the day. He left a young employee, T.G., in charge and went upstairs to lie down.

"I had not lain there long," R.R. recalled, "when I lapsed into a kind of feverish sleep. I had taken the aspirin, but I knew that my fever was pretty high. My wife was downtown shopping, and I wished that she would hurry and get home.

"I would drift off to sleep, then wake up, then drift off again. The next thing I knew, I seemed to slide right out of my body. I thought it was some kind of weird dream, and I felt kind of nonchalant about the whole thing. I remember thinking that I could slide right through the wall if I wanted to, and sure enough, I did.

"I slipped right down to the butcher shop, and I saw T.G. eating an uncooked weiner from the meat case. This was a bad habit of his, and I had got after him many times about this.

"One of his friends was in the shop, and he asked T.G. if the boss wouldn't get sore if he knew he was eating weiners again. 'Ah, he's upstairs sleeping,' I heard T.G. reply. 'What he won't know won't hurt him.' Then he offered his friend a weiner and they both ate two or three more.

"I wished that my wife would come walking in on them and give them what-for. The moment I thought of M., I was standing beside her in an ice-cream shop. I thought, 'Oh, baby, is this how you keep on your diet? You'll come home tonight and barely eat anything, and I'll praise you for sticking to your diet.'

"It was funny how everything I saw related to food, and even though I knew I couldn't really feel anything because I was passing through walls and people, I started getting kind of nauseous. I looked at M. scooping in that sundae and I got sicker. Then I had an image of T.G. stuffing an uncooked weiner into his mouth, and I got sicker still.

"Everything started spinning around and rushing past, and I seemed to land on my bed with a thump. I got to my feet and rushed to the bathroom, and later I felt quite a bit better. My fever was still plenty high, but I walked down to the butcher shop.

" 'Before you leave tonight,' I told T.G., 'you settle up with me for those weiners that you and O.A. were eating!'

"T.G. looked startled and so did the woman whose order he was weighing. T.G. started to say something, but I beat him to it, 'What he won't know, won't hurt him, eh?'

"When T.G. heard me say those words, he looked like he wanted a hole to dive into. To this day I know he's convinced that I've got some kind of two-way mirror or some electronic snooping device hooked up between my apartment and the butcher shop.

"When M. came home and found me lying sick in bed, she immediately set about fixing me some hot broth. 'You can join me,' I told her. 'It won't hurt you to skip a big meal after that big chocolate sundae you had downtown at K's.'

"I told my wife all about the experience, but I am certain she believed that one of my friends saw her shopping and tattled on her for eating the big sundae. But I know these experiences were real, and I feel I received proof enough to convince me that I wasn't just dreaming. Somehow, I was really there."

An associate of mine showed me a letter from a correspondent who was a prisoner in a state penitentiary in the Southwest. In the letter the convict told how, after acquiring some literature on the subject of astral projection, he had become proficient in projecting his consciousness.

Quite the opposite of Ed Morrell, the tortured prisoner who experienced out-of-body travel only in the throes of intense pain (see chapter 4), this convict projected best when lying on his cot in a state of general well-being. At that time, when conditions were just right for attaining a projection, the convict would slip out of his physical envelope and pass through walls as if they were nonexistent.

In the letter I read, the prisoner stated that he had been projecting himself about the city, then began to drift back toward the penitentiary. As he hovered above the guard's catwalk, he paused to watch the officer on watch march back and forth. The sober expression of one particular guard struck the prisoner as being so humorous that he began to laugh out loud. At that instant he found himself back on his bunk.

The February 1967 issue of *Fate* carried a brief article, "A Scotsman's Astral Projection," by spiritual healer Olga Worrall, which told how a Scotsman's reputation for penury resulted in an out-of-body experience during sleep.

Mrs. Worrall had left a light burning when she retired, because a neighbor had advised her that a number of houses in the neighborhood had been broken into during the night. She had been asleep for only a few hours when she saw the image of her husband, who was staying that night in another town, looking down at her.

"Put out the lights! Put out the lights!" he seemed to be saying as he lowered his face until it nearly touched her own. Mrs. Worrall acknowledged her husband's presence, clicked out the light and went back to sleep.

When her husband returned from his trip several days later, he immediately told her of the dream which had resulted in his projection. He had "dreamed" that he had entered their parlor; then, assuming she would be in bed at that late hour, he walked up the stairs to the bedroom. As he mounted the steps, he noticed the light burning in the bathroom. At this point he wondered, "Now why is she wasting money leaving the light on?"

According to Ambrose Worrall, he promptly headed for the bathroom to put out the light, but as he touched the switch, his hand went through the wall. "Startled, I went into the bedroom and began to call your name. I kept sending the thought, 'Put the light out! Put the light out!' "

The moment he heard his wife acknowledge his presence and his message, Worrall found himself back in the hotel bed.

In a fairly common type of out-of-body experience during sleep, the agent projects to a place he or she will one day visit. Mrs. W.M. of Georgia wrote me that she lay down one night to take a short nap after dinner and felt herself suddenly outside her body. Thinking it only a very realistic kind of dream, Mrs. W.M. relaxed and allowed the "dream" to carry her consciousness along through the night sky.

Suddenly she was in a hotel room.

"I knew that it was a hotel room the moment I 'landed' there," Mrs. W.M. wrote. "It just had that feel to it. I took note of the furniture, the bedspread, and I read the rules for overnight guests tacked behind the door. The room had been freshly carpeted and appeared to be very modern, but I was surprised to see that it had an old-fashioned bathtub...one of those with the legs shaped like claws gripping balls.

"I looked out the window and I could see a neon light flashing on and off to the right. It was advertising a milk product from a certain dairy.

"I was just beginning to feel a bit uneasy, like maybe all this wasn't a dream, when I felt a strange sensation along the entire length of my body, as if something were pulling at me. I imagined that I felt very much like a nail being attracted by a magnet. There was a rapid rush of images, and I was back on my couch.

"My husband and daughter were standing above me with strange smiles on their faces. They teased me about being such a sound sleeper. They had been trying to awaken me for several minutes without success.

"About a month later, my sister-in-law was involved in an automobile accident in another town, and I went to be with her, as my brother was in the service and was stationed overseas. I visited her at the hospital and I promised her that I would stay for another two or three days until she was feeling better. A nurse recommended a hotel, and when I checked into my room, I was not at all surprised to find the room of my most unusual dream. The bathtub with the funny legs, the neon sign flashing off to the right, the furnishings—all things were just as I had seen them during my peculiar after-dinner nap."

When he was called into service on September 5, 1917, Milton Watson was like so many young doughboys of World War I, but in a September 1967 edition of *Fate*, he told how his homesickness set him apart from his comrades.

On April 13, 1918, his company boarded a train for Camp Upton, New York, and prepared to sail to England. When he had been in Romsey, England, for thirteen days and still had not had any mail from home catch up with him, Watson remembers that his homesickness had reached a most painful level. It was just before his company was transferred to Southampton to sail for France that Milton Watson had the most peculiar dream of his life.

He dreamed that he left the tent in which he was quartered, went to Romsey, caught a train for Liverpool, then boarded a ship for New York. Step by step the strange dream traced the actual course which Watson would take if he were actually going home. He could see himself stowing away behind some large trunks in the hold of the ship. After the vessel docked in New York, he watched himself buy a train ticket at the Pennsylvania Station.

No one was there to meet him when he got off the train at the home depot, but he walked the quarter mile down the dirt road that took him directly to his parents' front gate.

In his dream, he lifted the noisy latch, closed the gate, walked up the front porch and opened the door. He looked around, saw that everything at home was just the way he had left it . . . then the sound of the bugle woke him up.

When he wrote to his sister to tell her of his strange dream, he received a most amazing reply: " . . .she said that my brother Perry and my nephew Charles Evans, sleeping in my old bedroom, both had hopped out of bed the night of my dream, rushed into the front room and told the family I was home. They said they had heard me open the gate and enter the house. The folks had a hard time convincing them I was not there."

According to Helen Louise Utter's article in the December 1967 edition of *Fate*, when she was growing up in Wilkes-Barre, Pennsylvania, a financial tragedy resulting from a bad investment in a mine affected many of the city's residents, including her own family.

Her sister Ann, fourteen years her senior, moved out of Wilkes-Barre when her husband and his father decided to move to Idaho to start a hotel. Helen and her parents moved to Sayre, Pennsylvania, where she married Leon Utter; but after her father died and her mother left for France, Helen began to feel the separation from Ann and her seven nieces and nephews more acutely than ever before.

Then on a night in September 1913, when she was feeling particularly lonely, she had a most unusual dream. She found herself in a strange city, walking up an alley off a main street. She saw a large barn and an old car up on blocks. A beautiful pine tree stood halfway down a path to a house. On one side of the path she saw lovely gardens of flowers; on the other, lush vegetable gardens.

She entered the house through a large enclosed porch. Helen walked into the kitchen and was shocked when she recognized Ann's Crown Vista china from England. She was in Ann's house! In all of their correspondence, Ann had never described her home. Now Helen was getting a firsthand tour via her dream.

She carefully noted the floor plan of each room, taking delight when she discovered a familiar object, such as the tea wagon, one of grandmother's paintings or the Oriental sword and hammered brass pistols which had been the gift of a Chinese student Ann had taught in New York. She looked up the staircase and knew that Ann, her husband and their seven children lay asleep in their bedrooms.

When Helen awakened, she told her dream to her husband, who convinced her that, though vivid, the experience could only have been a dream and nothing more.

A few years later Helen had her first baby, and when the child was but three months old, Leon became seriously ill. Physicians advised the Utters to move to a different climate, and Helen's sister insisted they try Idaho. On May 30, 1916, they began the train trip to Sandpoint.

When they were at last met at the station by Ann and her family, they all piled laughing and talking into their new Buick and turned off into an alley which led to their home. As they turned, Helen said to her husband: "Look! Remember my dream?" There was the large barn. "We turned and there sat the old Buick on its blocks, the pine tree, and gardens...."

She turned to her sister and told her that she had "been there before."
She went on: "I can tell you just how your house is planned and furnished,
where the pictures hang. Is the table in the breakfast room set with the pink
dishes from England?"

Helen Louise Utter states that her sister's house was precisely as she
had seen it in her vivid "dreams."

On a hot summer night in 1919, Jane Barrett (*nee* Babrowicz) was left
alone in her house in Westford while her parents attended Aunt Lucy's
funeral in Amsterdam, New York. A confident twelve-year-old, Jane
shunned her parents' offer of a babysitter.

As she lay in her bed trying to summon sleep on that torrid night,
Jane hung suspended "in that limbo between wakefulness and sleep." Then
she seemed to feel herself rising toward the ceiling. Could she be dying?

She floated through the roof, out into the summer night, "propelled
by some unknown force."

She saw a light in the distance and seemed to be moving toward it.
When she reached the light she was surprised to find herself in a room that
seemed somewhat familiar. "Among the people in the room were my Uncle
Harry, my grandmother and others I did not know, all standing around
quietly talking. Then I saw my own mother and father and I knew where I
was—at Aunt Lucy's funeral."

When her parents returned, Jane told them what she had seen. She
described the arrangement of the casket, the color of Aunt Lucy's dress, and
the style in which the deceased woman's hair had been fashioned.

"Not without some alarm, my parents confided that I was correct.
Everything had been just as I described it. In a dream I had attended Aunt
Lucy's funeral." (*Fate*, June 1908)

Perhaps the most striking out-of-body experience during sleep—and
perhaps the most convincing, because it is supported by objective
testimony—was reported in Volume VII of the *Proceedings* of the Society
for Psychical Research. It has been often quoted and many readers may be
familiar with the case, but I would be remiss if I did not include the
experience of S.R. Wilmot here.

Wilmot, a businessman from Bridgeport, Connecticut, sailed on the
City of Limerick in 1863 from Liverpool bound for New York. The vessel
ran into a stretch of very stormy weather during which no one got much
rest. Wilmot records that when they at last passed through the storm, he

took advantage of the calm to sink into sleep. Toward morning he dreamed he saw his wife, whom he had left in Connecticut, come to the door of his stateroom. She was in her nightdress and as she stepped into the room she saw Richard Tait, the other occupant of the stateroom, and hesitated.

After a moment, Mrs. Wilmot advanced to the side of her husband, stooped down and kissed him. Then, after gently caressing him for a few moments, she quietly withdrew.

Richard Tait had watched the whole proceedings with a wide-eyed stare of astonishment.

He had been startled when the form of a woman in a nightdress suddenly appeared in the doorway of their stateroom. When the shock of the impropriety of it all had subsided, Tait had at first assumed that the bold woman must be Wilmot's sister, Eliza, who was also on board ship. Perhaps some crucial errand had sent Eliza in her nightdress to their stateroom. Tait was about to become a bit more tolerant of the situation when he saw that the woman who had just stepped into the stateroom was a complete stranger to him.

Tait saw the woman hestitate when she caught sight of him, and he fully expected a word of explanation or apology from her. But she seemed to choose to ignore his presence and walked brazenly to the bedside of Wilmot and began to kiss him.

Tait was too dumbfounded to utter a word. With what kind of Casanova had he the misfortune of sharing a stateroom? Wilmot seemed an ordinary enough fellow. What strange and mysterious hold did he exert over women that would cause them to risk their reputations by a romantic visit to his stateroom?

The mysterious woman in white seemed so magnetized that she did not even mind fondling Wilmot in front of a witness. At last the woman withdrew from the stateroom.

Tait leaned over Wilmot's bunk and stared at him until he awoke.

"You're a pretty fellow," Tait told the puzzled Wilmot, staring at him fixedly. "You're a pretty fellow to have a lady come and visit you in this way!"

Wilmot pressed Tait for an explanation, which his indignant cabinmate at first decined to give. Finally, after many assurances of innocence, Tait related what he had seen while lying wide awake on his berth. Wilmot was amazed to hear that his cabinmate had seen exactly what he himself had dreamed.

Tait, however, was not satisfied with such a farfetched explanation. The next morning he confronted Miss Eliza Wilmot and asked her if she had come into her brother's stateroom the night before.

"I'm shocked that you should ask such an improper question, Mr. Tait!" Eliza stormed. "And why would you need to ask such a question? You and he share the same stateroom, so you should have known the answer to such a question before you asked it!"

"I didn't think it was you," Tait said, making a feeble apology, "but I swear that I saw some woman dressed in a white nightdress walk up to your brother's bunk and kiss and fondle him. Your brother says it was a dream of his wife, but I insist that I was wide awake and had full view of your brother and the woman on the bunk below mine. I confess to being a very puzzled man."

The moment Wilmot reached his home, his wife asked him if he had received a visit from her a week previously on Tuesday night. "It seemed to me that I visited you," she said.

Mrs. Wilmot had been very anxious about her husband's safety because of the violent sea storms, and on that most extraordinary Tuesday night she had lain awake thinking of him. As she thought of her husband being tossed about by stormy seas, it suddenly seemed to her that she had the ability to go in search of him.

Wilmot reported the experience to the Society for Psychical Research in these words: "Crossing the wide and stormy sea, she came at length to a low, black steamship, whose side she went up, and then descending into the cabin, passed through it to the stern until she came to my stateroom. 'Tell me,' she said, 'do they ever have staterooms like the one I saw, where the upper berth extends further back than the under one? A man was in the upper berth, looking right at me, and for a moment I was afraid to go in, but soon I went up the side of your berth, bent down and kissed you, and embraced you, and then went away.' "

Wilmot testified that the details his wife described as having seen on the steamship were correct in all particulars, even though she had never seen the vessel. In her own statement, Mrs. Wilmot said that she had experienced a "...very vivid sense all the day of having visited my husband; the impression was so strong that I felt unusually happy and refreshed."

The following technique is one that my wife Francie and I have employed with great success in assisting men and women to achieve projection during the sleep state. We use an altered-state relaxation procedure, coupled with a guided meditation, when we are working personally with a single subject or when we are conducting seminars and workshops consisting of several participants.

You may utilize the following exercise in several different ways. You may have a trusted friend or relative read the induction and the guided imagery to you as you lie in your bed preparing for sleep. You may memorize the steps as best you can and slowly lead yourself into an altered state of consciousness. You may prerecord your own voice on a tape cassette so that you can serve as your own guide through the process. I recommend the use of New Age music, such as any of Steven Halpern's compositions, as a strongly evocative background to your experiments.

Begin by making yourself as relaxed as possible, taking a number of deep, but comfortable breaths, then visualize the following through any of the three methods mentioned above:

You are walking toward a soft, green area of countryside—a beautiful, tranquil place.

You select a lush, grassy area on which to lie down. You place a fluffy spread on the softest area, and you nestle down into it.

You know this is a perfect place to rest, to find peace, to enjoy nature. It is, oh, so lovely, so peaceful.

It is so lovely, so peaceful.

Lie down, stretch out, take a nice, deep breath, and relax here in your grassy bed.

The sound of a nearby bubbling brook adds to the beauty of this place. The trickling water lapping over the rocks will help lull you to sleep.

Small birds whistle and sing melodiously, and they are, oh, so lovely as they flit from tree to tree, from bush to bush. The soft sounds they make are so peaceful, so relaxing.

As you lie on your back gazing upward, you notice that the sky is the clearest blue, with fluffy, white clouds spotting it now and then. Some of the clouds hang as if suspended. Some appear to be moving slowly across the arc of blue sky. It is all so peaceful, so lovely, so wonderful.

It is all so peaceful, so lovely, so wonderful. Relax, your body is gently falling asleep.

You are becoming more and more relaxed, and you find yourself breathing deeper and deeper.

A fresh, comfortable, cool breeze makes breathing so easy, and you find yourself breathing deeper and deeper.

Your taut muscles expand—then gently relax.

It is oh, so peaceful, so wonderful. The breeze carries the faint, sweet fragrances of lilacs, a spring garden with a bouquet of aromas.

Your body responds to this place with a great desire to sleep. Your breathing becomes deeper, deeper, slower, slower...

Your breathing is more measured now...you are slowly breathing, so soft...with long, deep breaths...

Your body begins to fall asleep...peacefully asleep, asleep.

But your mind will remain aware of all the beauty around you...

While your body falls gently asleep...deeper and deeper into a gentle, peaceful sleep.

The soothing, gentle warmth of an afternoon sun feels like loving, warm fingers soothingly massaging your body and helping you to sleep.

You can feel the soft, warm sun caressing, soothing the muscles in your feet.

Feel the muscles in your toes relax. The warm fingers are moving in a massaging-like motion, gently relaxing the balls of your feet, relaxing the arches, sliding over and moving into the heels of your feet...relaxing you.

The warm, relaxing, gently massaging fingers move over all the muscles of your feet, then move up your ankles, relaxing them, relaxing them.

Now the warm, relaxing, gently massaging, liquid-like fingers are relaxing the muscles of your calves, warming, soothing, relaxing all the muscles.

The liquid-like fingers move upward, relaxing the muscles of your knees, going deep into the joints...with healing, warming, soothing energy. You are, oh, so relaxed.

Continuing upward, the wonderful, gentle motion relaxes and warms the muscles of your thighs, going deep into the large muscles...and you feel them stretch out as if in a soothing sigh...as they relax.

You are so relaxed and so peaceful as the soothing warmth works so gently into the muscles of your hips, going deep into the joints, healing, warming, releasing...

You are relaxed and so peaceful as the soothing warmth moves gently into your abdomen, deep into the lowest part of your back...and the healing warmth is relaxing you, permitting your body to fall into a gentle, deep, deep sleep.

From the front of your body now, the warmth slides gently into your waist, then continues to move around your body into your spine. All the muscles of your waist relax, totally relax. You breathe deeper, deeper, and in a soothing, gentle manner, you are letting your body fall deeper and deeper asleep, asleep.

Yet the mind remains fully aware, aware of all the warmth and beauty around you.

Any sounds that you hear will not disturb you, but will serve to take you deeper and deeper into a more beautiful sleep.

Every sound that you hear will help you to drift deeper and deeper into a very peaceful sleep.

Whether it is the sound of a passing car...a closing door...a cough...the sound of someone's voice...any sound and every sound will help your body to go deeper and deeper asleep, while your mind stays aware of the sound of my voice...

And the soothing lull of the forest sounds...

The sound of my voice and the forest sounds will permit your body to go deeper and deeper asleep.

Now the soothing warmth of the sun slides up your spine and warms and relaxes every muscle of your back...massaging, gently massaging...

That same soothing, massaging warmth is now relaxing your chest, calming and relaxing every muscle, every fiber, every cell.

Every muscle, every fiber, every cell of your lower back, your upper back, and your chest is now so wonderfully, so soothingly, relaxed. All tensions in your back and your chest have been released.

You have been totally soothed and relaxed in every muscle of your body, and now that wonderful warmth moves into your shoulders, down into your arms, to the very tips of your fingers...soothing, massaging, gently relaxing every muscle, every fiber, every cell....

Your body sleeps so peacefully. Every muscle has been soothed and relaxed. Your body sleeps, while your mind remains aware...all knowing. Your body sleeps, but your mind is aware.

Now you enjoy the soothing fingers of the warm sun, warming, relaxing every muscle in your neck and moving up to your scalp.

It is oh, so wonderful, as the massaging, soothing, warm fingers relax all the muscles in the back of your neck, releasing all tensions, calming you, calming you.

And it is, oh, so wonderful as the warm, relaxing fingers gently massage the back of your scalp, the area above your ears, your temples...relaxing all muscles...releasing all tensions.

All the muscles of your scalp relax to the very top of your head as the warm, gentle fingers move lovingly over your forehead, your eyes, your cheeks, your nose...massaging and soothing your mouth...

The warmth moves deep into the jaw muscles, releasing all tension. Your jaw becomes slack, relaxed...oh, so comfortable. It is so restful to be at peace....

Your body is totally at peace...asleep. You are in a soothing, restful sleep. Yet your mind is still aware of the beauty of this garden setting.

Nothing else disturbs you...nothing bothers you. You will only enjoy the wonderful beauty of this tranquil place.

You are at peace, sleeping in this enchanted garden. Your body is going deeper and deeper asleep, yet your mind is aware...aware of the garden setting and my voice...

Aware of the garden setting and my voice...

You are so peaceful, so beautifully relaxed. You glance up into the blue, blue sky and you pick the most attractive cloud that you see. It is a rather small cloud, but is is perfectly formed.

It is a beautiful cloud with magnificent peaks of fluff on it. The cloud is exquisitely formed.

You feel deeply at peace looking upward at its fluffiness, its thick, rich fullness.

It is soft and white, and it appears to be glowing...a warm, comforting glow, as it catches rays of sunlight and shines with beautiful, prismatic colors.

As you watch the cloud, you wish that you might ride upon it, knowing that this special cloud would hold you safely in space.

If you can ride the cloud, you will be able to soar above the trees, the towns and cities, the Earth itself, and move into the heavens themselves. You can enjoy the beauty of the twinkling stars.

You can move so close to the stars, it will be as if you can reach out and touch them. As you move higher, you will be above all pollution. The air will be fresh and pure; it will be a new world, a higher dimension up there. All will be so wonderful.

The cloud appears to be growing larger and larger...larger still. You wonder if it might not fill a very large room. You notice it appears to be floating toward you. You are happy within....

Perhaps someone up there heard your wish, for the cloud is lowering itself to you. You know that you will soon be able to climb aboard.

The cloud settles down ever so lovingly on the garden ground without even pressing against the soft flowers. You know that you can now climb aboard.

You easily step over a full, puffy rim into the soft, fluffy center of the cloud. It is so comfortable on the cloud, so peaceful. And you can lie back as if you are lying down in a very comfortable reclining chair.

Your cloud is so soft, so strong, so secure.

A ray of light shines forth from the heavens and touches your strong and fluffy cloud. It causes your cloud to glow softly.

The radiance that is coming from the heavens is different from any other light you have ever experienced, for you can feel it as well as see it.

It feels strangely wonderful and it causes you to become very happy within.

You know that you have felt this sensation before. Sometime in your life it has touched your heart.

It is the warmth of love...a beautiful, touching love.

You feel so at peace, so happy, so loved, and you begin to rise...floating slowly, gently, so very safely.

You know that you are protected by love from a higher power beyond.

You begin to drift...drift and float...gently bobbing along like a cork in a pond.

As you drift...drift and float higher, you glance easily down toward the Earth. You watch the trees...the countryside...the cities and towns growing smaller and smaller until they look like tiny toys on a colorful blanket.

Now that you are drifting and floating, you know that you have the ability to travel anywhere you wish...instantly. You have but to think of the location, the destination, and you will be there...instantly.

Think of a loved one whom you have not seen for a long period of time. You know where that loved one is. Now...project yourself there...instantly.

You see that loved one now clearly before you. You see what the loved one is doing. See clearly the eyes, the nose, the hair, the face of this loved one.

Know, with complete certainty, that you are really there beside this one who means so much to you.

You cannot touch this loved one, but you can attempt to project a mental message to him or her. Do this now. Project the warmth of unconditional love...then form the message that you wish to convey.

Now that you have conveyed the message to your loved one, you are once again soaring through time and space. You know that you have the ability to travel anywhere you wish instantly.

You know that you have the ability to visit a particular geographical location...a city...a country...a forest...an ocean...anywhere.

Go there now. See the Earth below you becoming a blur as you soar through space with a speed greater than sound, faster than light. At the count of five, you will be wherever you wish to be. One...*moving faster*...two...*coming closer*...three...*closer and closer*...four... *nearly there*...five...*you are there!*

Become fully aware of this environment. Know this place. Know the climate, the atmosphere, the colors, the sounds, the smells. Understand the individual and peculiar characteristics of this place. Feel this place with your Essential Self.

You have the ability to move wherever you like in this place. Nothing will harm you. Nothing will distress you. Nothing will disturb you in any way.

You may wander here as long as you like. You may see whatever you wish to see.

When you have satisfied your wishes and your curiosities, you will return safely to your body. You will enter a deep, deep sleep...a deep, deep, normal sleep. And you will awaken completely refreshed, feeling better than you have for weeks, for months. You will awaken feeling completely refreshed at your usual time of rising.

8

Projection at the Moment of Death

Whenever a parapsychologist is asked to describe the areas of human experience that present the most favorable climate for psi phenomena, he or she is certain to include, somewhere near the top of the list, the moment of death.

Among the most common and yet universal of all psi phenomena is the "crisis apparition," that ghostly image which is seen, heard or felt when the individual represented is undergoing a crisis, especially death. It may be at the moment of death that the essential self is freed from the confines of the body and is able to soar free of time and space and, in some instances, make a last, fleeting contact with a loved one. These projections at the moment of death evince something nonphysical within us, something capable of making a mockery of accepted physical laws and even surviving physical death.

Canadian broadcast-journalist Robert Cummings and I once appeared on a show with program host Gary Kirker over CKTB radio, St. Catherines. During the call-in part of the program, a member of the audience called to share a typical crisis projection. Her voice quavered with emotion as she related the experience that had provided her with her own proof of survival.

According to her account, she had been sleeping for a few hours when she was awakened by the form of her brother standing at the foot of the bed. She woke her husband, but by the time he blinked his eyes into wakefulness the image had disappeared.

The woman insisted she saw her brother standing in their bedroom, and described in detail what his apparition was wearing. She particularly noticed that he wore a plaid shirt which she had never seen before.

No sooner had she completed her description than the phone rang and the woman was given the news: her brother had been killed. When she and her husband arrived at the morgue to identify the body, both of them were startled to see the corpse attired in the plaid shirt she had described.

The crisis apparition is as universal as death itself, and follows this pattern: A percipient, perhaps preparing for bed or going about some daily task, is suddenly and unexpectedly confronted by the image of a loved one. The apparition is clearly identified and often gives some sign of parting or affection. Within a short time after the apparition has faded from view, the percipient receives word that the loved one whose image he or she has just seen has passed from life to death.

In 1915 the *Journal* of the American Society for Psychical Research reported the case of Margaret Sargent, a certified nurse and the principal percipient.

Mrs. Sargent was caring for a young woman in Augusta, Georgia when, about eleven one evening, the patient took a decided turn for the worse. The doctor did not want to waken the patient's mother for fear of further upsetting her.

"We knew, however, that the patient ardently desired the presence of her mother," Mrs. Sargent wrote, "but since she had become unconscious, we did not think it necessary to satisfy that desire."

The doctor and nurse observed the final symptoms setting in, and they stood solemnly by the bedstead awaiting the moment of death.

Mrs. Sargent was sitting at the foot of the bed when she looked up to see ". . .a white form advancing, a robed form, although I could not see the face because it was turned in the opposite direction. The form remained for a moment by the inert physical body, then passed swiftly past the doctor and glided toward me, but always turning its face in the opposite direction."

The white-robed form passed through the wall to the room of the sick woman's mother, and as it passed the doctor struck him a smart blow on the shoulder.

Startled, the doctor turned around, saw nothing, then said to his nurse: "Something hit me on the shoulder!"

"It was the woman," Mrs. Sargent managed to explain, somehow overcoming her astonishment. "It was the woman who just passed you."

"What woman?" the doctor asked. "There's no woman in this room but that poor dying young lady on the bed. But someone just struck me. What does this mean?"

Before either of them could offer explanation of the phenomenon, the patient began to speak in a feeble voice. To their astonishment, the young woman had recovered her senses. She remained completely conscious for another 24 hours before she died with her head resting lovingly on the arm of her mother.

"It is our absolute conviction," Mrs. Sargent wrote for the *Journal,* "that, at the time when death was imminent, the soul of the young girl, who idolized her mother, left its own body for the moment to make its last adieu and then returned to its own body again. . . . One must at least admit that a *spirit* was manifested to us that night, that it was visible to me and that it signaled its presence to the doctor by striking him upon the shoulder. . . ."

In *The Phenomena of Astral Projection* by Sylvan Muldoon and Hereward Carrington, the authors use Mrs. Sargent's case to illustrate the reality of out-of-body experience. Carrington theorized that the blow the doctor received from the spirit may have been a physical act of revenge for his refusal to arouse the dying woman's mother. Again we have a case in which the agent, finding the normal sensory channels of communication blocked, has such an intense desire to contact a loved one that it sets in motion an out-of-body experience.

A case from Volume VIII of the *Proceedings* of the Society for Psychical Research offers an illustration of a man who encountered his moment of death, experienced out-of-body projection and somehow returned to continue his temporal existence.

Dr. Wiltse of Skiddy, Kansas thought he was dying and so said good-bye to his family and friends. Dr. S.M. Raynes, the attending physician, later testified that Dr. Wiltse passed four hours without pulse or perceptible heartbeat; although, Dr. Raynes stated, he may have perceived an occasional very slight gasp.

Dr. Wiltse meanwhile had regained a state of "conscious existence" and discovered that he no longer had anything in common with his body. In that new state of consciousness, he began to rock to and fro, trying to break connection with the tissues of the old cumbersome body. He seemed to ". . .feel and hear the snapping of innumerable small cords," and he began to retreat from his feet toward his head "as a rubber cord shortens."

Within a short time Dr. Wiltse "felt" himself in the head, emerging through the sutures of the skull.

"I recollect distinctly," he said later, "how I appeared to myself something like a jellyfish as regards color and form."

As he emerged from the skull, Dr. Wiltse floated up and down and laterally, like a soap bubble attached to the bowl of a pipe, until he at last broke loose from the body and fell lightly to the floor. At this point, he slowly rose and expanded to his full stature.

"I seemed to be translucent of a bluish cast, and perfectly naked." Dr. Wiltse writes.

He decided he should exit at once, and headed directly for the door. When he reached it he found himself suddenly clothed. Two of his friends stood soberly before the door and were completely oblivious of his presence. To Dr. Wiltse's surprise, he found he could pass through them and out the door.

"I never saw the street more distinctly than I saw it then," he recalled.

It was also at this time that Wiltse noticed he was attached "... by means of a small cord, like a spider's web," to the body in the house. Then, as if propelled, the doctor soared into the air and found himself surveying various locales and scenery.

He had just begun to enjoy his new freedom when he found himself on a road which had steep rocks blocking his journey. Dr. Wiltse tried to climb around them, but at that moment "a black cloud descended on me and I opened my eyes to find myself back on my sick bed."

About this time, you may be asking yourself why is it that a projection of one's essential self usually appears fully clothed rather than naked?

I have a series of letters from two individuals who are currently conducting experiments in astral projection. They refer to one session in which the agent appeared unclothed to the percipient. However, almost without exception the agent, along with any chance percipient, views his or her body as being clothed or draped in some manner. Crisis apparitions, as we have noted, are also in characteristic dress, or at least adequately covered, when they are perceived by the contacted loved one.

It is my theory that since out-of-body experience involves the essential stuff of human personality and is therefore a psi phenomenon, the projected mind may, in cases when the agent sees a "body" rather than some kind of wispy substance, "create" the clothing by exercising the same kind of mental machinery used in dreams. I think the case of Dr. Wiltse is most revealing and provides us with a good look at the mechanics of out-of-body experience.

When he first projects from the skull, Dr. Wiltse perceives himself as "something like a jellyfish as regards color and form." Then, because his mind has been conditioned on the temporal plane to think in terms of body concepts, the jellyfish expands into the full stature of a naked man.

Primitive men and women may have been content with such an appearance in their out-of-body experiences, but Dr. Wiltse, upon confronting his sober-faced friends at the door to his bedroom, suddenly finds himself clothed. A lifetime on earth and in a particular culture had conditioned the doctor not to conceive of himself going about in the nude.

I think it is quite likely that once one has made the "ultimate projection," one learns to discard temporal-plane concepts of "body" and "clothing" and becomes quite satisfied with the "shiny cloud," "bright ballon" or "something like a jellyfish" forms of one's soul or essential self. It is also worth noting that the experience terminated when the doctor confronted steep rocks which blocked his journey.

Generally speaking, there seem to be two types of environment for out-of-body experiences: (1) the environment of Earth, in which the projected personality observes people's actions and actual occurrences in faraway places, which he or she can later substantiate; and (2) the environment of other planes of existence, or dimensions of reality, in which the projected personality may encounter entities, which he or she interprets as "angels," "masters," "guides" or the "spirits" of loved ones who have passed away. The geography of these various planes or dimensions seems to be almost precisely that of the Earth, and is often (depending upon the religious views of the projector) interpreted as Heaven.

The "rocks" that halted Dr. Wiltse's advance may indeed have been rocks of another plane of existence, or may have been formed by the doctor's own mental machinery as a symbol that he was not to travel farther, but was to return to his body. Whether such solid symbolism is necessary after one has become acclimated to another plane of existence, we of course have no way of knowing. We are able to base our theories only on the testimony of those who have not yet made the "ultimate projection" when death severs the "silver cord."

H.H. Price, a former president of the British Society for Psychical Research, put forth the view that the whole point of life on earth may be to provide us with a stockpile of memories out of which we may construct an image world at the time of our death. Such a world would be a psychological world and not a physical one, even though it might seem to be a physical world to those who would experience it.

In Volume 5, Number 1 of *Tomorrow*, Price conjectures that the other world "...would be the manifestation in image form of the memories and desires of its inhabitants, including their repressed or unconscious memories and desires. It might be every bit as detailed, as vivid and as complex as this present perceptible world which we experience now. We may note that it might well contain a vivid and persistent image of one's own body. The surviving personality, according to this conception of survival, is in actual fact an immaterial entity. But if one habitually *thinks* of oneself as embodied (as one well might, at least for a considerable time), an image of one's own body might be, as it were, the persistent center of one's image world, much as the perceived physical body is the persistent center of one's perceptible world in this present life."

Not long ago a friend let me see some correspondence from a woman who wrote that her elderly mother's out-of-body experiences had helped her overcome a fear of death. The mother, a frail woman in her late seventies, had been brooding about the inevitable approach of death and had become increasingly morbid in her attitude toward life. Then, one day, upon awakening from a brief nap, the aged woman's outlook had completely changed.

"Mother said that she had seen herself step out of her body and walk about in her bedroom," the woman wrote. "In this state, she was able to see the forms of her husband, a son who had been killed in the service, her parents and many of her old friends. They all seemed happy, and they told her that they were waiting there near her in order to help her 'cross over' just as painlessly as possible."

"How wonderful it is," the old woman had said to her daughter, "to know that all my dear ones still care and love and are right here around me now, just waiting to help me join them."

Whether or not the skeptic wishes to assess the experience as an old woman's dream rather than a glimpse of the world unseen, the out-of-body experience provided great comfort to the letter-writer's mother and allowed her to pass from this life in an attitude of peace and hope.

Dr. Robert Crookall, author of a classic work on out-of-body experince, *The Study and Practice of Astral Projection*, reports a case first published in the *Moscow Journal* in 1916. The subject of the OBE was a Russian who had rejected any idea of survival.

The subject remembered feeling dizzy during a stay in the hospital. He called for a doctor, then, strangely, became aware of a "certain state of division" within himself. He was conscious of himself, yet at the same time he had a feeling of indifference toward himself. It even seemed as if he had lost the capacity for feeling physical sensations.

"It seemed as if two beings were manifesting in me: one, and the main part of me, concealed somewhere deep within; the other, my body, external and less significant."

He felt the "main part" of himself being drawn somewhere with irresistible force. He felt as if he were being pulled back to an earth that was reclaiming what it had allowed him to use for a brief period. At the same time, he was filled with the conviction that his essential self would not disappear.

The entire medical staff seemed to be crowded around his bed. The "main part" of himself moved forward and saw his physical husk lying there on the bed. He tried to grasp the hand of his body, but his spirit hand went through it.

"Struck by this strange phenomenon, I wanted someone to help me understand what was happening."

He called to the doctor, but the air did not seem to transmit the sound waves of his voice. He tried in every way he could conceive of to make his presence known, but none of the medical staff seemed aware of his real self.

Had he died?

He found this inconceivable, for death meant the cessation of life, and he had not lost consciousness for even one moment. He was as aware of himself as ever. He could see, hear, move, touch, think.

Even when the doctor declared, "It is all over," the perplexed Russian refused to accept the idea of his death.

A nurse turned to an icon and asked peace for his soul. The words had scarcely been uttered when two angels apeared at his side.

"[They] picked me up by the arms...carried me right through the wall into the street. We began to ascend quickly."

He noticed certain remarkable features of life in the spirit body. Although it was dark he saw everything clearly. And he was able to perceive a much greater expanse than he would have with his ordinary vision.

On the ascent, they were suddenly surrounded by "a throng of hideous beings, evil spirits" which tried to snatch him away from the angels.

In what must have been a remarkable experience for the Russian, he found himself praying for deliverance. To the nonbeliever's astonishment there suddenly appeared a "white mist which concealed the ugly spirits."

Their ascent was halted when an intense light appeared before them and a voice thundered: "Not ready!" At once, the angels began to descend with him.

"I did not understand the real sense of the words...but soon the outlines of a city became visible...I saw the hospital...I was carried into a room completely unknown to me. In this room there stood a row of tables and on one of them, covered over, I saw my dead body. My guardian angel pointed to my body and said, 'Enter.'"

The Russian felt at first as though something were pressing close about him. He felt unpleasantly cold. A sensation of increasing tightness continued, and just before he lost consciousness he felt very sad, "as though [he] had lost something."

When he became aware of his surroundings, he was in the hospital ward. The head physician sat at his bedside, astounded by the medical miracle the staff had just witnessed.

"They failed to understand...but there is no doubt in the veracity of that which I have written—my soul temporarily left my body and thereafter returned to it."

When Larry Exline finally got a two-week vacation with pay in August 1954, his wife Juliette was overjoyed. Larry had been working so hard without relaxation, and this would give him a chance to go fishing with a friend.

On the evening of the fourth day of her husband's absence, August 29th, Mrs. Exline awakened in a cold sweat. She was certain she heard Larry's voice calling her. The voice was faint, as if it were coming from a great distance away, as if it were in pain and suffering, but it was Larry's voice.

Mrs. Exline fought back the fingers of icy terror, slid out of bed, turned on a night light and stepped into the hallway. At its far end she saw her husband:

"He was clutching at the wall, trying to stand up, and his clothes were drenched in blood."

She screamed, rushed toward him. "Don't touch me," he warned her with a sob. "I must return."

She begged him to explain: Where must he return, and why? She told him to wait, that she would call a doctor.

At that instant the telephone rang. It was a sheriff from Ely, Nevada calling to inform Mrs. Exline that her husband had been killed instantly in an automobile accident.

" 'Oh, no,' I said. 'My husband's here!' I hurried back into the hall—but Larry wasn't there. He indeed had 'gone back.' " (*Fate*, July 1969)

In the summer of 1913, Stella Rife (nee Libby) was separated from her cousin and friend, Bernice Moore. Bernice was Stella's "double cousin." Bernice's father was Stella's brother, and her mother was Stella's father's sister. The two girls had been fast companions and confidantes until the Libbys moved to Jackson, Michigan.

Three years later, on the evening of December 19, 1916, Stella and a girlfriend were home alone getting ready for an evening out with some friends. Stella had left her room and was descending the brightly lit stairway when she suddenly froze:

"Standing in the bright illumination stood my cousin Bernice. She looked terrified. I saw her clearly, yet I knew she could not be there."

Stella ran hurriedly down the stairs, brushing past the apparition and out the front door.

She did not stop until she was a block away from the house. Her girlfriend at last caught up with her, and Stella tried her best to salvage her dignity.

When they met their friends, one of the girls, who worked for the telephone company, appeared to be troubled, and asked Stella if she were aware their phone was out of order. Lansing, Michigan had been trying to call them, and when the message could not get through the operator said she would deliver the message personally since she would be seeing Stella soon.

"The message was that Bernice Moore had died suddenly that evening." (*Fate*, February 1968)

9

Masters, Teachers and Guides

It must be admitted that a discussion of masters, guides and spiritual entities is almost totally alien to Western culture since it is concerned with materialism, technological advance and scientific proof. The philosophies of the beatniks in the 1950s and the hippies in the 1960s may have brought the West a few bits and pieces of Eastern religion and some names of Oriental holy men, but for the most part such information has been presented in a manner the average person finds offensive or bizarre.

When the experienced psychical researcher hears references to the masters and to spiritual guides, he or she is immediately flooded with thoughts and theories that speak of "collective consciousness," "archetypal figures" and the universality of the patterns of psi phenomena. There are Tibetan holy men living in hidden monasteries who are rumored to possess incredible mental powers. But can these adepts possess the power to move unhindered through time and space?

And if these gurus have the ability to appear in their soul bodies at great distances from their physical bodies, how do they accomplish such a feat?

Perhaps it is the compulsion to always ask how that makes everything so difficult for the Westerner. Perhaps the Westerner would live a much fuller existence if he or she would learn to accept the facts of a situation without wondering if the situation were really possible.

Nonetheless, references to spiritual guides often seem esoteric to the average person who is steeped in Western culture, and a large number of semi-skeptics are ready to dismiss them as foolish prattle or hallucinations inspired by Tibetan and Indian lore. These cautious individuals, who may be willing to keep an open mind toward accounts of out-of-body experience, refuse to give credence to reports that mention masters, teachers and guides. They charge that such accounts smack too strongly of occultism and are a charlatan's device to prey upon the credulous.

I always recommend caution when receiving any accounts of alleged paranormal activity, and I confess that I usually regard personal confrontations with masters and guides as subjective mental mechanisms. However, throughout this book I recount repeated references to spiritual guides by people who had not the slightest knowledge of occult or esoteric literature, who were not in any way familiar with the tenets of spiritualism and who were not, before their out-of-body projection, interested in the paranormal. Entities are often referred to as "mentors," "angels," "guides" and "old guys" by those percipients who obviously did not have the requisite knowledge and vocabulary to speak of spiritual masters.

The mind travellers in this casebook have come from all social classes, educational backgrounds and cultural influences. The fact that a medical doctor in England, a schoolteacher in Idaho and a motorcyclist in Nebraska all speak of etheric guides who stood ready to assist them in out-of-body projection is discomforting. It suggests many possible explanations—one might be that OBE is a universal hallucination which occurs in stress situations and is peopled with the same hallucinatory figures whether one is in Italy or Indiana, or it may be that OBE is a very real part of the human condition and the "masters" are actual etheric entities.

In *The Phenomena of Astral Projection,* Hereward Carrington and Sylvan Muldoon record the case of Percy Cole of Melbourne, Australia, who sent them an account of his meeting spirit guides during an out-of-body projection which occured when he was having teeth extracted.

Cole wrote that before the surgery he had a dream in which he saw a nun and a doctor dressed in army uniforms. Cole, a pharmacist, thought the nun was handing him a prescription, but he could not read what it said. When he asked the doctor for clarification, the physician told him it meant he had "mitral regurgitation."

Memory of the strange dream persisted after Cole awakened, and he interpreted the appearance of the nun and doctor as a kind of warning. The pharmacist had scheduled an appointment with a dentist to have several teeth extracted, but now he decided he should have a complete physical examination before submitting to surgery.

Normally Cole would have consulted his family doctor, but on a sudden whim he went to a Dr. Bender for his examination. Dr. Bender detected a slight heart murmur, but assured Cole it was nothing to be concerned about. Cole asked the doctor if he would personally administer the anesthetic, and Dr. Bender agreed to schedule the operation whenever Cole was ready.

Three weeks later, Cole lay on the operating table while Dr. Bender administered the ether and Dr. H.N. Johnson stood by to do the tooth extractions. Cole could feel himself struggling against the anesthetic; then he let himself go.

"When I woke again," Cole wrote, "I was standing in the corner of the room, near the doorway, with two other people whom I at once recognized."

One was the nun and the other was the spirit doctor, Cole said, but this time he was not dreaming. He could see his unconscious body on the operating table, and he could see the doctor and the dentist working over him.

The nun berated him for submitting to a general anesthetic. They appeared to warn him of mitral regurgitation. Why had he chosen to ignore them? Cole pointed out that he had gone to Dr. Bender and was told that his heart was all right.

The nun explained that they had sent him to Dr. Bender because the doctor was a man of immense physical vitality, which they were drawing upon at that moment to keep him alive. Cole's regular doctor, whom he would have had administer the ether, was a fragile man of slight build.

"Your heart trouble is masked," the nun told him. They had hoped that Dr. Bender would have found it, but it was too late. They informed Cole quite frankly that they were not certain he would live through the dental surgery.

As seems to be typical of those who experience out-of-body projection, Cole said that he had ". . .no feeling of alarm, but was quite calm and detached." He could "hear" the thoughts of the doctor and the dentist before they spoke "so that the spoken word seemed like an echo."

The two medical men were chatting about real estate values as they went about their work; then Cole noticed Dr. Bender begin to look very anxiously at his body on the table. Cole had stopped breathing.

Somehow, Cole remembered, although he could not explain it, he managed to make his chest lift in his physical body. "You will have to go back now," the nun said. "We cannot help you; you must fight to go back yourself."

Cole saw on his left a bright light, while on his right there was a dark tunnel of swirling shadows with a small light at its far end. "I struggled instinctively toward it, while shadows rushed past me.... It seemed a long time before I managed to reach the light at the end...then I was physically awake again."

While he was recuperating, Cole interrogated the doctor and dentist as to the details of their conversation and the events of the surgery. Both men corroborated his experience.

Some months later Cole underwent a medical examination by a prominent specialist, who detected that the beat of his heart was masked by a portion of his lung which overlapped it. "This confirmed in part, at least, what I was told by the spirit lady when out of my body," Cole stated.

A personal account given by Mrs. Nancy B. records her continued progress in achieving out-of-body travel.

"One night last week I lay down on my bed and began to practice the exercises I have found to be of great assistance. Within a short period of time, I felt myself leave my physical body. I have projected several times now, but I never quite get over that momentary sensation of strangeness that comes when I look back on my body lying there on the bed. Perhaps when I am more experienced, there will no longer be that chill of fear that runs through my consciousness.

"On this night, I remember entering a large room that made me think at once of a splendid palace. In the middle of the room was a man sitting on a throne. He wore an aqua robe, and a jeweled turban sat atop his beautiful grey hair.

"'Welcome, my child,' he said, smiling radiantly. 'You may walk about as you wish, but do not become too enamored of this plane. It is not yet time for you to remain. You have responsibilities which must be met and obligations which must be fulfilled before it will be your time.'

"As I wandered about the palace and looked out its windows, I had the strangest feeling that I was actually in another place on this planet. At first I had thought I had projected to a higher spiritual plane, but the longer I was there, the more I became convinced that the dawning sun I saw reddening the eastern sky was of this dimension, that the stone floors beneath me were solid rather than etheric, that the morning noises I heard coming from the surrounding stone houses were those of real people. I wonder if I might not have projected to one of the secret and sacred cities of this earth."

Paul N., a college student in Oklahoma, writes that he had begun to study certain books which discussed out-of-body projection and which provided instructions whereby the reader might conduct his or her own OBE experiments.

"One night I nearly made it," he told me. "I had just begun to feel my astral body rise when I distinctly saw a man, dressed in what I would imagine a Tibetan monk would wear, appear floating above me and shout: 'You fool! Go back! You don't know what you are playing around with!'

"My astral body seemed to drop back into my physical body with a thud, and I sat up rubbing my eyes. My Tibetan monk was nowhere to be seen, and I was suddenly very nauseated, as a person sometimes gets when he jumps out of bed too fast after waking. I haven't experimented with out-of-body projection since that time."

Had the young man's subconscious fears of astral projection dramatized themselves into the image of the scolding Tibetan, or had a master from another plane actually appeared to warn the collegian that he was toying with forces he was not physically able to control?

However you view the concept of the spiritual guide in your own personal cosmology is unimportant for the effectiveness of this exercise. The idea of having a guide to look after you as you soar free of time and space is a most useful mental mechanism.

I personally am well aware of my own guide, Holeah. I have heard her voice on many physical occasions, and I have seen her complete body image on numerous out-of-body travels. Whether guides and masters are a part of your reality is beside the point in this technique, which my wife Francie and I have used with marvelous success in disspelling fear from those who, in spite of their great desire for astral travel or to be regressed to prior life experiences, cannot conquer feelings of apprehension toward the inner journey.

In this exercise you may employ the assistance of a trusted friend or relative to read it to you, you may memorize the sequence of procedure or you may prerecord the suggestions and serve as your own guide. You may use the relaxation method I described earlier if it was effective for you, or you may use the following technique.

Visualize at your feet a blanket the color of ROSE. The color of rose stimulates natural body warmth and induces sleep. It also provides one with a sense of well-being and a great feeling of being loved.

Now you see that the blanket is really a kind of auric cover, a rose-colored auric cover. Imagine that you are willing the blanketlike aura of rose to move slowly up your body. Feel it moving over your feet, relaxing them; over your legs, relaxing them; over your stomach, easing all tension; moving over your chest, your arms, your neck. Now, as you make a hood of the rose-colored auric cover, imagine that the color of rose permeates your psyche and does its part in activating your ability to travel out of the body. Once you have done this, visualize yourself bringing the rose-colored aura over your head.

The color GREEN serves as a disinfectant, a cleaner. It also influences the proper building of muscle and tissue.

Imagine that you are pulling a green, blanketlike aura over your body. Feel it moving over your feet, cleansing them; feel it moving over your legs, healing them of all pains. Feel it moving over your stomach, ridding it of all pains. Feeling it moving over your chest, your arms, your neck—cleansing them, healing them. As you make a hood of the green-colored auric cover, imagine that the color of green permeates your psyche and does its part in activating your ability to project your astral body. Once you have done this, visualize yourself bringing the green-colored aura over your head.

GOLD has been recognized as a great stengthener of the nervous system. It also aids digestion and helps you to become calm.

Visualize now that you are pulling a soft, beautiful golden aura slowly over your body. Feel it moving over your feet, calming you. Feel it moving over your legs, relaxing them. Feel it moving over your stomach, soothing any nervous condition. Feel it moving over your chest, your arms, your neck. As you make a comfortable hood of the golden aura, imagine that the color of gold permeates your psyche and strengthens your nervous system so that your body-brain network will serve to better project your essential self. Once you have done this, visualize yourself bringing the GOLD-colored aura over your head.

Researchers have discovered that RED-ORANGE strengthens and cleanses the lungs. In our modern society with its problems of pollution, our lungs become fouled whether we smoke cigarettes or not. Yogis and other masters have long known that effective meditation, effective altered states of consciousness, can best be achieved through proper techniques of breathing through clean lungs.

Visualize before you a red-orange cloud of pure oxygen. Take a comfortably deep breath and visualize some of that red-orange cloud moving into your lungs. Imagine it travelling through your lungs, cleansing them, purifying them, bearing away particles of impurities.

Now visualize yourself exhaling that red-orange cloud of oxygen from your lungs. See how soiled with impurities it is. See how darkly colored it is.

Take another comfortably deep breath. See again the red-orange cloud purifying your lungs of the negative effects of exhaust fumes, smoke, industrial gases. Exhale the impurities, then breathe again of the purifying, cleansing red-orange cloud.

YELLOW-ORANGE will aid oxygen in moving into every organ and gland of your body, purifying them, cleansing them. Imagine before you now a yellow-orange cloud moving through your body. Feel it cleansing and purifying every organ. Feel it cleansing and purifying every gland. If you have *any* area of weakness or disease *anywhere* in your body, feel the yellow-orange energy bathing it in cleansing, healing vibrations.

As you exhale all impurities and inhale again the pure, clean yellow-orange cloud of oxygen, visualize the cleansing and healing process throughout your body. As you exhale and inhale, see your body becoming pure and clean. See now that the cloud that you exhale is as clean and as pure as that which is being inhaled. You have cleansed and purified your lungs. You have cleansed, purified and healed all of your body and all of its organs.

The color of VIOLET serves as an excellent muscle relaxant. Violet is a tranquilizer. It is a color of the highest vibration.

Imagine that you are pulling a violet, blanketlike aura over your body. Feel it moving over your feet, relaxing them. Feel it moving over your legs, relaxing them, soothing them. Feel it moving over your stomach, removing all tensions. Feel it moving over your chest, your arms, your neck—tranquilizing them, relaxing them. Now, as you fashion a hood of the violet-colored auric cover, imagine that the color of violet permeates your psyche and does its part in activating your ability to use your psychic powers. Feel the color violet attuning your psyche to the highest vibration. Feel the color violet connecting your psyche to the God-Energy. Once you have done this, visualize yourself bringing the violet-colored aura over your head.

BLUE is the color of psychic ability, the color which increases visionary potential.

Visualize a blue blanketlike aura beginning to move over your body. Feel it moving over your legs, soothing them. Feel it moving over your stomach, your chest, your arms, your neck—soothing them, relaxing them. As you make a hood of the blue-colored auric cover, imagine that the color of blue permeates your psyche and does its part in activating your ability to meet the spiritual guide who can most completely assist you in achieving the most important out-of-body experiences. Once you have done this, visualize yourself bringing the blue-colored aura over your head.

You are now lying or sitting there totally wrapped in your blue-colored auric cover. You are very secure, very comfortable, very relaxed. Your mind is very receptive, very aware. You feel attuned with a Higher Consciousness. You feel as though your awareness has been expanded. You feel prepared to explore deep, deep within you, deep, deep within you....

Fully secured in the color of blue, going deep, deep within, you are now becoming aware of a presence. You are becoming aware of a presence that is approaching you in a violet-colored aura flecked with gold. You know that violet is the highest spiritual vibration, the God-Energy, and you are completely filled with the feeling of unconditional love. You know that within that violet-colored aura is one who loves you completely, totally, unconditionally.

As this energy approaches you, you feel your essential self being transported to a very special place that is beyond time and space. This will be a place that is especially important to you on the soul level. It may be a crystal city of other worldly beauty. It may be a majestic temple high in the mountains. It may be a peaceful, contemplative garden. It may be a restful forest clearing at the edge of a bubbling brook. It will be wherever you most wish it to be.

And now that you are in your special place, your very special place of spiritual power, you are becoming more and more aware of the presence within the glowing, violet-colored aura. You are sensing the presence of an intelligence that you have felt around you ever since you were a child.

Now that violet light begins to swirl into form and substance. You see the shape of a body...a face...a beautiful smile. And look at those eyes. Feel the love, the unconditional love flowing out to you from those eyes. And now, standing there before you, you see your guide.

Your guide's eyes are filled with love; and a firm, but reassuring, hand stretches forth to take your own hand. Feel the love flowing through you. Feel the love from one who has always loved you...just as you are.

You know that you will be able to soar through time and space and to explore other worlds, other universes, safely under the protection of your guide. You will be able to travel anywhere you wish in your astral body, your essential self, secure in the aura of your guide.

You may now travel anywhere you desire, knowing that you will always be protected and returned safely to your physical body. Go now...wherever you wish. You know that you will awaken naturally when your journey is completed.

10

Conscious Out-of-Body Projections

T.T., a dairy farmer from Wisconsin, began to achieve out-of-body projections as a young boy.

"It started when I was just a kid," he writes. "Maybe we'd be putting up hay, and I'd sneak a little nap after the noon meal. I'd start to get a numb feeling in my toes that would spread up my legs and pretty soon all over my whole body. It's really funny it didn't scare me the first time it happened, because I've always been pretty concerned about my health.

"But I still remember lying there that first time, getting that numb feeling all over; and pretty soon there was a little crackling noise and another *me* was standing outside of my body. I didn't really know what had happened that first time, but I caught on pretty soon, and I've been slipping in and out of my body for many, many years now. I know that these experiences have not been hallucinations, because I've been able to check out lots of things."

In this chapter we will take a brief look at some of those people who have had a number of conscious out-of-body experiences. Many of these individuals, such as our Wisconsin dairyman, could qualify for the chapter on the "old pros," but the majority of people who have such conscious projections do not make a regular practice of popping in and out of the body. Emotional stress and psychic need seem to play as large a role in these experiences as they do in the cases of spontaneous and unconscious OBE.

The June 1963 issue of *Prediction* translated an episode from G.W. Surya's reminiscences of World War I.

Surya related how a German soldier, who could voluntarily project his astral body, was able to use OBE to spy on the divisional headquarters of the nearest French unit. When the soldier returned to his physical body, he reported to his officer that the French had scheduled an attack on their sector for eleven o'clock on the following night.

The German officer was understandably skeptical of such intelligence, and when the soldier revealed his source of information the officer's eyes bugged out in rage.

"But he really does have this gift," a number of the soldier's friends testified. "He really can leave his body and see things. It is a wonderful gift from God."

The German officer arched a skeptical eyebrow. "Then prove it to me," he challenged.

"But sir," the soldier protested, "I have just returned from the French headquarters with valuable information, and you will not believe me. How might I convince you?"

"Very simple," the officer replied. "You will project yourself to an area we can check—our own headquarters. It is several kilometers away from us, and we have absolutely no natural way of knowing what is going on there. We have a telephone with which to contact headquarters, of course, but we cannot see what is going on there."

"This is true," agreed one of the young soldier's friends. "If you can project yourself to our headquarters and describe what is going on there, our officer can check the information by telephone. Go ahead," he urged, "Prove it to him!"

The young solider lay down in the dark bunker that had been dug into the earth of the trench. While the officer watched, the soldier seemed to lapse into a deep sleep. When he stirred some minutes later, he awakened with a broad smile on his lips.

"An Austrian general has just arrived at our headquarters," he said. "He relayed an order, and here is what he said..."

"Not so fast," the officer said, trying to take notes as the soldier recited the general's order word for word. As soon as he had copied the message and a description of the Austrian general, the officer telephoned headquarters and asked them to substantiate what the young soldier had just told him.

The officer was unable to complete the message before excited voices were shouting at him over the telephone:

"How could he possibly know the order, the officers at headquarters had just moments before received from a general?"

What leak had there been in the security? What explanation did the officer have for all of this? The astonished officer told headquarters everything. "And now listen carefully," he said. "Our ghostly spy has also been dropping in over at the French headquarters. He says that they plan an attack on our sector for eleven o'clock tomorrow night. We must receive reinforcements if we are to hold!"

Evidently the convincing demonstration was not enough for the skeptical officers at German headquarters, for G.W. Surya tells us that the trench was taken that next night by the French at eleven o'clock.

After the publication of *The Projection of the Astral Body* in which Sylvan Muldoon provides lengthy directions by which the reader might attempt to produce OBE, the author received numerous testimonials from individuals who had been successful in carrying out his instructions. In *The Phenomena of Astral Projection*, Muldoon and Hereward Carrington published a letter from Mrs. E.C. Connelly of Herne Hill, London, who relates her experience in achieving OBE.

Mrs. Connelly writes that each night after retiring she would lie and concentrate upon the instructions Muldoon relayed in his book. She had begun to ask herself if she would ever be able to accomplish astral projection, but she resolved not to allow herself to become too anxious.

"**Then one night about 12:30** P.M.," she writes, "I heard a voice distinctly say: 'Now—you are ready—go ahead.'" At this point Mrs. Connelly states that she went out "...consciously, right from the head, rising upwards, then over my body...I looked down and I could see it plainly...Then turning, I started to travel through space at a high rate of speed...."

Mrs. Connelly writes that she was directed to her mother's house, and after spending some time there, the thought occurred to her: "How shall I go back?" No sooner had the question arisen when Mrs. Connelly "... slipped right back into my body, as a letter slips into an envelope." After a "strange" sensation, the woman lay wide awake, satisfied that she had accomplished what she had set out to do.

One of the most famous cases of producing a "ghost" on demand is to be found in the casebook *Phantasms of the Living* (1886), authored by Edmund Gurney, Frederic W.H. Myers and Frank Podmore, who gleaned this account and numerous others from the early records of the Society for Psychical Research.

On a Sunday evening in November of 1881, Miss L.S. Verity and her younger sister had retired in the front bedroom of their home at 22 Hogarth Road, Kensington, England. Miss Verity slept fitfully, and after only a few hours she found herself wide awake.

Her first reaction upon seeing the form of a man standing in the bedroom was that she was dreaming. But as she continued to look at the approaching figure, she realized that she was very much awake and that the intruder was her fiance, Mr. S.H. Beard.

Miss Verity began to scream at the outrage, and her screams awakened her sister. When the younger girl saw Mr. Beard standing beside their bed, she too began to scream.

At the sudden chorus of screams, the image of S.H. Beard began to fade.

After he had vanished completely, Miss Verity was filled with a terrible sense of foreboding. Perhaps something dreadful had happened to her fiance, and she had just been sent a portent.

Three days later, much to Miss Verity's relief, Beard called on her. He sat in silence while she told him the entire incident, then he confessed that he had willed the occurrence.

On that Sunday evening he had been reading a book that told of the great power the human will is capable of exercising. Setting the book down, Beard resolved with the whole force of his being that he would be present in spirit in the front bedroom of the second floor of the house at 22 Hogarth Road.

Beard's first experiment had been the result of a sudden decision to test the limits of the human will. He was quite as astonished as Miss Verity that he had been able to project his spirit to her bedroom. Psychical researcher Edmund Gurney became interested in the case, and he spent a great deal of time interviewing both the agent and the two percipients.

According to Miss Verity, there had been nothing ethereal or ghostly about the apparition of Beard. The form had appeared to be quite solid until it had begun to dissolve before their eyes.

"I woke my sister by screaming," she told Gurney, "and she saw the apparition herself. . . . It was some time before I could recover from the shock I had received, and the remembrance is too vivid to be ever erased from my memory."

Under Gurney's cross-examination, Miss Verity's sister substantiated all that she had told the researcher and her fiance. Gurney was convinced that the incident had not been a hoax, but he expressed the investigator's regret that he had not been in on the experiment.

"Let me know the next time you decide to do any testing," he asked Beard.

Whether he interpreted Gurney's request as a challenge or whether Beard would have tried again on his own is a moot question at this point. It is recorded in the annals of psychical research that the determined S.H. Beard again projected his astral self to the home of his fiancee. He tried twice on the same evening, each time falling into what he later termed a "Mesmeric sleep."

Unlike the majority of mind travellers in our casebook, S.H. Beard was never certain of the success of his projections until he heard from somebody at the Verity household. On the evening of his second experiment in directing the force of the will, Beard was seen twice in the house at 22 Hogarth Road.

Miss Verity was spared the shock of seeing her fiance materialize in her bedroom on this occasion. On each of his projections that evening, Beard was seen by Miss Verity's older married sister whom he had met only once, two years before. The sister was able to recognize Beard each time he appeared before her and subsequently faded away. No doubt she was impressed that she was about to acquire a most singular brother-in-law.

During his second projection that evening, Beard stood next to the woman's bed and bent over to stroke her long hair. Before the self-induced phantom had faded, he had taken her hand into his own. For some reason, the woman told Gurney, she was not frightened or nervous, but strangely excited by the remarkable episode.

On March 22, 1884, Gurney received a short note from Beard advising him that he would attempt another projection that same night. Once again, Beard wrote, his target would be the home of his fiancee.

Later, in a letter to Gurney dated April 3rd, 1884, Miss Verity testified:

"On Saturday night, March 22nd, 1884, at about midnight, I had a distinct impression that Mr. S.H. Beard was present in my room, and I distinctly saw him whilst I was quite widely awake. He came toward me, and stroked my hair. I *voluntarily* gave him this information when he called to see me on Wednesday, April 2nd, telling him the time and the circumstances of the apparition, without any suggestion on his part. The appearance in my room was most vivid and quite unmistakable."

After this projection, Miss Verity's nerves were so shaken that she was temporarily placed under a doctor's care. It is not known whether or not Beard attempted additional experiments, but it is quite reasonable to assume that he did not continue to use his fiancee as his target.

As you may have assumed, the method provided for sleep/dream projection in chapter 7 may easily be adapted to a conscious, or deliberate, out-of-body experience. I would like to share with you, however, an exercise that I have found marvelously effective in achieving profound projections for both men and women.

This is a guided meditation that makes use of a very special sound effect, that of the Peruvian whistling vessels. According to some theorists, the ancient inhabitants of the great mountain cities of Peru had perfected out-of-body travel by use of a sound technique achieved by blowing across the mouths of these unique vessels. Recordings of these actual instruments have been made and may be utilized in your own experiment [Write to Halpern Sounds, 775 Old Country Road #9, Belmont, California 94002 for further information], or you may simulate the vessels by prerecording the sound of your blowing lightly across bottle tops or into a flute, whistle or some similar wind instrument. In the latter case, of course, you would have to increase the suggestion in the meditation that one is truly hearing the Peruvian vessels. I must also state that if your powers of mental imagery are sharp enough, you may only have to suggest that you hear the vessels and not have to bother with any supplementary sound devices.

In any event, use either of the techniques of relaxation already provided and follow the instructions indicated in the exercises detailed in chapters 7 and 9. When you have reached a deep level of consciousness, utilize the following meditation for projection of the essential self.

You are seeing memory patterns before you. They may be your memories of a past life experience. They may be the memories of another. It does not matter. You are seeing them form before you now.

The memories are taking you to a faraway place, a faraway time on the vibration of the Eternal Now. You are seeing blue, blue sky. Mountains. A city made of stone. A large city made of stone high in the mountains. An inner awareness tells you that you are in Peru, ancient Peru. You are remembering the Andes, the Andes Mountains. You are remembering the ancient Incan city of Machu Pichu.

You are remembering that you were a student there, a very special student of a very special teacher—a priest, a master—who dressed in a magnificent robe fashioned of the colorful feathers of a hundred different jungle birds.

This priest, this master-teacher, has made you his prize pupil. You, more than any of the other initiates, have responded perfectly to the sound of the wondrous whistling vessels. When the master-teacher and other priests blow across the tops of these magic vessels, you are able to leave your body. When the master-teacher blows across the top of these vessels, hand-crafted and baked in a kiln, you soar free of your physical limitations. You soar high above the Andes. You soar free of time and space. You can go anywhere you wish—instantly. You have but to think it...and you will be there.

You are proud that you have become your master's special student. You are proud that of all the students in this great city of the Incas, you are the one who has been selected for the great demonstration.

And even now you are walking through the streets of the city, surrounded by the other students. It is night. There is a full moon. You are walking to a place in the mountains where you will give the demonstration. Look around you. Remember the faces of those nearest you. Remember the faces of those standing in the streets watching you. Remember the houses, the city walls.

Now you are approaching the area of the demonstration. It is a grassy place ringed by great rocks. You see your master-teacher, the High Priest is already there. He stands on one of the highest rocks, his robe of many feathers blowing gently in a mountain breeze. In each hand he holds a whistling vessel. On either side of him stands a priest. Each of the priests holds a whistling vessel.

Twelve students step forward from the crowd and form a circle around a blanket that has been spread on the grass. You step into the circle, advance to the blanket. You take a deep breath and lie down on the blanket. You look up at the full moon. A small cloud moves across its face. You lie quietly for a few moments, then raise an arm to signal that you are ready.

You lie down there on the blanket, on your back, looking up at the full moon. You are calm. You are relaxed. You know that when you hear the sound of the whistling vessel, you will soar free of your body. Your essential self, the REAL YOU that exists within, will burst free of the limitations of the physical body and shoot up toward the sky, toward the moon.

The High Priest, your master-teacher, lifts a vessel to his lips...and blows....

You feel yourself rushing, pushing, pulsating, spinning...bursting free of the body!

You, the REAL YOU, soars toward the moon. Down below you can see the students, the priests, your master-teacher. But your universe is only you and the sound, the sound of the whistling vessels.

Go with the sound. Go wherever you wish. You have but to think it and you will be there...INSTANTLY.

Think of a loved one...a loved one who is far away. You have but to think of that loved one and you will be there...INSTANTLY. You will be beside that loved one INSTANTLY.

Think of a place—a city, a forest, a desert, an ocean—anywhere. Think of that place, and you will be there. INSTANTLY.

THE SOUND TAKES YOU THERE. The sound takes you there. Go with the sound. Go with the sound!

11

Doppelgangers and Human Doubles

"This may sound crazy to you," a girl attending a southern university wrote, "but one night when I was studying, I looked up to see a mirror image of myself seated on my bed. I let out a little cry of surprise and the other 'me' smiled, crinkled up its nose, and after about six or seven seconds, disappeared."

The startled girl was having the uncommon, but hardly unknown, experience of seeing her double. The Germans call the human double a "doppelganger," but the phenomenon is technically termed autoscopy. By whatever name one chooses to call it, the experience of coming face to face with one's etheric double can be quite unsettling.

Guy de Maupassant once complained to a friend that whenever he returned to his home, he saw his double sitting in his armchair. The writer died in an institution for the insane, which poses the question of whether emotional disturbance caused him to hallucinate the double, or whether the constant reappearance of the double drove de Maupassant insane.

Writers certainly have no monopoly on doppelgangers, but the famous German poet and novelist Goethe had the remarkable experience of meeting himself as he rode away from a visit with his friend Frederika at Strassburg. His phantom wore an outfit—pike grey with gold lace—which the poet had never seen before. Eight years later, as Goethe was on the same road going to visit Frederika, it occurred to him that he was dressed precisely as his double had been on that earlier occasion.

In 1929, psychical researcher Sir Oliver Lodge received a letter from the Archbishop Frederic, who, on January 14th, had experienced a most singular evening. The clergyman had returned to his home feeling extremely tired, sat down in a favorite easy chair, and immediately began to doze.

"I was sharply aroused," he wrote in the letter, "in about a quarter of an hour (as I perceived by the clock). As I woke I saw an apparition, luminous, vaporous, wonderfully real, of myself, looking interestedly and delightedly at myself. Some books lying on a table back of my ghost I could see and identify.

"After I and myself had looked at each other for the space of about five seconds, my ghostly self vanished for a few seconds, only to return in a more definitely clear way...."

The phenomenon of viewing one's double must in some way be closely related to the projection of the astral self. Some researchers have observed that the doppelganger appears under the same physiological circumstances that seem to precipitate the projection of the astral body—fever, illness, extreme fatigue, headache and emotional distress.

In the April 1966 issue of *Fate*, Dr. Edward Podolsky presented a number of cases in which highly reputable people reported autoscopic hallucinations.

Mr. Harold C. of Chicago, Illinois, had a severe headache when he returned home after a hard day at the office. As he sat down to dinner, he saw an exact replica of himself sitting opposite him. As if it were a mirror image, the double repeated every movement Harold C. made during the course of the meal. Dr. Podolsky reports that since that time Mr. C. has seen his double on a number of occasions—each time after a migraine attack.

Mr. Samuel V. of Kansas City, Missouri, saw his double on Saturday afternoon as he was doing some gardening chores in his backyard. The double duplicated his every movement and was visible for about two hours.

When Mrs. Jeanie P. was applying make-up one evening, she saw an exact double of herself also touching up her features. The curious Mrs. P. reached out to touch the double, and the image reached out to touch her. Mrs. P. told Dr. Podolsky that she had actually felt her face being touched by the mirror image.

Dr. Podolsky presents two theories to account for such cases of autoscopy. One hypothesis holds that the phenomenon is due to some irritating process in the brain, particularly of the parieto-temporal-occipital area (the visual area). The other hypothesis, a psychological one, sees autoscopy as the projection of memory pictures:

"Certain pictures are stored in the memory and when conditions of stress or other unusual psychological situations arise, these memories may be projected outside the body as very real images."

But then there are cases in which a percipient witnesses the doubles of others. Who is doing the projecting in such instances, and how far can such animated mental marionettes carry on rigorous activity independent of their memory source?

Another question is relevant: How can it be memory dredged out of the past when the doubles are enacting a scene from the future?

When someone examines such a case as the following experience of Reverend W. Mountford, he or she must conclude that psychological and physiological explanations for autoscopy, while they may certainly be applicable in some instances, just do not satisfy the demands that must be made on any hypothesis about this enigma. You cannot put this phenomenon in a neat little pigeonhole.

Reverend Mountford of Boston was visiting some friends in Norfolk, when he happened to look out a window which faced the road. "I believe that looks like your brother and his wife coming," he said to his host.

"Yes," the man agreed. "And he's got old Dobbin out again. That horse is made of real stuff. He's barely limping after that bad accident he suffered."

Reverend Mountford later reported to psychical investigators that the two people in the buggy, Mr. and Mrs. Robert Coe, were clearly seen by all in the house. But to everyone's surprise, the two remained in their buggy, stared straight ahead, passed by the house, turned the corner and disappeared.

"Now that was strange," Reverend Mountford's friend said, reflectively scratching his chin. "Why wouldn't Bob pull in and visit? It's not like him at all to pass right by the house without stopping. And it's certainly not like either of them to just sit there without at least waving a hello. I think something's wrong."

The man had no sooner expressed these sentiments than his niece entered the house. The young lady was pale and excited.

"Oh, Aunt!" she explained, "I have had such a terrible fright. Father and Mother just passed me on the road and neither of them said a word to me. They just sat there and stared straight ahead and wouldn't pay the slightest attention to me. When I left home just fifteen minutes ago, they were both sitting by the fireplace."

While everyone in the house was theorizing about the reasons for the Coes' strange behavior, Reverend Mountford happened to glance out the same window and was amazed to see Mr. and Mrs. Robert Coe approaching the house in their buggy. Old Dobbin pulled them stalwartly with the same slight limp, and everything was precisely as it had been the first time—with one important difference. This time the Coes' stopped their buggy and went into the house to visit.

The man and woman were totally oblivious of the consternation they had caused their kin. They were emphatic in their statement that they had left their home only ten minutes before and had driven old Dobbin directly around the corner just minutes before Reverend Mountford saw them off in the distance, again approaching the house from the same direction in which they had just come. The confused witnesses to the strange occurrence could only conclude that they had somehow been given a preview of the Coes' arrival.

The vardogr of the Norwegians is also a type of spiritual forerunner that announces the arrival of its "owner." In my book *True Ghost Stories* (Para Research 1982), I wrote of my own experiences with the vardogr, and I refer the reader to that book for a more extensive treatment of the phenomenon. Because this noisy human double fits into our area of discussion in this book, I will quote Wiers Jensen, who, as editor of the *Norwegian Journal of Psychical Research*, wrote a series of articles on the vardogr as early as 1917:

"The vardogr reports are all alike. With little variation, the same type of happening occurs: The possessor of the vardogr *announces* his arrival. His steps are heard on the staircase. He is heard to unlock the outside door, kick off his overshoes, put his walking stick in place. . . . The listening 'percipients'—if they are not so accustomed to the prelude of the vardogr that they remain sitting quietly—open the door to find the entry empty. The vardogr has, as usual, played a trick on them. Eight or ten minutes later, the whole performance is repeated—but now the reality and the man arrive."

As a rule, the vardogr announces itself only by imitating sounds made by inanimate objects. There have been instances, however, wherein the vardogr has materialized into an exact likeness of its possessor. In these instances, the spiritual forerunner has truly tricked the percipients, who may have been anxiously awaiting the arrival of the individual whose form the dextrous vardogr so cleverly duplicated and whose actions it so expertly mocked.

Harry Hoffbower told of his deliberate projection of a doppelganger in the June 1968 issue of *Fate*. Hoffbower defines the doppelganger as being related to astral projection "...but unlike the astral body, the doppelganger is embodied, is solid to the touch, and is capable of performing tasks."

Hoffbower shares with his reader an interesting bit of his family background. It seems that he had an ancestor who achieved a great reputation as a witch because of her ability to travel outside her body. Because the woman had acquired this knowledge from a Cherokee medicine woman and because the totem of the Cherokee is the wren, local superstition soon had the woman flitting about in the form of a bird.

Humans must always create myths to explain what they cannot understand, and such a legend was the only way the residents of the Virginia village could explain how the witch woman could know so many things about so many people and be able to tell them about events in faraway places long before word had reached the village.

When Hoffbower was a boy, his family moved to Florida. it was here that he learned of "the Furneau boy," who was said to have the ability to send his shape out walking over the swamps. Hoffbower learned that Furneau was a brilliant college student who had a bent for the mystical.

With an admission of envy for the student, who could be heard in his room at his studies and seen walking about in the swamps at the same time, Hoffbower had a sudden inspiration. He headed for the college library and looked up the word "doppelganger." This eventually led him to the parapsychology section. He knew he was on the right track when he found Furneau's signature on many of the cards inside the books.

Hoffbower checked out the same books, and at last, in an obscure volume, he found an account by a man who claimed to have achieved out-of-body projection. Hoffbower studied the man's formula until the night when he felt he was ready to attempt a projection.

To his astonishment he seemed to burst free of his physical body and found himself above a bright blue sea and what looked like the city of Athens as it might have appeared two thousand years ago. He mingled with the people, smelled the exotic herbs, spices and perfumes, saw the Parthenon as it looked when it was new.

Hoffbower learned that he could travel wherever he willed, but he soon tired of romantic places and decided to drop in on his beloved grandmother, who lived in West Virginia. Thinking himself invisible, Hoffbower moved freely through his grandmother's home. Then he noticed the old lady's dog cringing in front of him.

His grandmother awakened, turned on her bed lamp, and cried: "Darling! Is it you? How did you get in? Is anything wrong?"

Hoffbower suffered a moment of terror, then blackness, and he awoke to find his mother dabbing at his face with a damp cloth. His parents took him severely to task for such an experiment. His mother worried that he had "found the way" of her ancestors and asked God to have mercy on his soul.

His father, however, scoffed at talk of witchcraft and concluded that if young Harry had got the information for out-of-body travel from a book, then anyone could practice such techniques if they had a mind to do so.

To his mother's promptings, which sought to learn what he had seen, Hoffbower said only that it had all been a flight of imagination. Then came the airmail letter from Grandmother: "I knew that if there had been an accident I would have been notified by telephone . . . but I thought I woke up and you were standing by the bed and the dog was taking on something terrible. I sat up and turned on the light and spoke, but you just looked at me and went into the other room. I just don't understand it. The light was on, and I got up to follow you but you were not there. I checked the doors and they all were locked . . . I thought you had died and had come to let me know. . . ."

Later his grandmother worked the truth out of him, and Hoffbower confessed that he had deliberately produced the doppelganger. He was surprised that her attitude was one of relief. She had feared that her mind was going.

Although she did not encourage any further experiments, she did tell him that a doppelganger could be used for good. Her great-uncle had once found a lost child by projecting his double. The search parties had given up hope of finding the lad, but Great-uncle's doppelganger had led the boy back to safety.

12

Teleportation and Bilocation

Of the two phenomena, teleportation and bilocation, bilocation—being in two places at once—is more closely allied to astral projection than teleportation—the actual transport of the body from one place to another. We know that teleportation has occurred throughout history from the myths and legends of earliest times to the well-documented and authenticated reports of today. In centuries past, men have been "taken up by the Lord" and carried from one geographical location to another; children, found in the most incredible places, have explained that "fairies" flew away with them; reports of modern poltergeists have shown instances in which infants have been transported from the nursery to other rooms, ostensibly through the walls.

The early date of the following case will cause some readers to doubt its authenticity, but be assured that the incident was thoroughly checked and substantiated by church officials.

In the bright sunshine of an October day in 1593, a strange soldier suddenly appeared among the sentries on guard at the Plaza Mayor in front of the palace in Mexico City. The befuddled soldier looked dazed and stared around as if in a dream. He was dressed in the uniform of a guard for the Governor's Palace in the capital of the Philippines.

When challenged, he answered: "My name is Gil Perez. I was ordered this morning to guard the doors of the Governor's Palace in Manila. I know very well that this is not the Governor's Palace and this is certainly not Manila. Why or how that may be, I know not. But here I am, and this is a palace of some kind, so I am doing my duty as nearly as possible."

When Perez was told he was in Mexico City, thousands of miles from Manila, he could not believe it. The Holy Office quickly jailed him as an agent of the devil, but they could not shake his testimony.

Two months later a galleon arrived from the Philippines. On board was an important government official, who at once recognized Perez as a palace guard and testified to having seen the soldier just before he embarked for Mexico. The Holy Office judged Perez to be an innocent victim of the devil, rather than a co-worker, and allowed him to return by ship to the Philippines.

On June 23, 1871 a seance was conducted at 61 Lamb's Conduit Street, High Holburn, London, by two famous mediums, Herne and Williams. During the seance another experiment in human teleportation was attempted and successfully accomplished.

On that Saturday evening, Herne and Williams, who had been in partnership since January of that year, commenced a seance, having in the orthodox manner, locked doors, a darkened room, clasped hands and earnest entreaties to the spirit world. The spirit guides who materialized from "the other side" were John and Katie King, a ghostly father and daughter, who often have been chronicled in the annals of spiritualism and the records of psychical researchers.

On that particular evening the lively Katie insisted that she wished to apport (materialize) something other than the standard fare of crucifixes, rings and semiprecious stones. Her spectral father cautioned her against such an extensive exercise of her ectoplasmic powers, but Katie insisted on having her way.

"Why not bring Mrs. Guppy?" laughed a Mr. Harrison, who was sitting in the seance circle that evening. The lighthearted suggestion brought a chuckle from the other members of the circle. Mrs. Guppy, a well-known London medium, was a woman of prodigious girth and weight.

"I will do it!" Katie said, accepting the challenge. "I will bring Mrs. Guppy!"

"Oh, come now,"spoke up a member of the circle, "you mustn't do that. You might do harm to the poor woman."

"I will do it!" the phantom said resolutely.

The unsuspecting Mrs. Guppy was seated by her fireplace, entering household accounts in a book. At the other side of the fire sat her friend, Miss Neyland, reading a newspaper.

The two women were chatting briskly when, in the midst of a remark, Mrs. Guppy seemed to give a short cough. Miss Neyland looked up from her newspaper to note with amazement that her friend had vanished. There was only a slight mist where Mrs. Guppy had been seated, working at her books.

Those sitting in the spirit circle that night later testified that no more than three minutes had elapsed between Katie's ghostly announcement and the heavy thud heard in the center of the table.

"There's a dress here," Mr. Edwards said excitedly. "I have my hand on a dress."

Someone struck a match and the confused Mrs. Guppy was seen standing in the center of the table, a pen and account book in her hands. her right hand, which held the pen, shaded her eyes, as if she were trying to shut out conscious knowledge of what had happened to her. She seemed unaware of the members of the seance circle, and did not respond to their questions.

The spirit voice of John King instructed the sitters to leave the woman in peace for a few moments. "She'll soon be all right," the phantom assured them.

The circle sat in silence for about four minutes; then Mrs. Guppy moved for the first time and emitted a high-pitched, sobbing wail of distress. As if in a rush of consciousness, she became aware of the presence of the sitters and the fact that she was attired in only a flimsy housecoat.

"I'm not at all dressed to go out," she complained. "I don't even have my shoes on!"

Mrs. Guppy's complaint had scarcely been uttered when her slippers fell from the ceiling. A bonnet was quick to follow, along with her boots, some articles of dress and, for good measure, four of her potted geraniums.

Such a remarkable achievement of human teleportation caused an understandable stir in both the popular and the spiritualistic press. Daily newspapers exploited the fantastic feat for all the sensationalism they could get out of it, and Mrs. Guppy's strange teleportation at once became the center of a controversy that rages to this day.

In his book on the phenomenon of teleportation, *Mind Over Space*, Dr. Nandor Fodor speculates that "...in a vestigial form, an electromagnetic power is hidden in the organism of the adult body. This is the only power that could accomplish the stupendous feat of human transportation. It needs the condition of trance or ecstasy for its literation, presumably because these states are the nearest parallels to the physiological and psychological status of the unborn. When the power is freed, it counteracts gravitation as in levitation, or affects space as in transportation. Sometimes this effect on space may be due to a blind discharge of fetal energies, at other times the power may well up in answer to tremendous unconscious needs."

If, as Fodor theorizes, a state of trance or ecstasy is prerequisite for teleportation, it should also be so for bilocation—the phenomenon in which a person is seen in two places at the same time. As the researcher investigates this particular manifestation of the human psyche, he or she finds that bilocation seems to occur most often to saints and spiritual leaders.

In 1774 while in prison at Arezzo, Italy, Alfonso de Liguori awoke one morning and proclaimed to his jailers that he had been at the bedside of the dying Pope Clement XIV.

The man was laughed at, and his declaration was attributed to a self-imposed fast. Subsequent investigation, however, produced testimony by those who had been present at the Pope's bedside that they had seen Alfonso de Liguori standing among them.

Another well-known incident concerns St. Anthony of Padua who was seen to kneel in his stall in church. While engaged in silent prayer, St. Anthony was also seen at the same time in another church taking part in the service there.

As many as 500 acts of bilocation are attributed to Sister Maria Coronel de Agreda, who was born in 1602. She began to have religious ecstasies when she was eighteen. During one series of bilocations, Sister Maria found herself in Mexico ministering to an Indian tribe. In another part of Mexico, as Indians began arriving at their settlement, a band of Franciscan monks were amazed to hear their reports of having been directed there by a mysterious woman who appeared out of nowhere. When one of the converts happened to spy a portrait of a Franciscan nun, he told the monks that the mysterious lady wore identical clothing.

In 1630 Father Alonzo de Benevides returned to Spain. Father Benavides, who was in charge of a mission in Mexico, told his superiors of the Indians who had been directed to seek baptism by a woman wearing the habit of a Franciscan nun. He further said that he and other clergymen in the New World were at a complete loss either to explain the circumstances of the woman's appearances or to know her identity. Father Benavides was then told to travel to Agreda to visit Sister Maria. As tradition has it, he did so, and was satisfied that Sister Maria, who seldom left her cell, and the Indians' mysterious lady were one and the same person.

Writer John Otto wrote in the August, 1966 issue of *Fate* of his teleportation from Niagara Falls to his home in Chicago.

Separated from his family for several weeks on business, Otto decided that a telephone call to his wife might help dispel his loneliness. As it happened, however, the sound of her voice only intensified the sense of being alone. So as he lay in bed, Otto began to visualize a trip home. As the mystics advise, he visualized every detail of the trip, step by step, omitting nothing. He visualized every step of the journey he had driven so many times in the course of his business from Niagara Falls to Chicago.

Then he stood before the entrance to his apartment building on the north side of Chicago. He entered and was puzzled to note that his son was not in bed. His reflection in the bedroom mirror startled him and he observed that the lights from the road cast his shadow over the bed where his wife and daughter lay sleeping.

Otto touched his wife; she reacted instantly. He sensed her fear and, filled with a desire not to frighten her, found himself back in his room in Niagara Falls.

Although he thought of the experience many times and spent many hours contemplating its significance, Otto did not discuss it with his wife until several months later when the two were at a party.

One of the guests was extremely interested in psychism and had, by coincidence, been doing some research on teleportation. Encouraged by the discussion, Otto told his story, but added that he had no way to validate his experience. It was at that point that his wife spoke up.

"Why didn't you tell me you had done that?" she demanded. "You scared me half to death. Why did you punch me so hard on the chest?"

Otto protested that he merely meant to touch her very lightly, to wake her.

Mrs. Otto told the guests that her husband had appeared as a solid form, not as a ghostlike, wispy image. She said she heard him enter the door whistling a tune. The footsteps sounded familiar, but she knew it could not be her husband, since he had just called her from Niagara Falls.

She decided to lie still. The next thing she knew she was punched sharply in the chest. When she sat upright, she found herself looking into her husband's eyes, just inches away.

Why had she been frightened, Otto wondered.

"One reads about people seeing a vision of someone," she told him. "Later they hear that someone has had an accident or something. I thought something had happened to you!"

Otto wanted to know why their son was not in his bed. Mrs. Otto explained the boy had spent the night at a friend's house.

"Could I have cast a shadow if I were not there *physically*? Otto asks, as he speculates about the reality of an experience in which a human body can be transported 500 miles in one instant, and return the next.

"I will always wonder," Otto concluded, "what would have happened if I had spoken softly to my wife instead of touching her. Would she have been frightened? Could we have conversed? Last but not least, will I have another opportunity to find answers to these questions?"

13

Encounters with Spirits of the Dead

We have already noted certain instances in which those who have experienced out-of-body travel have reported encountering spirits of deceased friends, relatives or people known to be dead. Such astral meetings seem to occur quite often during OBE and, depending on one's personal philosophy, may either substantiate the validity of spiritual travel or demonstrate that such experiences are founded in wishful thinking and inner longings and desires.

Because OBE is a part of the subjective personal experiences of certain individuals, tangible proof of such spirit encounters cannot be presented to the skeptic. Once again, all that can be done is to present these personal testimonies and suggest that the reader "weigh and consider."

Dr. T. has had a number of projection experiences, and although he is not a spiritualist, he has come to feel that he does have a spirit guide who aids him in getting in and out of the body. Dr. T. is convinced that he has travelled to another plane of existence wherein the deceased of this earthly plane continue to exist in much the same manner as they did in life.

"I have talked with loved ones, and I have met spirits of individuals whom I did not know in life. In many instances I have recorded their names and former addresses immediately upon returning to my body, and subsequent investigations have determined the reality of their lives here on earth.

"It is my belief that, upon death, one simply passes into another dimension, which coexists with our own."

In the fall of 1976 Carl V., a motorcycle enthusiast, went into a bad slide on some loose gravel and was knocked unconscious.

"I seemed to be spinning like a crazy top," he remembers, "and then this kind-looking old guy seemed to reach out and slow me down.

" 'Oh, God,' I said. 'I must be dead, and you must be Death himself.'

"He smiled at me and kind of squeezed my arm in a fatherly way. 'I'm not Death,' he said. 'You won't meet him for a while yet.'

"He told me that it was possible to leave your body and then go back to it. He told me to look down, and I could see my body—I mean my physical body—all scrunched up in the ditch. A car came along and some guys stopped and got out to look at me. One of them knelt and turned me over.

" 'Hey,' I yelled, 'careful! Don't you know you aren't supposed to move the body of an accident victim? You could be grinding my broken bones or driving splinters into my organs.'

"The old guy just smiled at me as if I was some little kid, and that's when I got the idea that he was Grandad A., who died when I was six or seven. I'm sure that's who it was. I remember him from some old pictures. I was about to ask him when I saw one of the guys in the ditch pull a flask from his pocket and shove it between my lips. The next thing I knew I was choking and sputtering on some cheap Scotch."

An interesting case was passed on to me recently in which a nurse was able to substantiate the projection claim and alleged spirit contact of a young patient.

Mrs. Helen C. was assisting a doctor in the pediatrics section of a county hospital. A seven-year-old girl had developed complications following a relatively minor operation and her fever had shot up during the night. About three o'clock in the morning, the girl seemed to lapse into a comatose state and Nurse C. spent some very anxious moments in the company of the girl's mother and doctor.

Day was just dawning when the girl's fever began to drop, and her eyes flickered open. She called for water, and Nurse C. placed a straw between her parched lips.

"You gave us a bit of scare, young lady," her doctor scolded in mock gruffness. "Are you going to be good now so your mommy can get some sleep?"

"You didn't have to worry," the girl told them. "I was in the garden with the other boys and girls."

"In the garden, eh?" the doctor asked, winking at Nurse C. and the girl's mother. "It must have been a bit chilly, wasn't it? December is no time to be playing in a garden."

"Oh, it was nice and sunny," the girl said, "and all the flowers and bushes were so pretty. The other boys and girls stay there all the time, but Alice said that I would have to go back."

Nurse C. wanted to know more about Alice. "She wore pigtails with yellow ribbons and her hair was black," the girl said. "And she said to tell you to give your mother a kiss from her and to let you know your daddy was all right."

Nurse C. was stunned. She had had a sister named Alice who had died of influenza when she was seven years old. She had often tied her black pigtails with yellow ribbons. In addition, her father had passed away just three months before this experience.

Was the girl's vision compounded of telepathy and a beautiful dream of a garden where happy children play, or did she travel to another dimension where she met the spirit of another little girl who had many years before made the final projection?

L.W., a lawyer, insists that he is not a spiritualist and that he had never really thought much about an afterlife. Late one night while he was doing research for a particularly difficult case, he happened to glance up and see what at first appeared to be a shimmering light in the corner of his office.

As he directed his full attention to the strange light, he was astonished to see it take the form of his deceased sister.

"I know I was wide awake," he said, "but suddenly it felt as if I were being pulled out of my body...as if my very soul were being drawn out through the top of my skull.

"My sister reached out her hand to me, and suddenly I was at her side, clasping that hand I had so often held in life. I looked back toward the desk and saw my physical body sitting bent over a book. My eyes were open, but I seemed to be staring at the book as if I were in a trance.

"I began to feel frightened. I did not know how such things could be. My spirit body seemed to spin and everything went black.

"When I regained consciousness, I was resting my head on my arms folded across the top of the desk. I attributed the whole episode—which couldn't have lasted more than fifteen or twenty seconds—to having dozed off for a bit. But the episode troubled me enough to do some reading on the subject, and now I'm not so certain that it was some kind of dream."

As might be suspected, mediums, and those who profess spiritualism, commonly encounter the spirits of the deceased during both deliberate and spontaneous out-of-body projections. One would immediately discount such testimony on the grounds that a professed spiritualist has been conditioned to expect to see those who have already "crossed over," if it were not for the spontaneous out-of-body experiences of those completely unsympathetic to these doctrines who have made the same claims.

For many mediums, astral projection is an integral part of living. Many have told me that they have practiced it since early childhood. Some have maintained that such projections served as a method whereby they received instruction from their spirit guides.

"I used to project nearly every night when I was a girl," one medium told me.

"At first two spirit guides would come to me and lift me from my physical body, but soon I was able to slip out of the body without their assistance.

"As soon as I was out of the body, I would receive instruction from spirit teachers. I suppose you could say it was like going to night school. During the day, I went to junior high school. At night, while my physical body slept, my astral body was taken up to a higher plane to attend a spirit school.

"Was such double schooling tiring? On the contrary, I used to awaken in the morning feeling completely refreshed.

"No, the spirits do not come for me in this manner any more. Now, of course, I have developed my abilities so that I am aware of my guides' presence, and often I can see them without the aid of astral projection."

Another medium told me that once when he was ill, he regularly had projected himself out of his body.

"I had been able to do astral projection since I was just a boy, so when I had that terrible period of sickness—I guess I was about forty—I made good use of my convalescence.

"I remember one time one of the nurses said I must have some kind of sleeping sickness, I slept so much of the time. I wonder what she would have said if I had told her that I had been in Paris that afternoon?

"Yes, that may sound a bit far-fetched to someone who can't project himself astrally, but I was able to prove it to a lot of my friends.

"They would come to visit me in the hospital, and I would tell them various things they had done that day. Sometimes really private little things that I just couldn't even have guessed. You know, things that would even embarrass them sometimes.

"Yes, I often met the spirits of friends who had passed on. Once you have learned how to do astral projection it soon becomes natural to be able to travel up to the planes where the spirits are. When the time comes to make the final projection, someone who has been doing astral travel already knows his way around. There is not that period of adjustment that most people have to go through when they leave their physical bodies behind in death."

It would seem, then, that the reason one might encounter the spirits of the dead in the course of an astral projection would be to receive counsel, guidance and redirection to the physical body.

According to some, when the time comes for the "final projection" spirit friends will be standing by to aid one in leaving the body and to calm the individual in the first moments of surprise.

A medium on the West Coast told me of a time when she had to aid the recent dead in making the adjustment that must take place before one can accept his etheric condition.

"Two young men had just been killed in a terrible accident near our home," she told me. "Not long after the accident, I could sense their presence around me. I projected myself out of the body and I could see them clearly.

"They were moving about wildly, in a state of panic. I tried to calm them and explain what had happened to them. I told them that they must accept what had taken place.

"But their thoughts were filled with earthly desires and frustrations. They were still of this earth plane, and I figure that that was why I could see no spirit guides.

"I feel that the spirits of these two young men had been directed to me, because the guides, in their wisdom, had known that these young men would not yet accept guidance from spirits.

"I talked to them, but they would not listen for the longest time. They did not want to leave the earth plane. Their girl friends would be waiting for them. They had plans for their lives on earth and they felt cheated to have their lives cut short. They truly were what is referred to as 'earth-bound spirits.' They did not feel the peace that comes to most souls when they leave our earth plane.

"At last I must have calmed them enough for the spirit guides to remove them to another plane, for suddenly they began to be pulled straight up.

"Such action on the part of the guides startled the two young men, and they emitted terrible screams of fear. There would still be much work for the spirit guides to accomplish, but at least I had aided them in their transference.

"When I projected myself back into my body, I became aware that my front room was filled with neighbors. I lay on my couch and one of my closest friends was bending over me and rubbing my wrists.

"They had all heard the terrible screams of the young men and had come to see if anything was wrong. I was amazed that they had been able to hear the screams, but I told them that I had just dozed off, and I tried to blame the screams on the television set, which had been left on in my front room. I don't know how many of my neighbors accepted this explanation, but they could certainly see that I was all alone in my little house."

After a person has been investigating and researching psychic phenomena, he or she seriously begins to wonder if you are ever really "alone." Even though these experiences are, for the most part, subjective in nature, you are struck time and time again by the universal pattern of OBE.

We would like to believe that somewhere there exists a physical law to explain OBE, ESP and all gradations of psi phenomena, but it would seem that such a law has not yet been included in the standard physics textbook.

14

The Old Pros

Oliver Fox's first published accounts of his astral projection appeared in the *Occult Review* in 1920. These, according to psychical researcher Hereward Carrington, were the first detailed, first-hand reports of a series of conscious and voluntarily controlled astral projections.

As with so many gifted with paranormal abilities, Oliver Fox was plagued with long bouts of illness during childhood. When he was as young as seven or eight, he began to have what he termed "the dream of the double." In these dreams he saw a double image of a dear one, usually his mother.

Young Oliver also suffered through a kind of nightmare which he called the "extension dream." In such dreams he experienced a strange sense of union with the inevitability and eternal nature of things.

Fox began astral projection when he was in school, and, although exhilarated by the wonderful sense of freedom, he morbidly imagined that he would one day perish by premature burial, heart failure or insanity if he continued.

It was in the summer of 1905 that a first romance really set Fox on the course that would lead him through many astral adventures.

Oliver's sweetheart, Elsie, learned of his "wicked" experiments and warned that God would be extremely angry if Fox were to persist in such studies. Fox told her she was a simple-minded young girl and could not possibly understand the true meaning of astral projection. He was surprised to see Elsie bristle at this pronouncement. She told him she would project herself to his room that very evening.

Fox laughed rudely at the girl. It was obvious to him that she knew no more about occultism than he knew about needlework. Nevertheless, she appeared to him that night in the middle of a "large egg-shaped cloud of intensely brilliant bluish-white light...her hair loose, and in her nightdress."

Elsie vanished at the sound of Oliver's voice, and the following evening the two young people met and compared notes. Elsie was able to describe his room in complete detail and list all the objects in it. She had never been in his home, Fox tells us, and they had no friend in common who might have been there and served as Elsie's source of information.

During that same summer Oliver returned the geture by appearing at Elsie's bed one morning when she woke up. He seemed so real and solid that the startled young woman thought he had, like Romeo, entered her open window.

Elsie could hear her brother whistling in the hall and her mother coming up the stairs to see if she were out of bed. The girl knew they would take a dim view of the eager lover in her bedroom. Then, just as her mother's hand rattled the doorknob, Oliver vanished.

Fox tells us that during these early experiments he often had the frightening experience of feeling solid hands grip and squeeze him until he gasped for breath. Once, his trance broken, he returned to his body and caught sight of a misty white shape dissolving at his bedside. On another occasion he encountered an entity that appeared as a conical mass of glistening "snow." The being had no features, but it did have two large blue eyes.

Fox also gives us a repertoire of the sounds of out-of-body travel. He describes "...crackling sounds suggesting electrical phenomena; roaring and whirring noises as of gigantic machines; a peculiar snapping sound...and sometimes voices calling."

Fox concedes that certain sounds might have been caused by variations in blood pressure, but he does not feel that all of them can be explained that way.

During a projection experience in 1913, Fox found himself in a woman's bedroom as she sat before her mirror. As the attractive woman studied her features in the mirror above her dressing table, Fox, standing behind her, noted that he was completely invisible.

Then, solely in the interest of experimentation, Fox assured his readers, he reached out to touch the woman. He distinctly felt the softness of her velvet dress, and "...then she gave a violent start—so violent that I in my turn was startled, too. Instantly my body drew me back and I was awake, my condition being immediately normal...."

In *Astral Projection: A Record of Out-of-Body Experiences,* Fox defended his action. Since he was invisible, he thought the woman would be unable to sense his touch. Since then, however, he has discovered that though he may be invisible to the people he encounters in his projections, they have responded readily to being touched.

As projection becomes more common, he says "...this question of one's right to intrude, even in an unseen body, upon the privacy of another person will have to receive serious consideration."

Fox was unable to see the "silver cord" that certain other projectors have described. However, he did state that he had often struggled against the pull of it, even though he had never been able to perceive it visually.

According to the experiences of Oliver Fox, there are two methods of producing out-of-body travel, the way of dreams and the way of self-induced trance.

The way of dreams is described as a more pleasant and less dangerous method, but, since it requires manipulating certain rare kinds of dreams, the experiences which result are never quite as vivid as the self-induced trance.

To achieve projection through self-induced trance, Fox recommends that the neophyte assume a comfortable position and then concentrate on an "imaginary trap door within his brain." Beathing should be deep and rhythmical, Fox instructs; eyes should be closed but rolled upward and slightly squinting.

Soon the student will feel a slight numbness that starts in the feet and travels up the legs until it eventually spreads all over the student's body. A muscular rigidity sets in, along with a mounting pressure in the head. The student will soon achieve the effect of "being able to see through closed eyelids, and the room will appear to be illuminated by a pale, golden radiance."

At this point Fox warns against the appearance of apparitions and terrifying sounds. One should ignore apparitions and be especially resistent to illusions that seek to interrupt the student and break the trance.

"And now the student will be experiencing the very peculiar sensation of having *two* bodies; the painful physical one and, imprisoned within it, a fluidic body."

The next step must be that of the student seeking to force his or her subtle body through the imaginary trap door in the brain by a supreme effort of will.

If the student is successful, Fox writes, "he will have the extraordinary sensation of passing through the door in his brain and hearing it *click* behind him." The student will be able to rise out of bed and walk away from the entranced physical body. The student will be able to walk through walls and travel through space at tremendous speed. The student will lose the sense of time almost completely.

"As to his powers of locomotion, he can walk, glide, levitate.... In short, he can behave as an ordinary man, if it pleases him, or as a superman as far as the astral currents will permit. If the experiment is terminated involuntarily, he will just flash home and find himself within his body almost instantly.... If the return is voluntary—accomplished by walking home or willing himself back—the approach to the body should be quite gentle...."

In *Practical Astral Projection,* a pseudonymous French author, Yram, tells how, in the astral body, he once embraced his physical body and discovered it to be warm and without muscular rigidity. Yram was able to observe the "silver cord" and wrote that it was his belief that the cord could be stretched indefinitely.

Yram's advice to the neophyte mind traveller is to experiment between four and five o'clock in the morning after a few hours' sleep. At this time there is less influence from the subconscious, and it is easier for the astral body to escape the confines of the physical body.

Sylvan Muldoon, mentioned often in this book, writes in *The Projection of the Astral Body* that he had his first out-of-body experience at the age of twelve.

Muldoon explicitly describes how to achieve astral projection, and theorizes about a "crypto-conscious" or super-conscious mind which is responsible for out-of-body experience. He believes this mind is influenced by the subconscious and is capable of accepting suggestions from the conscious mind. Therefore, Muldoon tells the student, certain principles practiced habitually can produce projection and out-of-body travel.

Muldoon describes a normal projection as one in which the astral body moves upward for several feet above the physical body, then moves into a vertical position and lands on the floor. There, due to the action of the silver cord (which, unlike Fox, Muldoon always sees), the astral body sways back and forth before it comes out of a trancelike state and is set free.

The late John Pendragon, a leading British seer and clairvoyant, believed that humans have a physical body, a spiritual body (or soul), an astral body and an etheric body.

"The physical body I liken to a base from which the others operate," the clairvoyant told me. "I would not say that they permeate each other, since each can act independently of the other.

"The astral body can travel of its own accord while man is asleep and can visit places and return. In this way a man may be able to describe scenes and conditions in parts of the world where his physical body has never been.

"The etheric body is one through which contacts are received on the channels that supply us with guidance, both spiritual and inspirational. This is the body that receives our impressions, refreshes our memory of the past, directs our emotions and is the center of our spiritual awareness.

"It is from the etheric body that the radiations known as the auric colors build up around the physical body and enable those who are psychically sensitive to see what the state of this realm of being denotes. It is exceptionally helpful in health diagnoses and in all psychological aspects of the person. It is also the most important adjunct to the earthly body, as it is the reservoir from which the mind draws much of its material. Again, let me state that it is the physical body which houses these other vehicles."

Pendragon is not alone in adding the "etheric body" to the strata of our being. Occultists' psychic dissection usually includes the etheric body, a strip of glowing ether; the astral body, which surrounds the etheric body and is more or less egg-shaped; the etheric double, which radiates positive and negative lines of force; and the physical body, which temporarily houses the more subtle bodies.

The terminology matters little. The out-of-body experiences the occultists describe are essentially the same as those reported by all who have undergone an OBE.

While I was collaborating with John Pendragon on various projects, the extraordinarily talented clairvoyant demonstrated his prowess at astral traveling on numerous occasions. Projecting himself over 3,000 miles to our home, he witnessed minor domestic tragedies, overheard conversations and perceived potential hazards. Upon his return he would immediately send me a letter detailing what he had seen and heard on a particular day. The postmark proved his experience at a particular time, and he was always thorough about dating the OBE and describing as many incidents and personalities as possible.

Pendragon, himself, felt that astral projection and long-distance clairvoyance are very closely allied, and well they might be. At this point all I can say is that whichever he was doing it seemed to work.

Pendragon protested that he had no technique to explain, and even though he could project himself easily and could see so much in various parts of the world, he could not always tell where he was, nor could he prove each instance. When I persisted in knowing a little of the "how" of his ability to project, he explained his out-of-body projections to my home. "I simply write your name on a note pad and put my finger on it. In a few seconds, I'm there."

For a more detailed description of the English seer's *modus operandi*, I shall quote two out-of-body experiences from his journals:

"Astral journeys are a common occurrence for me. A sort of free-wheeling process goes on. I get to places without any conscious volition.

"Not long ago I was seated reading a newspaper when, while idly glancing at the sports page, I saw a picture of a footballer unknown to me. Almost instantly I found myself projected into a back kitchen of a dingy little house where a young girl was pinning the same photograph of the athletic hero on the wall with some rosettes. In front of the fire sat a middle-aged woman preparing vegetables. I could see all the details of the room.

"Presently Father came in and washed himself at the sink. Then a young man entered, presumably the girl's brother. He said he had forgotten his cigarettes and asked his sister to fetch him some.

"By effort of will, I followed her out of the house to a dingy little shop at the top of this dingy little street. I saw the details of the iside of the shop and all the surroundings.

"The girl left the shop and spoke with a neighbor, and I knew all that was being said. Then I followed her home again.

"Tiring of the tableau, I concentrated on homebase and pulled my etheric body back to my easy chair. Where I had been and whom I had seen, I had not the faintest idea. . . ."

"One night a friend called at my room and we got to reminiscing about our school days.

" 'I wonder what became of old Franklin?' my friend wondered. 'He wanted so much to become an actor.'

" 'Yes, ' I nodded. 'Let's see if he made it.'

"I wrote Franklin's name on a scrap of paper and put my finger on it.

"There were a few seconds of blurred motion before I found myself on the top deck of bus. Seated in front of me was a man of my own age, whom I suddenly realized was 'old Franklin.' His ginger hair of youth was almost grey, but I recognized him.

"I was terribly upset to see that Franklin was enveloped in gloom.

"I wondered where I was, and by effort of will, I 'floated' out of the bus and looked at the destination board of the bus. I could not recognize any of the names, but I had the distinct impression that I was in a suburb of Birmingham, England.

"I willed myself back into the bus again, and presently Franklin got off, and I followed.

"Franklin went over to a theater that was empty. He unlocked a door and entered. All was dreary, and Franklin felt very miserable. Some sort of important project had failed. He went into an office and began packing some items in a case, quite oblivious to my etheric presence.

"After snapping the case closed, Franklin quit the place and boarded another bus.

"Once again, I sat next to him, but he never knew I was there. After a bit he alighted and I followed him home to his wife and two children.

"There he told her that all was over, and that he must have another try. It was obvious that something very big had gone 'bust' for old Franklin.

"I willed myself back to my room and my waiting friend, who had scarcely had time to smoke half a cigarette as he sat watching over my physical body. After I felt myself fully 'returned,' I told him what I had seen. We both hoped that 'old Franklin' would come out of his doldrums and attain the success he had so long been seeking."

A dear friend of mine is a businesswoman in a large southern city. She goes about her workaday tasks with the utmost practicality, and is quick to apply down-to-earth solutions to her career problems. Millie is also an accomplished mind traveller. None of her business associates are aware of her mystical bent, and I am certain that even her husband does not suspect that she practices out-of-body projection about as regularly as she drives to the supermarket.

One noon, while one of my children and I chatted over lunch, we were interrupted by the ring of the telephone. It was Millie, and, although she had discussed some of her experiences with me through private correspondence, I must confess to surprise when she repeated the gist of the conversation my child and I had just had a few moments before her call.

"Now do you believe I can do astral projection?" She laughed at my stunned silence.

On another occasion, when we had had some electrical wiring done and had installed some fire alarms, Millie called that evening to report that she had observed the electricians at work in our home. "It was about time you had that bathroom switch rewired," she said. "On one of my last trips up to your country, I was certain I could smell smoke coming from it!"

I know a publisher of several popular magazines who has been engaging in private out-of-body experiments for the past twenty years.

On numerous occasions he has witnessed tragic scenes on his astral flights, which he recorded the moment he returned to his physical body. Once he has written his account of the incident, he dates it and seals it in an envelope and gives it to a friend to hold. When the tragedy is reported in the newspapers, he has the previously written account to substantiate his experience.

In one instance during World War II, this man viewed a major sea battle and later recorded the name of the ships destroyed. He gave his report to a skeptical editor to hold until he asked that it be opened in the presence of witnesses.

Because of wartime security, a period of several weeks passed before the loss of the U.S. battleships was made public. The publisher gathered members of his staff around the desk of the editor and asked him to open the sealed envelope. The date and the names of the sunken war vessels, which the publisher had listed, coincided exactly with newspaper accounts.

The editor still was not convinced, however. He accused the publisher of a trick ". . .a mental trick like Dunninger does."

If this man were to set down his many experiments on paper, I am certain the volume would rival the accounts of Oliver Fox and Sylvan Muldoon in terms of variety of experience and graphic detail of out-of-body experience. When I last visited him he was conducting a series of experiments in which he invaded the dreams of certain staff members, planted suggestions, then received confirmation of the experiment's success when they passed on the key word or performed the key bit of action the next day.

For obvious reasons this gentleman requests anonymity, but perhaps someday I will corner him with my notepad and tape recorder and come away with accounts of several remarkable experiments in controlled OBE.

The late Paul Twitchell, who re-introduced the ancient spiritual science of Eckankar to the modern world, allowed me to see certain items of his correspondence with two "old pros." They achieved varying degrees of proficiency in OBE before they began to practice the methods of soul travel that he taught in Eckankar.

One elderly gentleman wrote that he had been practicing out-of-body projection since 1905.

"Some years ago I lived in a hotel where I had a place to practice certain techniques, but I could spare very little time because I was working then. The technique I used is quite simple, but a terrible strain on the eyes until you get some distance into the work for which it is designed.

"You need total darkness, a mirror, and a five-watt light. On your forehead, in the center, you place an orange-colored disc. You look at this disc for five minutes without winking, and this is to be practiced every night until you can do this.

"You increase your sitting to six minutes, then seven minutes, and so on, only when you have succeeded in making the previous time. Once while doing this, the wall suddenly disappeared and I found myself in a backyard garden. One thing was certain, it was no garden in the area of the hotel, but I was in the garden and back in my room at the same time!"

Here are excerpts from the letters of a very articulate young man who Paul Twitchell said "had it made" as far as soul travel is concerned.

"Once, while lying down, I began noting and discounting the various forms of consciousness—such as consciousness of body, consciousness of thought, feeling, senses—using this process of elimination to see what finally was left and what I could make of it. Suddenly I felt something like a force throughout me, and it seemed as if my mind was pulled forward into the vastness in front of my eyes. Then, out of the vastness, I could sense and visualize that very vastness flowing into forms, that is, forms suddenly coming into being out of nothing. Then there was a sense of oneness between me and yourself, which then took on the sense of oneness between me and what you might call everything.

"After that, my thought processes were exposed. That is, I saw thought in pre-thought form. This immediately seemed to be a flow of knowing above thought. I'd merely sense a question and almost immediately the answer of knowing would flow. This, then, broke down into what I am now calling a display of the primary function of mind: mind structure, perception, and, upon perception, the mind restructured itself and this restructuring was feeling and knowing. . . .

"At another time, I located the Real Self, that is, in the 'back of the head, observing.' I sense that this Real Self is what I am calling the 'control factor' and that there should be a shift of my 'identity' to this in due time. At the moment, when I am observing the Real Self, I am aware of a curious thing. First I note that I, the Real Self, am 'observing' the play of the sense, etc. Then, 'I' am literally watching the Real Self and then I wonder who or what is 'watching' the Real Self. There seems to be a multiple phenomenon going on that could be expressed as watching the observer observing the observer observing yet another observer, and so on, in a series.

"I have had the daring thought that as the consciousness moves along this series, the series is an ascendant one, and the consciousness ascends also until finally reaching God-consciousness.

"I am finding much better awareness and control when working from the soul plane. My practice now is to begin observing each of the bodies and work up to the soul plane. Each time I do this they are much easier to discern. Of course, I then attempt to see how they interrelate, and I find that a very subtle shift of identity is taking place. I am less body, personality . . . and more Real Self.

"I am now using God-realm postulates I hadn't used before . . . since my mind responds that way, I go ahead and use it. I figure that this will begin sensitizing me to those higher vibrations.

"My most recent development: Consciousness does not seem necessarily 'tied down' to any particular one of the bodies. Last night, after I had gone to bed, I found myself seemingly going to sleep while simultaneously shifting my consciousness to another state. This is actually a common experience for me, but each time it has happened I've been startled by it and I promptly wake up with a jolt. Last night I became fascinated with the phenomena, and I tried to control it. . . . I remember feeling quite astonished at how unattached to the body I seemed to be."

In the January 1964 issue of *New Dimensions*, W.E. Butler, author of *The Magician, His Training and Work*, told how his occult teacher freed his soul from his body.

There was no hypnotism, Butler assures us. One day he asked his teacher if he might not experience "spirit travelling," and the teacher told him to lie down on the couch, close his eyes and relax.

The teacher placed his hand on Butler's head. Then, after a minute or two, the student felt a peculiar tingling sensation. A painful pressure seemed to be building up within Butler's skull.

Just as he felt he could no longer bear the pain "...something seemed to snap in my head, and all consciousness left me for the moment. When I again became aware of things, I found myself standing by the side of the couch, looking down on someone who lay there where a short time ago I knew I had been lying."

Butler was not at all impressed with the appearance of his physical body lying on the couch, but there were so many new things to distract him that he spent little time examining his flesh-and-blood shell. He saw, for example, that his spirit body glowed with a blue luminosity and was connected to his physical body by a "pulsating cord of bluish-grey substance."

Before Butler could ask any questions of his teacher, a "mighty wind" seemed to catch him up and whirl him away.

"...I discerned glimpses of landscapes of mountains and lakes, and here and there the faces which I had loved long since and lost awhile."

The young student at last found himself in a place of perfect peace where he wished he might stay forever. A voice from far away called for him to return, but for many "ages" Butler refused to listen to it. Then he became aware of a powerful pull, and he began to descend from that place of perfect peace.

"Once again the melodies of heaven sounded around and within me; once again the vision of the light formed before me; and then, with an agonizing wrench, I was back in my physical body."

His teacher apologized for bringing him back so soon, but Butler claimed to have been gone for what seemed like ages. "You were out exactly three minutes by my watch," his teacher replied.

Olof Jonsson, who participated with astronaut Ed Mitchell in the famous moon to earth ESP experiment, is another "old pro" at mind travelling.

"In the midst of parapsychological investigators, I have succeeded in setting free my astral body," Olof agreed. "I have been able to give an account of happenings which were occurring at other locations at the same moment that my physical body sat under strict control. All these experiments in out-of-body projection have been carefully controlled, and my reports have been proved to have agreed with distant events. It has happened that a faint figure of my astral body, easily identifiable as me, has been caught on film."

When I pressed him for more information of such a startling bit of substantiating evidence—a photograph of a "living ghost"—Olof shook his head sadly. "The professor who took the picture died just a few years ago, and his wife, who had always detested his interest in parapsychology, burned all of his books, notes and effects. But some day, when the conditions are harmonious, I will do it again, *ja*."

Although that precious photograph no longer exists, a Swedish doctor tesstified that an image of Olof Jonsson once appeared in his home in Malmo. According to the doctor:

"I met Olof Jonsson at a friend's party and immediately, and perhaps rudely, I expressed my skepticism. Although Jonsson had never been in my home, he went into what appeared to be a very light trance and described numerous particulars in my residence. When he described the children's bedroom, I began to lose my skepticism, but when he went on to describe the children and give their names and ages, I became quite convinced of his abilities.

"One night some weeks after Olof had visited my home to verify his impressions and to meet my family, I was disturbed from my reading in the front room by my daughter's delighted laughter. I hurried to her bedroom to inquire after her, since it was past her bedtime. When I asked her what had amused her so, she replied: 'Oh, Father, that nice Engineer Jonsson was here smiling at us.'

"I telephoned Jonsson's apartment, but there was no answer. When I at last was able to contact him, I said: 'I understand that you carried on an experiment with us tonight. My daughter saw you plainly in her bedroom where she and her brother sat reading.'

"Jonsson admitted that he had been sitting in a theater earlier that evening, waiting for a somewhat uninteresting film to run its course. Since his companion found the film fascinating, while Jonsson was bored, he decided to turn off his conscious mind and allow his astral self to wander. For some reason he had found himself in our home, smiling at my daughter and son, who were both seated in their bedroom reading."

I asked Olof Jonsson how he controls his out-of-body experiences:

Jonsson: I can control such projection with my mind. First, I either lie on a couch or sit in a chair. Then I close my eyes and I concentrate on being outside of my body, looking at myself lying there. I *think* myself out of my body.

Steiger: You actually *will* yourself out of the body?

Jonsson: Yes. I do this by concentrating on being outside of my body, looking at myself. After a couple of minutes, I can see myself lying there. Once I am free of my body, I think of all the different places I would like to visit—Malmo, Stockholm, Copenhagen—and then I *wish* me there. When I think of Malmo, the scenery just changes, and I am there. I can see the people around me, but they cannot see me. I can just walk around unencumbered.

Steiger: Do you ever experience a rushing sensation or see multicolored lights?

Jonsson: No, nothing. I just feel completely harmonious . . . at one with the universe. I am in my *real* body, not my sluggish physical shell.

When I am doing astral projection, it is a very happy time in my life. I do not miss the earthly life at all. The cares and considerations of the physical plane mean absolutely nothing to one who is in his astral body. The Earth dimension does not mean one thing to him.

Steiger: Do you think that is what it will be like for you when you make the final projection, the final separation of mind from body?

Jonsson: Yes, I believe so. That final separation should be the happiest time in one's existence.

Olof Jonsson detailed his method for conscious out-of-body projection to me:

> I lie down in a comfortable position, close my eyes, and relax until I reach the stage between waking and sleeping. Even though I am now into this hazy, in-between zone of consciousness, I still have full control over my mind.
>
> After a few moments, I begin to visualize myself outside of my body. Once one has become adept at astral projection, it takes no more than a matter of seconds until one's spiritual essence is floating above the physical body. When my astral self has been freed, I then visualize where I would like to be, and I am there, instantly.
>
> It seems easier to visit family and friends when one is in the astral body. It appears quite evident that there exists some kind of force there to help draw one back.
>
> Hypnosis can be helpful in freeing the neophyte astral traveler from his body, but this method should be considered only if a good professional hypnotist of high repute and extensive experience in such matters is available.

"I have learned a great deal from my personal out-of-body experiences," Olof once reflected. "I have never used this ability to spy upon others or to attempt to learn things which others have decided to keep from me. And you can imagine how many times a man or woman has approached me to help them keep watch over the intimate lives of their spouses in order to gain evidence of disloyalty. I have never involved myself in such matters.

"No, what I have gained from astral projection is that calm and peace that can only come from being in harmony with the universe. I have learned to place the value of my fleshly body in its true perspective, and I have come to realize that the concerns and cares of the Earth plane are very insignificant indeed. To be free of the flesh, to soar to other cities and countries completely unencumbered by time and space—what a happy thing!"

"What is astral travel to you?" I once asked Louis, the famous seer of Orcas Island, Washington.

Louis: Astral travel is referred to by many labels. It has been called "soul travel," which is a misnomer, because in essence it is not. It has been called bi-location, which is perhaps a little better, more definitive. Even the phrase "astral travel" is not an exact label. I like the term "out-of-body experience" myself, because I think it gives it more latitude. For aeons, it seems that man has been leaving his body for many reasons—perhaps out of discontent, perhaps for purposes of study and visiting other dimensions. There are many recorded evidences of this in the Bible and all the writings of the great sages and prophets of old.

Steiger: Just exactly what takes place?

Louis: When one talks about this, one must get rather personal, because it is a personal experience.

I lie down, although I don't think that one would actually have to. I think any relaxed state would be all right. Then it is a matter of willing yourself, of mentally conditioning yourself.

You tell yourself, "I am going to be leaving the body, and I want to do thus and so."

You should have some motivation, some reason for going. I think the greater motivation, the easier it is to achieve this thing. I would not advise anyone to try to leave the body just for kicks, because it is not a thing that one does lightly.

Lie down, relax, close your eyes. The process is very similar to going to sleep. You have willed your invisible body to leave your physical body.

The sensation is rather interesting; the nearest I can describe it is that it is like taking your hand out of a rubber glove after you have been washing dishes. Your body feels like a very thin, yet at the same time, heavy rubber glove; and you can almost feel the sensation as you leave the body.

Steiger: I have been told that it is wise to leave by the head.

Louis: I have tried leaving the body at various other points, and have had rather unpleasant sensations.

For example, you can leave through the lower extremities of the body. You get a very confused vibration as you pull through this force field. It is not a pleasant experience.

You can leave through the solar plexus region. Here the sensation is very much like being on a merry-go-round; it is a very difficult way.

If you leave through the top of the head (the crown chakra), which is the area of higher consciousness or vibratory state, it seems to be much easier. It is as if you are pouring out very gradually, although the whole process takes only a few seconds. In many instances you find yourself suddenly floating over your body and looking down. I remember this happening to me when I was a child.

You are quite aware that you are you and where you are—yet you are quite aware that you are also you, "down there." The experience gives a different awareness of who you really are. If anything could convince you that you are not your body, this does.

You look down and see the body; then you find that the activator, or motivator, that propels this invisible you is caught. As soon as you think a thing, it is so.

Ordinarily, we are very concerned with taking steps and doing this and that. We find ourselves in a rather limited world; we are limited by how fast we can walk, how fast we can do things, and there are certain restrictions put on our activities. Suddenly you find yourself in an unrestricted world where there is no day or night, where there is an unlimited uniforce—unlimited, unhampered; and the physical world is no longer one of the boundaries.

Many people find themselves "going to school" when they leave the body. I have had this experience many times.

Steiger: Could you describe this?

Louis: It appears to be a round place, a circular room, shall we say. There do not seem to be any walls, and yet there is something there which appears to be very iridescent—like mother-of-pearl with changing colors. On these occasions, you usually leave the body within just a matter of a split second; you come popping up through the floor, and you find yourself in this place.

You find yourself sitting in a large circle. You and the others there are robed in loose-fitting garments. There are many people in this circle. Shortly, a person appears who gives a lesson or lecture. It is usually something very profound and with great meaning. In my own instances, it has generally dealt with something that I have need of in my life at that time. Many other people have had similar experiences.

I have also found myself visiting friends when I leave the body. In some instances they remember, in some they don't—it depends upon how perceptive that individual is.

Steiger: What is the purpose of this astral travel?

Louis: I think the purpose of out-of-body experiences, as of all life, is to grow, to expand, and to teach awareness. I don't think it has much point if you do it for frivolous purposes, but I think you can use it to enter into other realms, other planes of consciousness, and to study.

Steiger: I have read accounts of people who were incarcerated escaping from their situations by this means.

Louis: There have been many instances of people who were in jail and very unhappy about their situations who fled in this fashion. Madame Blavatsky, for example, got much of her information for her theosophical books, it is said, from certain volumes which were in a secret section of the Vatican Library. These books were unavailable to her in her mortal form, so she put the mortal form aside, went and did her research, brought back what she wanted, and used it in her writings.

Steiger: Do you usually re-enter the body at the same point you left?

Louis: Yes. My one thought on being about to return used to be: "My God, I have to come back to this heavy body." You feel a great weight; the body seems so heavy and coarse and made of lead; whereas your invisible body has no weight or substance—a very euphoric state.

Steiger: Some people think that astral travelling is actually meditation; that the goal of meditation is to leave the body.

Louis: No, meditation and astral travel are two distinct and separate things. Meditation is basically going within, whereas astral travel is going with-out.

Of course, it depends on how one uses the universe; and if you get to the point where there are no such things as within or with-out, you have a different problem, as far as your references are concerned.

Steiger: You mentioned a loose-fitting robe; do you usually wear clothes when you are astral-travelling?

Louis: Yes, usually there appears to be a garment of sorts on the body, though there doesn't seem to be any weight to it.

Steiger: Are you aware of sex or male and female?

Louis: Yes, you are aware of male and female, but not to the degree that we are aware of it on our ordinary mortal plane of endeavor. It doesn't seem to be as pronounced, and yet it does seem to be there.

Steiger: Are you aware of time?

Louis: No, time seems to be laid aside, and there is no such thing as space at that particular moment.

Steiger: You just will yourself to go somewhere, and you are there?

Louis: You are there immediately.

Steiger: Many people talk about the "silver cord" linking you to the physical body.

Louis: Yes, you are always aware of an attachment with the body and that there *is* a body asleep "down there" or someplace.

Steiger: If something were to happen to the physical body when one's consciousness were in the astral state, would the cord be severed—if the body were to be burnt in a fire or suffer a heart attack, for instance?

Louis: This is what happens at the moment called death—a separation of the invisible part of you from the visible or manifested part.

Also, if you are out of the body and someone shakes you or calls to you very loudly, you find yourself coming back into the body very suddenly. Many people who have had such experiences recall waking up in the morning with a great spastic jerk, almost jumping. This occurs when one has just come back into the body, and it is the muscle reaction to this experience.

Steiger: You say you feel no mass; nothing has weight.

Louis: Nothing has weight, but you are aware of the molecular structure of things. For example, if you are out of the body and you walk through a couch, you are aware of its molecular structure. You are not aware of its weight or density, but you are aware of the fact that it does exist.

Steiger: You mentioned that you are not aware of day or night. Does there seem to be a light, and if so, where does it come from? What kind of light is it?

Louis: The "air" (or surrounding medium) seems to be filled with light; there doesn't seem to be any day or night.

Steiger: Are you aware of electric lights?

Louis: You are aware of everything you are aware of in your ordinary manifested state; but there do not seem to be the same limitations as far as day and night are concerned.

For example, you wouldn't ordinarily walk down a dark alley during the nighttime, because you might stumble over something; out-of-the-body you don't have that sensation of night or darkness as a limiting factor.

Steiger: I heard you mention that you have been able to move a bell.

Louis: One thing that is sometimes very frustrating when you are out of the body and in a nonphysical state is that the same laws that apply to your physical state don't apply to your nonphysical state. Consequently, you are not able to pick things up as you do now; your hand goes right through them.

I was trying to contact some friends and asked them to put a bell up to see whether I could ring it. They put a bell up over their bed, and my hand just passed through it. Finally they got a very tiny bell, such as is used on key chains, and I found I could cause a molecular action that would ring the bell. I couldn't ring it in the ordinary sense, but I could cause it to ring by a thought process and could contact people that way.

Steiger: About how often do you do this travel?

Louis: Consciously, about once or twice a week. I find myself doing it at other times in an unconscious state; I just find myself out-of-the-body.

Steiger: Some people consider the experiences of astral travel as a status-giving accomplishment.

Louis: The only status that I think a person can achieve is how much he can give. If you are a giving person, you have a right to feel good about it. I don't think astral travel is a status thing. I don't think it is something that should be taken lightly or should be bandied about and played with. It is a real thing and a very serious thing.

Later, Louis asked his guide about possible evil influences or evil entities entering a body when a person is travelling astrally or is out of the body.

"If all is God, can there be else?

"Let us not concern ourselves with evil and thus have a two-edged sword. The way is narrow, the way is One, not Two.

"Man has been so concerned with good and bad, black and white, that he is very confused. Let us focus upon the Good, the Right, the True, the Real.

"Cast aside all these other shadows. They do not exist unless we want them to. If we want evil, we can have evil. If we want bad, we can have bad. But why would we want them?"

15

Some Experiments with Hypnosis

An enormous amount of literature deals with hypnosis and its possible effect on the functioning of various paranormal abilities. One need read little of the professional literature in parapsychology to learn that even the most cautious investigators concede that. Apparently a large number of subjects have displayed dramatic increases in paranormal skills while in an hypnotic trance. Researchers have not yet isolated the special qualities of hypnotic trance which facilitate "psi" functioning, but most of them conclude that the induced hypnotic state must in some way liberate the deeper levels of consciousness, wherein lies the transcendent quality of the human mind.

The earliest of the modern hypnotists, or mesmerists, conducted numerous experiments in which they bid an entranced subject to go somewhere mentally and describe what he or she saw.

A remarkable series of experiments was conducted in 1884 by French psychiatrist Pierre Janet. Distinguished physician Jean Martin Charcot presided at some of the sessions and one of his students, Sigmund Freud, may have been an observer. In one experiment in telepathy, Janet hypnotized a young woman fifteen out of twenty-five attempts while at a distance of one-third of a mile away from her.

In 1849, before Pierre Janet, the famous mathematician Augustus de Morgan worked with hypnotism and "travelling clairvoyance."

The mathematician records the following experience. While he dined at a friend's house, his wife remained home to treat a young epileptic girl by mesmeric therapy. When de Morgan returned home, his wife greeted him, "We have been after you." While in trance, the girl, who had demonstrated clairvoyant abilities on numerous occasions, had been instructed to follow de Morgan. The girl's mother said her daughter would never be able to locate the address Mrs. de Morgan gave. "She's never been so far away from Camden Town," she explained.

Within a few moments, however, the girl announced from the depths of her trance that she stood before the house to which she had been "sent." Mrs. de Morgan suggested that she knock at the door and enter.

The entranced girl replied that she could not knock at the door until she had entered the gate. Mrs. de Morgan was puzzled by this answer, and it was not until her husband returned that the mystery was explained. Being unfamiliar with the friend's home, Mrs. de Morgan was unaware that the house stood in a garden and that the front door could be reached only by entering at the garden gate.

But the mesmerist had told her subject to simulate entering the house and to continue to pursue de Morgan. Within a few moments the girl said she was inside the house and could hear voices upstairs.

She "walked" up the stairs and gave a detailed description of the people assembled, the furniture, the objects, the pictures in the room and the colors of the drapes and curtains.

De Morgan, admittedly awed, verified that each detail given his wife by the entranced subject was accurate. He was even more astonished when the girl repeated conversations she had overheard. As further testimony she correctly described the dinner menu.

Had Mrs. de Morgan really turned up the power of the girl's latent clairvoyant ability, or had the hypnotist somehow freed the girl's mind and enabled it to move uninhibited by time and space?

Experiences are termed clairvoyant when they deal with information about people and things at a distance from the percipient, and provide the percipient with knowledge he or she could not receive via normal sensory channels of communication. Certainly Mrs. de Morgan's subject provided "clairvoyant" information about her husband, but had she not bade the young girl to "follow" Morgan while she was in the trance state? Perhaps the girl's etheric self had taken the command literally and the induction of the trance state permitted the astral body easy escape from her physical body.

In a paper entitled "On the Evidence for Clairvoyance" (Volume VII, *Proceedings*, Society for Psychical Research), Mrs. Henry Sidgwick discusses a vivid example of an OBE which was hypnotically produced.

Dr. F., who was experimenting with "travelling clairvoyance," placed a woman named Jane into hypnotic trance. The doctor arranged to have one of his patients, Mr. Eglinton, stay in his apartment that night so the woman might clairvoyantly call on him. Jane had never met Mr. Eglinton, who was thin and weak after a serious illness, nor had she ever been to the district in which he lived.

After the hypnotic trance had been induced, Jane was told to "travel" to Mr. Eglinton's apartment. She accurately described the approach to the house, the knocker on the door and the furnishings in the room; but when she described the appearance of Mr. Eglinton, Dr. F. thought the experiment had failed. According to Jane's description, Mr. Eglinton was fat and had an artificial leg.

Dr. F. recalled Jane, puzzled that she should go completely astray on his patient's appearance when she had described everything else so exactly.

The next day Dr. F. discovered that Mr. Eglinton had grown weary waiting for the experiment and had fashioned a dummy of himself to maintain a vigil in the sitting room. He had stuffed his clothes with several pillows and had propped the manikin up beside a glass of brandy and some newspapers. Hence, the "Mr. Eglinton" Jane had seen in the apartment was indeed fat and possessed of artificial limbs.

This case has often been cited as a successful experiment in clairvoyance. However, it seems to me that, if the experience were one of true clairvoyance, Jane would have known that she was viewing a dummy of Mr. Eglinton and would not have reported the information incorrectly. It seems to me rather that Jane's mind had travelled to the apartment and had mistaken the manikin for the man, much as anyone might do if he or she were granted a peek into a strange room under rather unusual circumstances.

It can be argued that whenever clairvoyants say they are "seeing" a faraway scene, they are in reality projecting their astral selves to that scene. Some researchers theorize that OBE may explain nearly all psi phenomena. Although I believe that all psychic occurrences may have a common source in some as yet unknown or unexplained set of natural laws, it does seem to me that there are gradations of psi abilities, at least as they are demonstrated by individuals.

I have been and still am in close communication with a number of people who conduct regular systematic experiments in induced astral projection. Some use hypnosis; others prefer concentration or various exercises prescribed by adepts. In my years as a college instructor, I strongly advised students against entering carelessly into such experimentation, but, as might be supposed, my warnings were often ignored.

Two young fellows, Ted and Rob, gave me the details of a hypnotically induced astral projection that appears to have been authentic. Through lengthy experimentation Ted learned to hypnotize Rob and to send him on out-of-body excursions. One night they decided to test Rob's alleged travels to see if they could substantiate his mental journeys. Previously, Ted simply hypnotized Rob and then allowed him to relate what he observed on his mind trip. Several experiments had produced impressive recitations, but the fellows realized that all the descriptions could have been produced in Rob's own subconscious. One night they decided that Rob should try projecting to the apartment of Jim, a friend who had graduated from college and lived in a city several hundred miles away.

Ted quickly placed Rob into trance, then suggested that he find himself on the way to Jim's apartment in Chicago. Neither had ever been to Jim's apartment, and though the three of them corresponded regularly, the decor of Jim's rooms had never been discussed. When Rob said he saw Jim sitting in a chair reading a book, Ted placed a long-distance phone call to Jim.

"Hi, Jim, this is Ted. What are you doing?"

Jim, unaware of the experiment, expressed pleasure at hearing the voice of his friend, then answered casually that he was just sitting in his apartment, catching up on some reading.

Ted muffled the receiver and asked Rob what Jim was wearing. "A turtleneck..." came his slightly hesitant answer. "A yellow turtleneck sweater."

"Hey, Jim, are you wearing a yellow turtleneck?"

"Why, yes, I am," Jim replied with a chuckle. "Is this some kind of guessing game, or have you suddenly taken an interest in my wardrobe?"

Ted turned to the entranced Rob, asked him to describe the apartment—pictures, furniture, rugs, vases, anything at all he might see. As Rob named various objects and their relative positions in the room, Ted relayed the description to Jim.

"What's going on?" Jim demanded. "Yes, I've got a picture of Paula on my nightstand. A lucky guess. But how did you know about the bullfight poster over the dresser? And how did you know it covers a stain on the wallpaper that I accidentally made with some oil? What kind of business are you giving me?"

Ted handed the receiver to Rob and told his hypnotized friend to speak directly into the mouthpiece and describe Jim's room to him. As Jim was confirming all that Rob was saying, there was a knock at his apartment door. Jim set the receiver down, then came back to it with a challenge: "Okay, you guys, describe who just came in the door!"

Ted, who still had an ear pressed to the receiver, translated Jim's challenge into a hypnotic suggestion for Rob.

"He is tall, thin, wears a tweed jacket. He has a six-pack of beer in the sack he carries. . . ."

Jim again confirmed Rob's description of his friend. He demanded to know what kind of crazy ESP experiment the two of them were up to, but Ted told him they would write it up for him in a letter.

I have received other reports from people who have experimented with hypnotically induced OBE and who have also used the telephone to substantiate instantly a percipient's description. Ironically, the telephone, a relatively recent technological aid to communication, is used to prove the latent existence of what may have been humankind's most archaic method of communication.

Some experimenters argue that they prove clairvoyance by such demonstrations; others maintain that they project the astral body. But of one thing we can be certain: some manifestation of mind phenomena is at work.

The subjectivity of such experiences prohibits researchers from pronouncing with certainty precisely which facet of psi phenomena is being demonstrated. When an entranced subject claims that his or her "astral self" has broken free of physically imposed barriers of space, time and dimension, and he or she is able to describe people and places that do demonstrably exist in an actual location, then it seems that the subject is undergoing an OBE. On the other hand, many accomplished clairvoyants, who do not undergo any kind of trance experience, claim simply to "see" things as they are in a faraway place, and make no mention of projecting in the astral body.

In certain cases of hypnotically induced OBE, I wonder if hypnotists and the controllers of the subjects, might not complicate the issue. Although the cases discussed in this chapter seem to indicate out-of-body experience, perhaps in some instances the subject has verbalized the experience in terms of astral projection because the hypnotist has envisioned such a process taking place during the experiment. In other words, I am suggesting that a hypnotist could unconsciously or telepathically influence his or her subject to describe a clairvoyant experience in a language of other planes, dimensions and an astral body.

I had regarded cases in which astral travel was induced by hypnosis as being less reliable than those out-of-body projections which occur spontaneously and independently of a second party. Then, in July, 1968, I began a series of tests and experiments with hypnotist Loring G. Williams, which forced me to amend my opinion of hypnotically induced OBE.

We were conducting sessions on hypnotic regressions to previous lives and medical diagnoses via entranced subjects, when I asked Williams to indulge my desire to test certain hypotheses concerning OBE. Williams was quick to oblige, as astral travelling constituted an integral part of his medical diagnoses experiments. A friend of mine volunteered to serve as the subject. While in trance, she was sent on out-of-body jaunts across the continent from coast to coast, north to Canada and across the ocean to England. Descriptions of people's homes, medical symptoms and physical appearances were verified by witnesses observing the experiments or by long-distance telephone calls to the individuals visited.

I still maintain that caution must be exercised in such experiments to guard against the reseacher-hypnotist becoming a participant rather than a recorder and guide. In the Williams experiments, I feel that we provided adequate safeguards against such participation.

Nevertheless, Williams' experiments left me in awe at what a valuable aid hypnosis can be to the psychical researcher. Not only is it efficacious in cases in which the investigator might wish to regress a percipient of the paranormal occurrence in order to recreate an incident in the past, but it may liberate the essential stuff of the subconscious to soar freely through time and space.

The late Loring G. Williams was not a psychic. Thirty years of interest and research in the realm of paranormal phenomena had brought him a few personal experiences that many people might consider a bit unusual, but generally, when it came to seeing ghosts, gaining clairvoyant impressions or peeking into the future, Williams readily admitted to being a "dud."

Early in life, however, "Bill" Williams became convinced that men and women are endowed with what writers of book-jacket blurbs and others enamored of catch phrases refer to as a "sixth sense." What Williams meant is that some people—probably all of us—are gifted with certain abilities which, although not everyone talks about them, must be considered paranormal. Basically, Bill argued—as do I—that there exists a nonphysical capacity within men and women, and that we are more than chemical reactions, glandular responses and conditioned reflexes.

After thirty years of study and research, a reflective, thinking person cannot avoid coming up with personal theories concerning these unusual abilities—this "sixth sense" that prophets, pseudo-priests, politicians and public relations people are so fond of crediting to themselves whenever they hit upon an idea that did not seem to come to them from their own memories or thinking mechanisms. Williams decided that his research was based on three principles.

> *One:* Psychic ability is inherent in all people. Although it may once have been as useful as sight, smell, taste, touch and hearing, "psi" ability has been blunted and, in most people perhaps, become dormant because of the demands of contemporary civilization on the physical senses.
>
> *Two:* The subconscious mind is the governor of psychic ability within each individual.
>
> *Three:* Each person's subconscious mind is linked to, and may be attuned with, a Universal Mind. This Universal Mind knows no boundaries of time or space and is in harmony with all of the knowledge in the universe.

Throughout this century, especially the last forty years, there was enough card-guessing, dice-throwing, billet-reading experimentation and documentation of psi phenomena to convince any open-minded, thinking person and even the skeptical and narrow-minded (if they took the trouble to examine the evidence) that such things as telepathy, clairvoyance, precognition and psychokinesis do exist. Williams felt it was not enough merely to conduct experiments just to prove something exists. One may know that the telephone exists, he pointed out, but if one does not know how to dial, what good is it?

Williams, ever the Yankee pragmatist, pondered, "What good is there in psychic abilities if they cannot be directed at will? Most people who have had spontaneous psi experiences—such as telepathic transfer, a glimpse of the future or out-of-body experience—have had them only once or twice in a lifetime. These most likely occurred at completely unexpected times, and the percipients, the subjects, had absolutely no control over the situation. Such experiences as spontaneous OBE are interesting, but, in most cases, what value are they?

"I feel that man is not given such powers unless they are intended to be used in a regular, productive, rewarding manner," he told me.

Williams' first goal in his research was to find a method by which he might contact and direct psi abilities at will. If his basic premises were correct, it would first be necessary to unlock the subconscious mind. The best key available, in his estimation, was hypnosis.

Drugs might have been used, but Williams believed they might produce undesirable side effects and unpleasant aftereffects. Another negative aspect of drug use was the required time for induction and retraction.

Hypnosis, on the other hand, can be almost instantaneous. There are no side effects and, when induced by a responsible agent, hypnosis leaves no aftereffects. As a bonus, the subject invariably feels better after hypnosis than before the induction of trance.

As Bill Williams conducted his preliminary experiments with hypnosis and psi phenomena, he was soon to learn that the tree of psychic knowledge has many branches. Try as he might to limit himself to the study of one phenomenon, the interrelationship of these wonderful powers of mind became increasingly obvious. Such interrelationships continually presented new challenges, forcing him to attend to the other branches of the ever-spreading tree.

"So it was," Williams remembered, "that my first experiments in hypnotic regression and cases suggestive of reincarnation thrust me into contact with such phenomena as ghosts, spirit possession, the viewing of past and future events and astral projection, mind travel."

Controlled out-of-body projections seemed to offer him an intriguing and rewarding area for intensive study and experimentation. Astral travel, a term we borrow from the Theosophists, suggests the movement of one's astral body, or essential self, through space and time to a specific place. Although there are numerous cases on record in which the astral traveller became visible to those startled individuals being visited, Williams' experiments with controlled out-of-body experience produced no such shadowy or vaporous apparitions. Williams preferred to term his hypnotically controlled projections "mind travel," because he believed there was a distinction between the results of his experiments and the phenomena of self-controlled, or spontaneous, astral projection.

Like so many of his discoveries, Williams' first experience with mind travel came about in a most unexpected manner. He had taken a young neighbor of his, George Field, from New Hampshire to Jefferson, North Carolina to investigate what appeared to be George's previous incarnation as a Civil War victim. Williams' friend, Professor Charles Hapgood, was planning an archeological expedition to Kentucky at about the same time. Williams had agreed to telephone Professor Hapgood in Kentucky when his research in Jefferson was completed and make arrangements to join him at his archeological dig.

As soon as they had substantiated the incarnation of Jonathan Powell (George Field) in Jefferson, Williams tried calling the number in Kentucky where Professor Hapgood said he could be reached. However, the person who answered the telephone told Williams he did not know when to expect the professor.

Bill was faced with the dilemma of whether or not to wait there in Jefferson and continue calling Kentucky, or to drive directly to Kentucky hoping to meet Hapgood there. Then too something may have altered Hapgood's plans, forcing him to remain at home in New Hampshire. The only certain thing was that Professor Hapgood had no way of contacting them, since they were camping.

"Then I received an inspiration," Williams recalls. "Why not try to send George, under hypnosis, through space to find Charles. I knew that he had a sister in New York City. At my command, I instructed George that he would be in the apartment of Charles's sister."

When the suggestion had been made, Williams asked George what he saw.

George described an apartment.

Did he see Charles?

No, George said, he was not to be seen.

Williams told him to leave the apartment in New York City and drift through space to Charles' home in Richmond, New Hampshire. George described Charles Hapgood's home perfectly, even though he had never been there before.

Williams asked George if there was anyone there. "Yes," he answered, "Charles is here, reading a book."

The next day, on the strength of George's mind travel experience, Williams and his companions began to journey home to Hinsdale, New Hampshire. Upon their arrival Williams called Professor Hapgood's home. The professor answered the telephone at once and explained that last minute events had forced him to cancel the expedition to Kentucky. He said he had been home all the time, making the best of his change of plans by catching up on his reading.

And so, by chance and a bit of inspiration born of desperation and confusion, Loring G. Williams had conducted what appeared to be a successful first experiment in mind travel.

Although the single projection in itself hardly presented enough conclusive evidence to make an orthodox scientist desert the miscroscope and test tubes in favor of a study of hypnotic mind projection, the experiment had seemed to produce accurate information. And it served to spark Williams' curiosity and to provoke him into an intensive exploration of this strange phenomenon of mind.

Perhaps the next milestone in Williams' mind travel experimentation was marked with the shards of a shattered mirror.

A personal friend of mine, whom I shall call Rita, volunteered to cooperate with Williams in some experiments in hypnotic regression. Although Rita was able to go back in time to her days as a schoolgirl and, it appeared, even to the birth experience, she could not seem to form any clear articulation of those impressions that could be memories of a past life. There was one briefly observed scene of a young girl walking along a dark country road and being frightened of a horse and wagon approaching, but that could have been almost anything, from a snatch of a story told by Grandmother to a bit of hypnotically provoked fantasy.

Then Bill said: "Let's try Rita on some mind travel." He pointed at her and told her to fall into a deep sleep.

We decided Rita should "travel" to the home of an editor friend of mine and look in on him. Bill gave her the man's home address (a home neither of us had ever been in) and directed her to soar through space "...over Iowa, Indiana, Ohio.... Look down at the fields, the lights of cities. And now you're approaching New York City. Have you ever been there before?" Rita shook her head no. "Look below you. There's Times Square...the Empire State Building.... Now go to this address." (Bill repeated it slowly, firmly.) "Do you have it?"

"I—I think so," Rita said, her brow furrowing in deep concentration.

"Can you see our friend?"

"I see a man," Rita told us.

"Describe him, please."

Her description of my editor was, in my estimation, exceedingly exact. But could she have picked up this information via mental telepathy? Bill then asked Rita to see my editor in "x-ray" form.

"Now you can see through him, Rita," Bill instructed her. "You can see if he has any injuries or diseases, any old scars or wounds."

At this point, Rita described some old injuries and gave her analysis of his present-day health condition. To my amazement, but not to Williams', who had a great deal of experience with hypnotically directed mind travel, my editor verified Rita's complete examination of both his past and present health during a subsequent long-distance telephone call which I made to him the next morning. Although I had worked closely with this man for some time, we had never discussed matters of personal health. We always used our time together discussing book projects, not swapping symptons and discussing old operations.

The real clincher to this particular experiment came when my editor told me about his mirror. The lovely antique looking glass had shattered at the precise moment we had been "looking in" on him via mind travel.

There is a whole system of occult practice and lore concerning mirrors. Whether or not there is the smallest germ of truth to the eerie tales I have read and heard about occultists using mirrors to work their esoteric rites, I do not know. I can only offer this rather unfortunate evidence—a highly valued antique mirror shattered when a young woman was sent to flit about in the ether near the mirror.

Later that same evening we sent Rita travelling to Niagara Falls to look in on some friends. She described the Falls by night in such lavish detail that the impression remained deeply etched in her consciousness after she had been awakened from trance. Her word-pictures were so colorful that she and her husband decided to visit Niagara Falls and the East on their vacation and postponed the trip they had been planning to make to Yellowstone National Park.

Mind travel did not work for Rita's husband, however. Although he had at first expressed a fear of being in an hypnotic trance, he became so intrigued by his wife's experience that he almost demanded to be hypnotized. But nothing happened. His psyche simply would not budge from his body. He definitely was not fighting Williams' will. He may have been trying too hard, that is true, but this was a situation which I have since witnessed on several occasions.

It seems not everyone can be hypnotized easily. At least not in one session. Williams maintained—and I think most hypnotists agree with him—that anyone, with the exception of the very young and the insane (their attention spans are too short), can succumb to the state of hypnosis. If not in one session or two or three, then eventually after a definite program of hypnosis has been established as part of a daily or weekly regimen.

Had I actually witnessed a soul, a mind, taking leave of its physical shell, bursting free of the physical limitations of flesh and, astoundingly, space?

Mind travel is not a new phenomenon, nor was Loring G. Williams the first person to experiment with out-of-body projection via hypnosis. In the literature of psychical research there is no dearth of accounts of hypnotists attempting to send entranced subjects out of their physical bodies.

"The question a lot of good, hard-nosed materialists always ask is, what is the point of all this mind travel experimentation?" Williams repeated, recognizing full well that the whole world is not lying awake nights awaiting the results of a study of mind projection. "People want to know what practical things can be gained from such work. They wonder if it isn't something that is weird, far-out—something that might better be left alone?"

Williams felt that to answer these questions he had to do a great deal of self-analysis. He realized that simple statements of faith would not satisfy the cynical and the skeptical.

"To answer fully such a question as why it is important to study such a thing as mind travel, one must analyze both himself and the universe in which he has his being," Williams said. "In our Western civilization it seems to be the accepted thing that we should progress in the fields of science, the arts, creature comforts and the ability to kill huge numbers of our fellowmen. At the same time, we are told that our knowledge of our inner selves, of our souls, terminated with the teachings of Jesus two thousand years ago.

"We live, however, in a universe of law. All around us we see the effects of natural laws. When Galileo stood atop the tower of Pisa back in the seventeenth century and dropped those two stones, it was the law of gravity which caused them to fall. The law of acceleration caused them to drop at the rate of thirty-two feet per second. If we were to repeat this same experiment today, precisely the same thing would happen, because the law of gravity is a natural law.

"I believe that there is a force within our universe greater than we. This force orders our lives, keeps the world revolving once every twenty-four hours, causes stones to fall when they are dropped from towers, and so many other things which we can but barely perceive. At the same time," Williams remarked, "I feel that our universe is progressive, as is our civilization. We do not, we cannot, hold to the standards of hundreds of years ago. We must grow and evolve with time."

As Williams saw it, we, as individuals, have only one true asset—our minds. "We are nothing, we have nothing, except that we know and think. We are the product of our thoughts."

What about the question: Why experiment?

"We are but mortal men," Williams said. "We must experiment in order that we may learn. I believe that there are many natural laws—such as the law of gravity—which have yet to be discovered. These laws react in specific ways to specific stimuli. It remains for us to determine the action of the laws and the stimulus required to make them operative. To achieve this requires experimentation. If we do not continue the experiment, we stagnate. We only exist in a mental living death."

But Williams wanted to go a step further than "psi" research had gone in modern times. He wanted to do more than simply prove that such phenomena exist.

"I want to find out *how* and *why* these things work," Williams declared. "These studies are not 'far out' or 'weird.' Psychic phenomena generally occur spontaneously, on a hit or miss basis. Let us find a control so that we may turn on such abilities of mind at will.

"Man in his normal, harried, conscious state does not seem to have the ability to see beyond himself. On occasion, certain people—perhaps thousands—have flashes of precognition or clairvoyance, but generally, the majority of men and women journey along through life seeing only the very narrow path before them.

"On his subconscious level, however, man's mind seems to be ever-alert and above all boundaries. The subconscious can, if man permits it, keep him posted on events going on all around him.

"Hypnosis allows us to tap into the subconscious, and together with the subconscious, we can achieve mind travel."

But by now the skeptical must be asking "All right, the idea of mind travel is fascinating, and a discussion of the pros and cons of its existence may provide many hours of provocative conversation, but is there any possible value to man's being able to consciously leave his body?"

Williams suggested that we look ahead to the year 1990 and suppose that an established science of mind travel has been accepted by the government and by the general population.

"Remember a few years ago when one of our U-2 pilots was shot down on a flight over Russia?" Williams asked. "Our government suffered global embarrassment because they had to admit that they had been spying. In 1990, if mind travel is accepted scientifically, we could have some well-trained hypnotists working with some excellent subjects. These subjects could, mentally, be sent anywhere in the world. They could survey the military might of any of the world's powers without risk of detection or danger. These mind travelers could tune in on high council meetings; they could mentally search through political archives; they could slip inside the minds and the physical bodies of any nation's political and military leaders. No longer would it be necessary for our agents to endanger their lives by spying around the world."

Williams earnestly hoped that by 1990 peace would have come to our world and that mind travel would never have to be applied in such a manner. There are so many more positive benefits other than psychic surveillance of one another which could accrue to man if such a science were perfected.

"Today, any illness is expensive," Williams noted. "Long gone by is the day of the country doctor who would drive miles to treat illness and deliver babies for fifty cents or a few eggs. Today we have specialists, x-ray technicians and fifty-dollar-a-day hospital rooms. The diagnosis of illness can require extensive hospitalization and the services of many specialists and technicians. The cost can mount to hundreds or thousands of dollars in a few days.

"With the use of hypnotic mind travel, a skilled hypnotist and a good subject may be able to diagnose and pinpoint the cause of an illness of a patient anywhere in the world in just a few minutes. This information could then be given to a medical doctor, who would then be able to act immediately, using this hypnotically gained information to supplement the findings of his own observations and diagnosis.

"Hypno-diagnosis can pick up minute physical problems in their early stages, and their true (and not always obvious) causes can be determined. In this way, earlier and more effective treatment can be provided. Everyone would be able to afford frequent, inexpensive hypnophysical examinations as preventive maintenance for their bodies."

Williams also suggested that police departments could employ hypnotists to seek out lost persons and to examine the scenes of crime through mind travel. Detailed accounts of the movements of known criminals could be recorded, and the scene of any crime could be "visited" within a few moments after the report had come into headquarters.

"The human mind has been endowed with more power, more abilities, than we can possibly conceive of in today's orthodoxy," Williams believed. "Perhaps we may be thousands of years late in comprehending the lessons once taught by the great leaders and prophets of the past. Could it be that if we were to devote as much time to our mental, our psychic, development as we do to our technological development that we might yet have the perfect world?"

In another experiment with Rita, Bill asked those witnessing the session to suggest places where she might travel. At this point, Rita had made a good number of controlled out-of-body projections and seemed to have become more proficient with each mental "trip."

One woman asked Bill to send Rita to a city in Kentucky to look in on her mother. Bill agreed to this and asked the woman to write down the specifics.

In each test the same general *modus operandi* was followed: a target place or person was decided upon and the subject was put into trance and told to travel there and to describe the target. Once this had been accomplished, we attempted to substantiate whether we had chalked up a hit or a miss by telephoning the target who of course knew nothing of the test.

In cases where we attempted projections to Europe, we dispatched airmail letters to the persons named as targets and asked them to substantiate whether or not we had indeed looked in on them via mind travel.

In all cases, the hypnotist gave the subject the target's complete name and address before the subject was projected. If someone witnessing the experiments provided us with a target, then he or she was asked to give in writing the complete name, address and detailed physical description of the person volunteered as a target.

The following transcript of one of Rita's astral flights to Kentucky serves more completely to inform you just how such a session of controlled mind travel was conducted. Note that I use assumed names to insure the anonymity of certain individuals who took part in these experiments, especially to protect the privacy of those people who unknowingly served as targets.

Bill: Okay, Rita, deep sleep, deep sleep! Now you are going to travel to the home of Mrs. C.B. in Owensboro, Kentucky. You are travelling over the plains, over the cities, over rivers, you are coming closer and closer, closer and closer to Owensboro, Kentucky. When I count three, you will be there. One...coming closer...two...nearer and nearer...three...you are in Owensboro. Are you there, Rita?"

Rita: Yes, I think so...[She named a landmark or two and the witness who provided the target nodded her head affirmatively. In some cases subjects will indicate they are not yet in the prescribed area or that they are uncertain. The hypnotist must then place the subject in deeper trance and intensify the suggestion.]

Bill: Now you must go to (complete address) and see Mrs. C.B. When I count to three you will be standing outside her home. One...two ...three. Are you there?

[Rita indicates that she is there and describes the house on the request of the hypnotist. The witness who provided the target indicates that the home the subject is describing is indeed the home of Mrs. C.B.

Bill tells Rita to go inside the home and find Mrs. C.B. Rita does this and describes a woman who is tall and dark-haired, with streaks of gray. The witness who provided the name emphatically shakes her head in the negative. Bill looks at the description of Mrs. C.B. which the witness has provided: "Pale red hair, almost white. 76 years old. Five-foot-three. 135 pounds. Wears glasses (high heels, jewelry and earrings as a rule). Usually very smartly dressed—chic."

Rita continues to describe the woman in Mrs. C.B.'s home. She tells how the woman is cleaning the house, dusting, preparing to vacuum.

"She has the right house," the witness concedes, "but that is not my mother."]

Bill: You have the wrong woman, Rita. When I count to three you will leave the house and find Mrs. C.B. You will find Mrs. C.B. wherever she might be. One...two...three...

Rita: I have her now. She is playing cards with three other women.

Bill: Describe Mrs. C.B. for us, please.

Rita: She's kinda shortish. She has red hair but it is nearly white. She has quite a bit of makeup on and some big earrings. She's a little bit plump.

When Rita went on to describe each of the other women in the card circle, the witness smiled and said that she recognized the ladies as close personal friends of her mother.

Rita was asked to go outside the home and describe its physical appearance. After she had done so, the witness was able to name which of her mother's friends was hosting the card party.

Later, when the witness telephoned her mother, she learned that she had been at a party in the home of Mrs. ——— and that the tall dark-haired woman whom Rita had first described in Mrs. C.B.'s home was a cleaning lady who always came in on the afternoons Mrs. C.B. played cards.

It was during this session that a rather interesting phenomenon took place. My secretary, Jeanyne Bezoier, was eager to see if Rita would be able to project to her home in Edina, Minnesota, so she pressed a slip of paper into Bill's hand which gave her parents' full home address. Without giving

Rita a chance to rest and to "come back" to my office for a moment or two (generally this does not seem to be necessary), Bill uttered the command and began the countdown which would send Rita travelling to Edina.

Jeanyne nodded her head vigorously and smiled excitedly when Rita "entered" her parents' home in Minnesota and began describing the front hall. She almost squealed her approval as Rita described the furnishings in the dining room, but then when Rita entered the living room Jeanyne's face suddenly rumpled with surprise and confusion. "She's certainly walking around in our house," she whispered, "but that is most certainly not our living room!"

"But it *is* my mother's!" said the witness who had asked Rita to travel to Owensboro, Kentucky. "That's her floral design carpet that she is describing right now!"

And so it went. Rita would walk into one room in Edina, Minnesota, pass through it naming objects and furniture correctly, then enter the next room in Owensboro, Kentucky, and call off details of its arrangements and its artifacts.

Was Rita's psyche actually in one city while she clairvoyantly saw the details of a house in another city more than a thousand miles away?

Or had her mind somehow found a way to be in two places at once? Three places, if you wish to maintain that a part of her essential stuff still sat there in the easy chair in my office directing the brain of the physical Rita.

Whether by clairvoyance or by out-of-body experience, Jeanyne and the other witness testified that, somehow, Rita was really there in each of their parental homes. Astoundingly, Rita was even able to read the brand names of furniture and appliances as she psychically toured two homes in two different sections of the United States at the same time!

Admittedly, a good many readers are going to find such a report exceedingly difficult to accept. I did, yet there I was, sitting in my office listening to witnesses testify that my friend Rita was describing people and places hundreds, thousands of miles away—and in that one unusual instance she was describing two places in two different parts of the country at the same time.

For those who will immediately write off such phenomena as nonsense, or for those who steadfastly deny the existence of a soul, a nonphysical capacity of men and women, no amount of exposition will convince them that we all did not just get together and make it up. Such people are welcome to witness a similar demonstration at any time and see for themselves. But better yet, why should they not employ a good hypnotist of their own—I repeat, a good hypnotist of high principles who is jealous of his or her reputation, not a parlor Svengali who conducts his experiments with his forefinger on the directions printed in a how-to book on hypnosis. Then they should conduct their own experiments. One may not find a good subject among his or her first few volunteers, but there is no esoteric ritual to follow once a hypnotist has discovered a proficient mind traveller.

Those who do accept a nonphysical capacity of men and women, but who find controlled mind travel difficult to reconcile with certain of their own pet theories, most likely will attempt to explain away the dramatic results of these experiments by ascribing them to telepathy or clairvoyance.

A telepathic facet of "psi" ability might indeed explain these sessions of mind travel if the subject described only those situations and events that were known to one or more of the witnesses observing the experiments. Such, as the reader has clearly seen, has not been the case.

Since the reach of the subconscious while in trance may be limitless, however, I do not suppose one can ever completely rule out clairvoyance. Still, one might argue that when one "sees at a distance," that is, engages that psychic ability known as clairvoyance, he or she is really projecting his or her essential self there to see the events and the people described.

The night that Alice McGregor served as subject, I decided to try another test to determine whether or not the mind, the soul, actually left the physical body.

Again, those who cherish orthodoxy will throw up their hands in despair, but I invited two friends, Faye and Mary Clark, to observe the reaction of the subject's aura to hypnotically induced mind travel. Both Faye and Mary had the unique ability of being able to observe the human aura with the naked eye—at least that was their claim. Neither of them ever gave me any reason to doubt their word in other areas of their lives. At that time they were a strikingly attractive middle-aged couple: Faye was soft-spoken, scholarly. Mary, who died recently, was poised, almost regal in her demeanor. There was nothing of the kook or crackpot about their nature.

The aura, according to occultists and those with extrasensory talents, is a glowing ring of psychic emanations which surrounds the human body. Some sensitives maintain that it is the astral body that transmits this radiation. Readers of this text will either accept or reject the ability to view auras depending on their own biases; however, for those who are interested in what two sensitives, who claim they can see auras, have to say about experiments in mind travel, I record the following:

Bill placed Alice McGregor in a deep hypnotic trance and asked her to travel to his home in Hinsdale, New Hampshire. He had recently purchased the house from the village doctor. While it was a veritable mansion, it was in great need of repairs and remodeling. Bill had joined me for these experiments when he should have been home spurring on his son Jack and a young friend, who were, he hoped, busy at work with hammer, wood paneling and carpet tacks. Bill wanted Alice to see how the boys were doing.

As Williams gave Alice the "deep sleep" command Faye and Mary observed that her aura began to withdraw, or fade out. And as Alice moved through the home and described the young men's progress (later verified by telephone), Faye and Mary noted that Alice's aura, which had once extended for several inches, was now but a mere outline around her body. At the completion of Alice's mind travelling, her aura was once again restored to its full radiation.

In short, it appeared to the Clarks that mind travelling did seem to bring about either a projection or an intense utilization of the aura. The aura did not disappear, for life remained in the physical body; but it seems, according to their analysis, that a major proportion of the aura's glow, or radiation, did withdraw to travel along with Alice's astral body.

16

Visiting a Haughty Lady from Old Scotland

Among the greatest out-of-body experiences may be the soul's journey back through time to a previous existence. Although this may not have some of the classic trappings of the spontaneous out-of-body experience, past-life regression is valid none the less. It fits into the category of controlled astral projection. Whether or not one accepts the validity of past life recall while under hypnotic regression, it cannot be denied that a great deal of paranormal material has been relayed during such experiments.

In the summer of 1969 while Loring Williams and I were conducting a number of experiments in controlled out-of-body projection, one of our guests came to us with a mystery. On the first night of her stay she had inexplicably lost a ring while she slept. She had searched her bedclothing exhaustively, and conducted a minute examination of the entire room. Strangely enough, although the ring seemed to have vanished without a trace, the ring's jade liner remained on her finger.

The woman, whom I shall call Joyce, suggested that she be hypnotized in an effort to recreate the circumstances under which the ring had disappeared. Williams placed her into trance quickly enough, but nothing evidential could be learned. We both noted, however, what a good hypnotic subject Joyce was.

Joyce was awakened and asked if she would consent to being placed into deep trance so that we might attempt a regression.

She quickly granted permission and, at Williams' "deep sleep" command, we were travelling back in time and space...hundreds of years...back until Joyce saw herself doing something....

Then, with a slight change in voice, suggestive of a high, aristocratic clip, rather than a low, common brogue, we found ourselves talking to a haughty lady from Scotland at about 1500.

We picked the woman up on the meadow of a large estate. When asked her name, she became upset because she could not remember. Williams told her not to worry, that it would come back to her.

"Who is your husband?" Williams asked.

"Lord Riven" (phonetically) was her reply.

The entity told us her estate was in the highlands and that she had two sons, David and Jamie. The estate was very large and they had a good number of servants who were part of the estate.

"How do you feed so many servants?" Williams wondered.

"Ha!" she laughed bitterly. "They probably eat better than we do. They steal us blind!"

The entity groused a bit about the light-fingered ways of her servants; then she seemed to become quite distressed because she had ridden away from the estate:

"I shouldn't be here," she said, her voice quickening, "but I used to love so to run this way."

Williams learned that she was expecting another child and that she had been criticized for pursuing her love of horseback riding. "But a little exercise is good, isn't it?" she asked, hoping for an ally.

The entity informed us that she had been born on the Cromie estate, the daughter of Alexander Cromie. She named villages and landmarks, some of which still exist, some of which may have disappeared ages ago. She distrusted the Campbells and was proud to be allied with the Stuarts.

She described her tartan shawl: "Aye, it is pretty. Every tartan tells a story. It tells everyone that I'm proud to be a Scotsman. Its thickness also tells everyone that we live in a bad climate!"

But she still could not remember her name.

Williams told her that at the count of three she would be able to recall her name and write it on a sheet of paper. This request was not beyond her capabilities because she had already explained that she had a rudimentary education typical of ladies of that time.

I handed the regressed subject a red nylon-tipped pen. She accepted it, began to write, then stopped, horrified. "It writes with blood!"

Williams took the pen from her before any trauma could set in and substituted a black pen. "Here is a good, old quill pen," he told her. "Write with that."

In a flowery, elegant script the entity wrote that she was "Fiona Riven, lady of Lord Riven."

Fiona went on to confess that she had always been considered a bit unorthodox and unconventional. To our way of thinking, the haughty Scottish lady sounded like a suffragette born several centuries ahead of her time. One priest in particular had given her a bad time.

"He has heaped penance upon me and made me suffer," she complained. "He says it is unseemingly if I go to the games where they throw the great weights and engage in feats of strength. He says a lady should not like to ride as much as I do. He admonishes me to take only the coach and never to sit on an animal's back."

"What color is your hair?" Williams inquired.

"It is the color of the devil and brings his own curse upon it because it so attracts attention" Fiona replied. "Father [meaning the priest] tells me that it [red hair] is Satan's mark upon me. Father cares not at all for women, but I think he has an eye for the men! I will no longer send my son to lessons. [Her voice became very concerned and she grimaced.] He keeps touching them.

"And Father laughs and drinks with the men. They don't see him the way he really is, because they are too often drunk and in stupor.

"Father gives me penance and advised my husband to put me away!"

We learned how Fiona's marriage to Lord Riven had been arranged when she was a girl of sixteen. Riven was considerably older than she, but she regarded him as a "bonny, brae man."

By moving Fiona backward and forward in time we deduced that we had first picked her up when she was about twenty-nine years of age. Once again attaining this age level, we moved her ahead five years.

We found Fiona seated at her sewing, embroidering a tapestry. She told us that she no longer rode. Such pastimes were behind her, regardless how much she had once loved it. She had now borne four children. One, a girl, had not lived. Another, a boy named Andrew, had been born with a "crooked back." And, Jamie and David were growing into strapping young men.

Fiona became visibly upset when we inquired about her husband. In a voice thickly edged with hurt and disgust, she told us that Lord Riven now concerned himself primarily with clan feuds and wenching, not necessarily in that order.

A short move into Fiona's future found her still sitting at her sewing, but we were startled to see the contorted manner in which she raised and used her hands. She had been hurt by a man, by many of them. Fiona grimaced in such obvious pain that Williams "counted" the pain away and encouraged her to tell us about the experience.

Lord Riven had been away fighting the Campbells. Fiona had been at home on the estate with the servants and the two younger sons. Men, whose faces she did not know, broke into the great house and demanded to know the whereabouts of Lord Riven. When Fiona refused to disclose this information, one of the men grasped her tightly by the wrists and beat her elbows on the table. Old Robert, a faithful manservant, was killed, and the serving girls were molested.

"But I wouldn't tell them," Fiona said softly, proudly. "I wouldn't tell them where my husband was."

The marauders, whom Fiona was certain must have come from the Campbells, destroyed the Abby and drove off most of the servants. The lady bemoaned the leaks and the draughts, but she expressed her determination to do what she could with the two lads and the few faithful servants.

"Wee Andrew does what he can with that crooked back, but he is but a babe," Fiona told us. "Jamie tries to work at the land a bit, while David, the older lad, is off fighting with his father against the Campbells. Jamie may make a good landsman, but already Andrew is good with the numbers. His back is crippled, but his mind is sharp."

Williams moved Fiona ahead another five years, and we found Riven Hall in the midst of a celebration. The clan wars had been over for a time, and David had returned sound in body to claim himself a bride.

Strangely enough, Fiona, the mother of the bridegroom did not seem to be present at the celebration proper; rather, she seemed to be merely reporting the festivities. When Williams questioned her about this, Fiona replied that she was watching the celebration from behind the curtains of a recessed balcony. She had been crippled from the waist down when the Campbells invaded the Great Hall in search of her husband. When she had refused to talk they had smashed her elbows as she had previously described; then, when the marauders saw they could not break her resistance, they slammed her against the stone fireplace and broke her back.

The proud and lusty Lord Riven, with his ever sharp eye for a comely wench, had hardly repaid Fiona's loyalty upon his return from the clan wars. When he beheld his broken and misshapen wife, he had her set aside in a secret room in the mansion and conducted himself as if she had died. Fiona had not even been granted the right to meet the young woman whom her David was marrying.

"They have told everyone that I am dead," Fiona said in a voice heavy with great sorrow.

"What of your sons?" Williams asked. "They come to see you, don't they?"

"They don't bother with me," Fiona sighed. "At least Jamie and David don't."

Andrew, the crippled lad, with whom she could now so easily identify, was the exception, however. Fiona and her youngest son, who was at this time about ten years old, had formed a firm bond of love between them. To insure that Andrew's bright mind would receive the proper amount of formal education, Fiona had sent the lad to her father, Alexander Cromie.

Williams moved the entity who called itself Fiona ahead another five years.

Williams: What are you doing?

Fiona: Nothing.

Williams: What do you feel?

Fiona: Nothing. I just seem to be floating. [It appeared as though Fiona's death experience had occurred sometime in the interim between the hypnotist's selected stopping points.]

Williams: Okay, Fiona. We'll go back to your last day as Fiona. One, two, three. What are you doing now?

Fiona: I'm lying down.

Williams: Who is there with you?

Fiona: (bitterly) My great, brae husband!

Williams: How is he?

Fiona: Not as good as he will be before the day is over!

Williams: Why?

Fiona: Because he wants to be free of me.

Williams: What does he have to say to you?

Fiona: Die! Die, damn you, die!

Williams: What of your sons? Are they there?

Fiona: Jamie is married. Davy has wee bairns. But they do not come to see me.

Williams: Not even Andrew?

Fiona: Andrew will be along directly. They told my husband that I was dying, so Lord Riven came into my chamber for the first time since before the wars. He wants me to die so that he can move my body out and move his wenches into this back room.

It is not enough that he has fouled my home with his ragged troops and his wenches, now he wants to bring his whores into my very bedchamber!

[Williams moved Fiona through the death experience. She described the serving women wrapping her dead body "in a cocoon" of cloths. Fiona was amazed that she could be "floating up here" and still see herself lying "down there" on the bed.]

Fiona: Why am I not roasting in the fires? [The entity suddenly screamed this question and began to verbalize a great deal of distress and confusion.]

Williams: Why would you roast in the fires?

Fiona: Because I've cursed my husband. And I've led my poor Andrew astray. He is going to set fire to the house. At the moment of my death he is going to burn Riven House to the ground, then there will be nothing for the great Lord to gloat over.

Williams: Before you died, you made Andrew promise to do this?

[With the information now discovered about the mother–son plot to destroy Riven estate, we realized for the first time that Fiona was not expecting to see hell's fires, but, rather, the flames of vengeance set by young Andrew, who, at that time, would have been fifteen.]

Fiona: Yes, yes. I made the lad promise to put the torch to Riven House. There they are! Oh, here come the flames! Beautiful! Beautiful!

Williams: Now what is going on?

Fiona: Everything! Everything is going to go! (She begins to laugh in between ecstatic cries of "beautiful, beautiful.")

Williams: Where is your husband?

Fiona: In the great hall, drinking and drunk! He will soon be baking in the fires of Hell! (terrible laughter) Beautiful! Beautiful! Curse his drunken soul!

Williams: We'll move on now a bit later. Has your husband been killed by the flames?

Fiona: Doesn't look like the flames got to him, but he is dead.

Williams: What are you doing?

Fiona: Floating.

Williams: Where is your husband?

Fiona: He is there (puzzled frown) and here.

Williams: Does he speak to you?

Fiona: I can see him, but I don't think we can speak to each other.

After a few moments, we moved Fiona through time toward the present until a yawning Joyce awakened in the easy chair before us. The story the emergent entity told was both compelling and greatly detailed. Since Joyce was spending the week assisting Williams and myself with the controlled OBE sessions, we asked her if she would again permit us to regress her to the Fiona personality.

Two nights later, Williams again gave the "deep sleep" command to Joyce, and she began to drift back in time and space to old Scotland. It was my plan to take over the questioning and try my best to trip up Fiona in regard to the details about her life.

This is an edited transcript of our second session with the haughty lady from Scotland:

Steiger: What are you doing today, Fiona? [I had asked Williams to place Fiona in the same year in which we had picked her up during the first session.]

Fiona: I am counting the linen, sir.

Steiger: Why do you count them?

Fiona: To make sure that they are all here. [Fiona had previously mentioned her distrust of the help, but it seemed this time she was only checking for torn linen which would have to be replaced.]

Steiger: What are your servants' names?

Fiona: There's Lucy, Mary and a new girl.

Steiger: Is old Robert still with you?

Fiona: Why, certainly.

Steiger: And there is faithful old Peter. [This was a ploy.]

Fiona: Peter? I know of no Peter on this household staff.

Steiger: Perhaps I am mistaken. Maybe he is the servant of another estate in the area. I have been visiting several other clans in Scotland. Perhaps Peter works for the Campbells. Are you a friend of the Campbells?

Fiona: You have come from the Campbells? [A quaver of disgust slightly distorts her voice.]

Steiger: I am just travelling around the area. I like to visit people as I travel. The Campbells seem to be very fine people.

Fiona: A lot of things seem to be something that they are not!

Steiger: Don't you think the Campbells are good people?

Fiona: No, I do not!

Steiger: What have they ever done to hurt you?

Fiona: I am busy today. [Her air becomes brusque, an aristocrat dismissing an annoying commoner.]

Steiger: Don't you want to discuss the Campbells?

Fiona: I thnk I have made myself clear. [At this point Fiona would answer no additional questions from me. I was forced to move her back to an earlier time in her life and begin the interrogation anew.]

Steiger: Fiona, at the count of three, it will be 1430.... Where are we now?

Fiona: Cromie.

Steiger: We are in the house of Cromie?

Fiona: Certainly.

Steiger: I knew a man once named Matthew Cromie. [This was a deliberate attempt to mislead the entity.] Was he your father?

Fiona: No, my father is Alexander. [She had stated this in the session before.]

Steiger: But I was certain that Matthew was lord of the house of Cromie. Are you quite sure that your father's name isn't Matthew?

Fiona: His name is Alexander. [She goes on to describe her father as being a big man, "broad with sandy hair aged with white."]

Steiger: I cannot see too well, but you seem to have black hair. [She instantly corrected and reaffirmed her "satan's mark," her red hair.] How old are you, Fiona?

Fiona: How did you know my name?

Steiger: I stopped and asked the servants at these fine gates, and they told me that you were one of the master's daughters. What is your sister's name?

Fiona: Dierden.

Steiger: How old is she?

Fiona: Nineteen.

Steiger: And you are a few years older?

Fiona: No, I am not.

Steiger: You seem older than nineteen. How old are you?

Fiona: Do I look nineteen to you? [She began to giggle girlishly at the flattery.] Goodness! Let me then be nineteen. And what might your age be?

Steiger: I am quite a bit older than nineteen.

Fiona: A man is only as old as he acts.

Steiger: How old are you really, Fiona?

Fiona: I'll soon be fifteen, and that's grown.

Steiger: Do you have a boyfriend, a suitor?

Fiona: There are those who have asked my father about me. Some of them have fast changed their minds.

Steiger: Why would they change their minds? You seem like a bonnie lass to me.

Fiona: Have you spoken to my father?

Steiger: No, I am just interested in being friends with you. I have come from the Stuarts, and they seem to be kind people.

Fiona: Aye, they are the best.

Steiger: And I have also visited with the Campbells. They, too, seem to be kind people.

Fiona: (in disgust) You run the gamut, don't you?

Steiger: I am interested in meeting all the people in Scotland. What do you do for entertainment around here?

Fiona: Entertainment?

Steiger: What do you do for diversion, to pass the time? Fiona named a number of locales she considered to be of interest. When I asked what I could do at those places she laughed and said one should simply enjoy their beauty. I then inquired what I might do for physical activity. If I were a hunter, she advised me that there were a number of roe (deer) and partridge and other foul to stalk.

Steiger: How would I catch these fowl? Just run and snare them in a sack?

Fiona: (laughing) You aren't a gentleman are you?

Steiger: I try to be, but I am not yet familiar with the customs here.

Fiona: If you were a gentleman, you would know how to hunt no matter where you come from on this isle!

Steiger: Should I use a bow and arrow?

Fiona: (sharply) Are you a tradesman?

Steiger: Yes.

Fiona: Then I won't spend any more time with you, sir! [Again I had been curtly dismissed by the haughty lady from Scotland.]

Steiger: Fiona, I am going to count to three, and when I do, you will come with me to 1415. . . . What are you doing?

Fiona: I am in my chamber, sir, and the question is what are *you* doing in here with me?

Steiger: I am just coming in to check on you.

Fiona: Oh, yes. Have you now seen all you want to see, or would you be good enough to step outside?

Steiger: [I tried to placate her.] I am one of the new servants, and your father asked me to. . . .

Fiona: Will you get out of my chamber! [At this point she began to scream, and there was nothing to do but to remove both myself and Fiona from that particular scene. I counted to three again and set 1420 as the target year.]

Steiger: Why must we be quiet?

Fiona: We are at prayers.

Steiger: At the count of three, we will move ahead just a little bit in time until the prayers are over. You will want to talk to me and tell me things about yourself.... What are you doing?

Fiona: I am walking about the house after Matins.

Steiger: Do you enjoy going to Matins?

Fiona: I guess you are supposed to enjoy them.

Steiger: Are you a devout young woman?

Fiona: Certainly, sir.

Steiger: Do you listen carefully to what the priest tells you?

Fiona: Oh, I listen.

Steiger: Do you obey?

Fiona: Oh, yes.

Steiger: How often do you go to confession?

Fiona: Every Saturday.

Steiger: Does the priest ever lay penance on you for misdeeds?

Fiona: Some of the best ones I tell him he ignores!

Steiger: What are some of the misdeeds which you have committed?

Fiona: I don't trust my soul with strangers!

[I counted to three at this point and told the entity I was her priest and that she must confess her sins to me and confide in me all things.]

Fiona: Oh, Father, I do try to be good and to obey my father and mother, but sometimes it is so difficult.

Steiger: I understand, my child. Do you say your rosary every afternoon and evening?

Fiona: Yes, Father, and I say the whole rosary each time.

Steiger: That is fine, Fiona. Do you have any sins to confess to me?

Fiona: I caused the stable boy to be beaten!

Steiger: How was this?

Fiona: I told my father that it was he who rode the horse to sweat and did not rub her down.

Steiger: Ah, my child, you know better than to do such a thing!

Fiona: But I like to ride, Father, and I like to ride fast. I know you consider it unseemly for a young woman to ride, but it brings me so much pleasure.

Steiger: What other sins have you committed, my daughter?

Fiona: I listened to my sister's courting!

Steiger: You should have gone to the nuns for such instructions.

Fiona: Do you mean that they have such experience!

Steiger: It is given to nuns to know certain things.

Fiona: Ah, Father, then why is it not given to young ladies to know such things?

Steiger: You must wait your time, my child. Have you other sins to confess?

Fiona: I took off my skirts to go swimming.

Steiger: You went swimming in a common brook? Why would a young lady of such fine family do such a vulgar thing?

Fiona: I always do it, Father!

[With Fiona complaining that she had not asked to be born a girl and that she would rather have been born male, I moved her ahead to 1448.]

Fiona: I am waiting for my husband.

Steiger: Is he out working on the estate?

Fiona: I think they are having a meeting. They are always having meetings. It worries me.

Steiger: Doesn't he tell you about the meetingss?

Fiona: Sometimes he tells me it is for my own good that I don't know.

Steiger: Do you have any children, Fiona?

Fiona: I have had four. I only have three now. David and Jamie and the baby, Andrew.

Steiger: They all seem to be strong lads, especially the youngest.

Fiona: (at once on guard and curt in manner) What do you know of the baby? Nobody sees him.

Steiger: Why not?

Fiona: My husband says no one can see him. I am not to show him.

Steiger: Why?

Fiona: Andrew was born with a twisted back.

Steiger: Why does your husband feel so strongly about Andrew?

Fiona: He feels that a crippled child would reflect upon the strength of the Riven house.

Steiger: How do you feel about Andrew? Does his twisted back bother you?

Fiona: He is so sweet. His twisted back bothers me some, but it would bother me more if I didn't have the babe.

Steiger: Where is your fourth child?

Fiona: Her name was Caroline. She did not live.

[At the count of three, Fiona was moved ahead to 1456. I suggested that she would feel free to confide in me and to tell me things which she would not tell others. When we picked her up this time, Fiona was in pain with her injured hands, and Williiams temporarily resumed control to free her of the physical torment. Fiona once again described the raid by the hooded men and told us how she had been tortured and had her back broken against the hard stones of the fireplace. As she had told us before, old Robert had been killed trying to defend her, and she named a servant girl who had been so brutally abused by the marauders that she, too, had died. We moved ahead this time to 1460.]

Fiona: I'm in a bed chamber.

Steiger: Who is with you?

Fiona: I'm alone. I am always alone.

Steiger: Where is Davy?

Fiona: He is with his wife and his wee bairn.

Steiger: You have not yet seen your grandchild? Why not?

Fiona: They have never brought him to me. They conduct their affairs as if I do not exist.

[After determining the whereabouts of Jamie, I asked about Andrew. It was obvious that the two cripples, mother and son, had formed a firm alliance. "Andrew is twisted and ugly in his body," the entity told us, "but he has the bonniest face you've ever seen on a man!"]

Steiger: Why isn't your husband with you?

Fiona: I haven't seen the likes of him for quite some while.

Steiger: He doesn't come to see you anymore?

Fiona: (laughing bitterly) He doesn't like my looks.

Steiger: Is he ashamed of you because you are a cripple? But you were injured protecting him.

Fiona: You see it that way; he does not.

Steiger: Do you still love him, even when he has abused you so?

Fiona: Aye, but I hate him, too. What is love and hate?

[Fiona, at my request, described her bedchamber in minute detail. As a cripple, she had a great deal of time to do nothing other than lie and look about her room. She complained how her husband had gone through her money, as well as his own. "My father's dowry to this great ass kept him in armor for quite a while," she fumed. "My dowry outfitted a good many of his men for the wars!"

I interrogated her at great length concerning the weaponry of the era and, according to reference works, Fiona's names and descriptions were accurate for the period. Once when her memory failed her while she was searching for the proper word to describe a particular type of leather breast shield, I told her that I would count to three and she would remember the elusive term. At the count of three, she spoke the correct name. She considered this for a moment, frowned, then asked me: "How do you do that?"]

Steiger: Now we will move ahead to 1465, Fiona. One...two... three. What are you doing now?

Fiona: I...I'm lying in my bed. Feel as if...great weight has just been taken from me. Pain is leaving me. It is good to get away from the bitterness that has been eating at me.

Steiger: Bitterness toward whom?

Fiona: Toward that great, brae husband of mine.

Steiger: Has he come to see you now?

Fiona: He was up to see me a day or two ago, but all he did was spew his filth on me.

Steiger: Filth? To you, his wife?

Fiona: He says I have been no wife to him these past years. And I said to him, "Did you ever come up to ask me?"

Steiger: What was his reply?

Fiona: He said the pickings were more pleasant elsewhere.

Steiger: Has he been unfaithful to you?

Fiona: Is there any other way for a man to be?

Steiger: Let us move along now to another day. What are you doing?

Fiona: Waiting for Andrew. Waiting for him. The plan. He will work our plan.

Steiger: Tell me of the plan. You know that you can trust me.

Fiona: I've talked with the boy. It is not fair that I have had to suffer, that I have been humiliated, that I have been deserted. That proud cock is so ungrateful. He will pay for his ingratitude with the loss of this damned estate!

Steiger: How will he lose this?

Fiona: I will take it with me! Andrew will help me.

Steiger: How will a dying woman and a crippled young man accomplish this? [After eliciting my promise that I would not betray them, Fiona revealed this plan.]

Fiona: Andrew will fire the place as soon as I die. He has kept the books all these years, and all this time he has sneaked a little oil from the lamps. He has fixed it so it doesn't show in the books. He is going to sprinkle the oil around the place and set a torch to it.

Steiger: What will happen to Andrew?

Fiona: He will take some money that has been put aside and go to my father at Cromie.

Steiger: Let us move ahead another day. [I noticed a strange change of expression on her face.] What is happening, Fiona?

Fiona: Nothing is wrong. I am just dying.

Steiger: Are you in pain?

Fiona: Who cares?

Steiger: I care. I don't want you to be in pain.

Fiona: It will soon be gone.

Steiger: Where is your husband? Isn't he with you?

Fiona: He is down drinking with his men. Celebrating!

Steiger: What about Andrew?

Fiona: Andrew is about his business.

Steiger: The plan? [Although her voice had been growing increasingly weaker and more feeble, Fiona grew a bit more animated.]

Fiona: You know about the plan?

Steiger: Yes, you told me about it. But don't worry, I haven't betrayed you.

Fiona: But you didn't forget it, either.

Steiger: No. I remember it.

Fiona: Then get it from your mind. If they catch you, they'll get it from you!

Steiger: Let us move ahead just a bit further in time to the last time your husband comes to see you.

Fiona: (with great bitterness) Well, if it isn't the great, gay cock!

Steiger: What does he say to you?

Fiona: He tells me to hurry up with my dying. He says that he will rejoice when it is over, and if I take too much longer, he will be pleased to help me along.

Steiger: How do you answer him?

Fiona: Only with words of love. [Her voice breaks into gentle sobbing.] Only with words of love.

There seemed little point in forcing the entity to recreate the trauma of the death experience, so I decided to terminate the second session at this point. Everyone agreed that we had received a great deal of data dealing with daily life in Scotland in the fifteenth century, and that we had details regarding everything from linen preparation to weaponry.

We were also delighted with the quick wit of the entity and amused at the lively manner in which she responded to my questions.

And each of those who witnessed the second session were extremely impressed by the fact that Fiona's rapid responses were never incorrect. No matter how many times we moved her backward or forward, she always knew the ages of her children and other related trivia as they pertained to that particular time in her life pattern.

Our third session with Fiona, which took place two nights later, presented us with a surprise dividend which took us completely off guard and gave us an extraordinary glimpse of a most bizarre facet of the paranormal.

Williams had brought Fiona back to a time shortly after the child Andrew was born. When he turned the questioning over to me, he told the entity that she could trust in me as she would her very most inner self and that she would keep no secrets from me.

We began by discussing matters which would seem pure trivia if I were to set them down for the casual reader, but for research purposes, would allow us to compile more facts that might be substantiated. Fiona said that she was troubled by the sound of my voice. I counted to three, moved to the year 1441, and told her that she had no reason to be disturbed.

At the final count, we were listening to the music of bagpipes. I asked Fiona if she might hum or sing along with the music.

"It's got no words," she said, "but it stirs the blood, doesn't it?" Upon saying this, she began to hum a lively tune with a strong Scottish flavor.

Fiona told me that we now stood outside, listening to the sound of the pipes being carried on the wind. I asked her to describe the various kinds of flora growing around us, which she did without hesitation. Later, we determined that all of the plants which she named would have been growing in Scotland at that time.

"I want to thank you for talking with me, Fiona," I began. "When I count to three...."

"Oh," she interrupted, "there is someone else here!"

"Who?"

Fiona–Joyce squirmed in her chair. She appeared to be frightened and she was becoming more agitated by the second. "I don't know, but he is approaching us!"

"Relax. You need not feel any anxiety. When I count to three we will begin to move away from Scotland and 1441. We will move through time and space. One..."

"Brad!" Joyce screamed, "There is someone else here talking to me!"

Something had seized Joyce before I could finish the countdown that would have brought her back to 1969. Our control had obviously been broken, because that had not been Fiona with her soft Scottish brogue who had screamed for help. The voice was that of Joyce, and she was not calling out in her fear for assistance from a stranger, she was shouting for help from me, a friend, who stood by in momentary confusion.

"Brad!"

"Deep sleep, Joyce!" Williams commanded in his deep, reassuring voice.

Williams was, of course, the hypnotist who had been in control. It was Williams who, each session, would regress Joyce to her ostensible life as Fiona, then introduce me to the entity and allow me to do the questioning. Now, to our consternation, something had, in some manner unknown to us, managed to temporarily usurp Williams' control.

"You're in a deep sleep, Joyce," Williams told her. "It is 1969, and we are here in Brad's office. Who was talking to you?"

"I don't know."

"Do you want to see who it was? Do you feel fear? Do you want to wake up?"

Joyce indicated that she was frightened, but, somehow, she felt an obligation to attempt to contact the interloper.

"He cannot harm you at all," I told her, once again assuming control from Williams. "You must feel absolutely no fear or anxiety. You will be able to see this entity objectively.

"I am going to place a golden shield of protection around you. I will take the tip of a great Crusader's sword and trace a circle of fire around you. Nothing will be able to penetrate the circle of flame. Do you see my sword? [This was power of suggestion, of course. Joyce answered, "Yes."] It is going around and around you. Do you see the flames that it leaves in its wake? ["Yes."] It is now completed."

"I see him," Joyce said. "He stands very straight and tall. He carries his hands before him as if he is reaching out to me. He tells me to come closer."

"Go ahead," I assured her. "You can because of the circle of protection which I put around you. You need have no fear or anxiety."

"He smiles at the flames, and he speaks, but I cannot hear him."

I counted to three, and told Joyce that she would now be able to hear him distinctly.

"He is looking for one of those assembled here tonight."

"Ask him to whom he wishes to speak."

Joyce's forehead crinkled in concentration. "I—I can't understand him. I never heard...seen...anything like this. It is like he is speaking in geometric designs...like I can see these designs in cartoon-type balloons over his head."

"When I count to three," I told her, "you will be able to translate these designs as he releases them."

Joyce said that she still could not understand the entity. I directed her to convey that she wished to cooperate but that she could not until she could understand what he wished to communicate. If he did not wish to talk, I said, then she must tell him that we would leave him.

Joyce's next impression was that the entity wished to speak, but could not. Joyce described him as wearing a loose-flowing garment with a hood which shielded his face from her vision. The skin of his arms, which could be seen as he reached out toward her, was a dark, healthy brown.

"Brad." Faye Clark, who was witnessing the experiments that night, spoke up. "I think I know who this is, and I think that I am to be the recipient of the message. It is also my feeling that if you were to change the circle of fire to an aura of golden orange, he would be able to speak."

I did as Faye suggested, and Joyce said that the mysterious entity was now surrounded by swirling colors.

"Tell him that he is welcome here," I told her. "Ask him to speak if he desires to communicate with anyone here. We would like to hear from him."

"Someone here knows him," Joyce said.

"Mr. Clark says that he knows him."

At this point, the entity delivered a message through Joyce, which, judging by Faye Clark's response, had great personal meaning for him. Then, after a general message to all those assembled in my office that evening, the entity left us.

Afterward, as we sat around coffee cups analyzing the experience, I was interested in noting the spectrum of reactions and comments from those who had witnessed the unexpected communication.

First of all, our reluctant medium, Joyce, was completely stunned to hear from us what had come through her lips. She had never had any aspirations of becoming mediumistic, and she firmly expressed her wish that she would never again be "used" by an external entity.

Faye Clark told us that the entity had first contacted him years ago and that it had given him certain instructions which he had attempted to follow. This had been Clark's first contact with the entity since that time, and he had been pleased to receive certain admonitions which had been meaningful to him in relation to the previous teaching.

Rita, either because of her own sensitivity or because she may have become susceptible to my hypnotic suggestions, had seen clearly the circle of fire which I had drawn around Joyce with my "Crusader's sword."

Later when the entity took control of Joyce to deliver the message to Faye Clark, Rita saw Joyce's features become transfigured into those of a gaunt visaged man with a dark beard. She had become so upset by the metamorphosis that her husband had had to lead her from my office.

Williams and I were puzzled by the fact that hypnotic control had been broken. While neither of us would flatly deny the existence of entities, elementals and possessive spirits, we had never considered the possibility of such ethereal interference in our experiments.

Even after such a dramatic episode as that evening's, I do not believe that either of us would state that our placing a subject in hypnotic trance would open the subject to possession by "spirits." With an experienced, competent hypnotist at the helm and in full control of his or her subject, there can be little danger of any extraneous force, or will, influencing the entranced party.

If what happened that night really was the temporary invasion of an extraneous intelligence—and we did witness a most extraordinary phenomenon along with a dozen others who were in attendance that night—then we would have to suppose that the entity responsible for such an action was indeed a most powerful one.

As we listened to a playback of the tape for that evening, we were able to pick up at least three places when Fiona had become nervous or frightened and had told the control, me, that there was someone else present.

Although a regressed subject does not generally remember but bits and snatches of an experiment, Joyce, perhaps because of the strange, etheric "interference," did recall being watched from the trees by a hooded figure. As "Fiona," she had felt that it was her nemesis, the priest, spying on her in order to present another uncomplimentary report to her husband, Lord Riven.

Faye Clark told us that the entity which had spoken through Joyce that night had lived at approximately the same time, the fifteenth century, but on the other side of the globe. It seemed possible to Clark that, desirous of making contact, the powerful entity had somehow gained knowledge of our time travel back to that particular plane of existence and had "hitched a ride" back with Joyce as we began to count her back to 1969.

And all of this, the discovery of "Fiona" and the visitation by an entity from an ancient priesthood, had come about because Joyce had lost a valuable ring. Although under hypnosis Joyce was unable to re-create how she had misplaced the ring, it did return under most mysterious circumstances.

It was the day after the final session with "Fiona" and the surprise visitation had taken place—five days after Joyce's ring had disappeared—that we began to notice a disagreeable odor which seemed to be emanating from the downstairs half-bath. There were no sewer problems in spite of heavy summer rains, but I can remember spraying the bath with air fresheners several times that day. We were entertaining a good number of people who had come to volunteer for experiments in controlled out-of-body experience, and I was embarrassed by the terrible smell.

That evening, Williams was in my study explaining the scope of our experiments to a number of guests. My wife, my secretary and I had excused ourselves to prepare cold drinks. We were the only ones in the kitchen; everyone else was in the study.

"That smell!" My wife complained. "I'm embarrassed to have anyone come out in our kitchen with that terrible odor coming from the half-bath."

She picked up a can of air freshener, walked back to repeat the ritual of pressurized purification.

"Say," she snapped her fingers. "The smell seems to be coming from the children's sink in the hall. I've been keeping some potatoes under there. You don't suppose there is a rotten potato in the sack?"

"How could there be as often as you've been making potato salad this past week?" Jeanyne asked. "You haul that sack out at least once a day."

"Well, it won't hurt to check." My wife knelt, opened the door in the sink's cabinet, removed the potatoes.

We found no rotten potato, but we did find Joyce's ring. And almost at once, the disagreeable odor had gone.

"It appears that something may have been using the 'bloodhound technique' with us," I remarked. "It seems as though we have been led by our noses and our sense of smell right to Joyce's ring!"

Joyce was elated to have her highly valued ring returned to her, but she could not understand us when we described how we had found it.

She had never used the half-bath downstairs, and she was unaware of the small sink and cabinet in the back hall which we had installed primarily for the children's use.

But *where* and *how* we had recovered her ring did not matter at all to Joyce. She was only overjoyed to have regained possession of her keepsake.

And, I quess, her repossession of the ring is really all that does matter. Maybe too often we mortals insist on asking "why" and "how" when we should really learn to be more gracious recipients of gifts bestowed upon us.

17

Into the Time Tunnel

The romantic notion of being able to travel either forward or backward in time has teased our imagination for centuries. Devotees of science fiction never seem to grow weary of an author's attempt to come up with a new twist on the standard "time machine" plot.

It may be, however, that the concept of a physical machine constructed especially for time travel is an erroneous one. We may one day learn that the only mechanism capable of travelling unhindered through the space-time continuum is our own mind.

Professor Charles Hapgood told me how he and Williams used mind travel to investigate the histories of various archeological excavations. Professor Hapgood has said that a great deal of the information relayed by hypnotized subjects directed to these locations has since been verified by in-field expeditions.

As Professor Hapgood stated, the accuracy with which subjects uder hypnosis have described the social conditions of past times into which they have been sent has inspired him with a dream of far-reaching historical investigation. It is his hope, Hapgood has said, to have the resources to "...use a hundred hypnotists and five thousand hypnotic subjects for a really thorough investigation of how people lived in past times." Professor Hapgood has become convinced that it is from such hypnotized mind travellers that an investigator can acquire, and later confirm, the sort of fascinating details of everyday life that are "usually neglected in the history books."

Spontaneously, people have been inadvertently making sudden trips on the time track for centuries, and the processes of obtaining visions of the future (precognition) and re-creations of the past (retrocognition) have become recognized as another uncontrollable facet of psychic phenomena. If energy, like matter, is indestructible, then the impulse and vibration of every word and deed ever uttered or enacted might still be echoing and pulsating on some psychic ether. The same kind of paranormal mental mechanism that enables the emotions of certain individuals to permeate a room or a house and cause their "ghost" to be seen by those later inhabitants who may possess a similar telepathic affinity, may also cause certain emotionally charged scenes of the past to become imprinted upon the psychic ether and reactivated by those individuals with the proper attunement. At the same time, momentous and emotionally supercharged incidents from the future may somehow reverberate "back" into the present.

There are numerous classic cases of those who have experienced spontaneous trips on the time track. Anyone at all familiar with the literature of psychic phenomena has read accounts of the *Petit Trianon* incident, wherein two English school teachers, Miss C. Ann E. Moberly, principal of St. Hugh's College, Oxford, and Eleanor F. Jourdain, a member of her staff, found themselves, in 1901, traversing the grounds of the French tourist attraction as it existed at the time of Marie Antoinette.

Another oft-cited case is that of Miss Edith Oliver, who, on a rainy night in October 1916, observed a village fair, the like of which had been abolished in 1850, and drove on a particular avenue that had disappeared before 1800.

The famous "phantom battle of Edge Hill" was refought by spectral soldiers on several consecutive weekends during the Christmas season of 1642, and emissaries of the King, who had been sent to debunk the accounts, were able to recongize comrades who had fallen in the bloody fray.

On August 4, 1951, two Englishwomen vacationing in Dieppe, heard a violently audible re-creation of the ill-fated raid which had taken place nine years before and had resulted in the slaughter of nearly a thousand young Canadians. The record, which the women kept of the ebb and flow of the battle, was found to be identical to the minute with accounts of the raid which were held by the war office.

Anyone who chooses to take the time can find hundreds of testimonies from sober and sincere men and women who have claimed to have walked into offices from another era, driven on roads that no longer exist through lively villages long ago deserted, and who have witnessed everything from love scenes to fist fights from previous decades and centuries.

Author Russell Kirk told the *Los Angeles Times* how he glimpsed a quaint street one night in 1949 while he was exploring the ancient city of York between trains. He has since spent years trying to rediscover that short street beautifully lined with eighteenth- and seventeenth-century houses. Kirk has finally concluded, on the basis of available records, that he must have seen a section of the city as it once was before it was destroyed at the turn of the century.

In 1956, Leonard Hall reported to the St. Louis *Post-Dispatch* that he had seen Spanish *conquistadores* and Indians when he and a number of companions were fishing and camping on the Upper Current River in the Ozarks in August, 1941.

October 23, 1963, Mrs. Coleen Buterbaugh, secretary to the Dean of Nebraska Wesleyan College in Lincoln, stepped into an office as it must have been in the 1920s. Mrs. Buterbaugh told Rose Sipe of the *Evening Journal*: "I gazed out the large window behind the desk and the scenery seemed to be that of many years ago. There were no streets. The new Williard sorority house that now stands across the lawn was not there. Nothing outside was modern. . . ." With the help of old college yearbooks and a venerable member of the college staff, Mrs. Buterbaugh identified the apparition of a woman which she had seen in the office as the image of a music teacher who had died in that room.[1]

With Bill Williams' rationale, "if 'psi' phenomena is possible spontaneously, why not learn to control it," as our guiding principle, we conducted numerous experiments in mind travel into scenes of the past. For several of these sessions, my friend Rita served as the subject.

At this point I must concede that, regardless how fascinating the experiments were, we have not come up with any kind of conclusive evidence to convince the skeptic that we had actually found access to a "time tunnel." In most cases, however, the circumstantial evidence for at least some kind of clairvoyant reading of the past is most impressive.

I have been an avid student of history since childhood, and in more than one instance, I found my memory of a certain episode faulty when compared to Rita's psychic reportage, which I later verified by research in reference volumes. I do know that Rita has never been particularly interested in history, and I am quite certain that she had never heard of most of the incidents to which we "sent her back."

---

[1]These cases, and many others of a similar nature, are reported in greater detail in my *True Ghost Stories*, Para Research, 1982.

Professor Charles Hapgood, for many years professor of anthropology at Keene State College in New Hampshire, participated in a number of earlier experiments in time travel and past life regression with Williams. Hapgood is the author of *Earth's Shifting Crust, Great Mysteries of the Earth* and *Maps of the Ancient Sea Kings*. He is a Fellow of the Royal Geographical Society, the Museum of Modern Man and the *Union Internationale de la Presse Scientifique*. Here, in his own words, is an account of how he first became interested in research which his colleagues no doubt considered a bit bizarre:

"When people asked me whether I believed in reincarnation, I said I regarded it as merely an interesting superstition. Then one day Mr. Charles H. Cook, a trained psychiatrist, who was at the time president of the New Hampshire Society for Psychical Research, asked me if I would like to accompany him to a meeting of the society of Shaker Village, in northern New Hampshire. I accepted, and at the meeting, a Dr. Kenneth Lyons, who was president of the New England Society and a trained hypnotist, put one of the audience in trance and started regressing him backwards in time.

"I was amazed as I saw how, under hypnosis, the subject was able to recall every little detail of a day in his sixth year, his first day at school.

"I held my breath as the hypnotist said, 'Now I want you to go back to the last time you were on earth before this present life.'

"Then Dr. Lyons asked the subject (whose name was Fred) his name, and Fred answered, 'George.' Question after question brought out a complete description of George's life as an indentured servant in a country house in the early seventeenth century in Cornwall, England.

"As a lifelong student of social history, I was amazed at the accuracy of the description of the social customs of that time. It would have been impossible for the subject to have been familiar with the details of country life as he described them, or with the life of the thief in London, which this same George later became. But George made not one mistake.

"This experience shook me up, you may be sure. But I was not satisfied with the exhibition. I wanted to try it out for myself with my students, and so we did this many, many times.

"In one case we regressed a girl into a past life as the daughter of a fur trader in French Canada. She had never studied French, but in hypnosis she spoke fluent and faultless French, and she also took on the characteristic body gestures of a French woman. She described a method of curing hides that has not been in use for a hundred years. Later we regressed her furher back and got a detailed description of the life of the daughter of a feudal lord—with no mistakes.

"On one occasion I accidentally became hypnotized myself when one of my students was trying to hypnotize some other people. Seeing that I had gone into trance, he regressed me to the past, and I suddenly found myself in a Hindu Temple, and was able to describe the way of life of the monks.

"Soon we found that we could "progress" students into the near future, and we did this a number of times. In this case it was easy to check the results, for we had only to wait three or four days to compare what the subjects had experienced in trance with what actually happened. These experiments told us something about time travel.

"About this time I met Mr. Loring Williams, whom we all call 'Bill.' He enrolled in one of my evening courses at the college. He already knew a great deal at that time about hypnosis. Knowing that I had many archeological projects on foot, he suggested that we apply the principles of time and space travel under hypnosis to them. We got some interesting results. One case is especially interesting.

"Some years before a woman had written to me from a western state, and sent me a clipping that told about a floor made of well-shaped bricks or stones, underlying glacial material on the western slopes of the Rocky Mountains in Colorado. This, if it could be proved, would be of the greatest interest for archeology, for it would indicate that man had been building advanced types of buildings in America before the Ice Age, or perhaps 60,000 years ago, which, of course, according to the official views, would be an impossibility. That is just the reason why I wanted to prove it.

"My students finally located the floor, and we got photographs of it. We started organizing an expedition to go out there. We also made use of hypnosis.

"Mr. Williams put one of the students (and later myself) in trance and sent us out there "astrally" to observe it. I saw the floor. Bill asked me to go back to the time when I could see it being built. I did so, and I told him that it was being built about 5,000 years ago. This was a surprise, and something of a disappointment to me, because I expected a much greater age.

"It turned out that my vision in the trance was proved true. I had asked the United States Geological Survey to send an expert to the site of the floor to meet my party there and make a study of the geology of the deposits under the floor.

"When it turned out that we were unable to go (for financial reasons), the Geological party went anyway, and turned in an estimate of about 5,000 years for the age of the floor. The material on top of the floor was glacial, all right, but it had been washed out of a nearby glacial deposit and redeposited over the floor.

"The payoff in this particular case was that even after we had established the existence of the floor, and proved that it was probably several thousand years older than the oldest presently known stone structure in the Western Hemisphere, not a single professional archeologist was sufficiently interested to go to see it!

"On another occasion, when I was working on ancient maps (which led to the publication of my book, *Maps of the Ancient Sea Kings*), Williams hypnotized a high-school student and sent him to the Topkapi Palace in Constantinople to look at the collection of ancient maps there. The student correctly described the appearance of the palace from the waterfront—the interior rooms and particularly the map room, with the ancient maps on parchment rolls, a type of map the student had never seen! He then described a map that he said had actually been drawn in the time of Alexander the Great! However, I have not yet been able to get to the palace to confirm his finding.

"I must mention one matter that may have great importance for the future. The accuracy with which subjects under hypnosis describe the social conditions of the past times in which they apparently lived has inspired me with a dream of a far-reaching historical investigation. It is my hope that someday I shall have the resources to use a hundred hypnotists and 5,000 hypnotic subjects for a really thorough investigation of how people lived in past times. It seems that from hypnotic subjects we get precisely the sort of fascinating details of everyday life that are usually neglected in the history books."

Unless an archeological expedition brings back confirmatory evidence, as in the case that Professor Hapgood reported, there seems little way of substantiating a trip through the time tunnel back to ancient times. To revisit more recent historical events would only invite accusations that the subject or the hypnotist has at least second-hand knowledge of the incidents described.

The only way to "prove" mind travel into the past seems to be to allow scholars to select a certain incident which lies far enough back in time to be removed from the general subject's realm of knowledge, yet which has already yielded certain pertinent, and generally agreed upon, data to those who have made the historic episode a part of their scholarly expertise. Once such an incident has been selected by a panel of scholars, a hypnotized subject might then be sent back to describe the characters and the activity for the academicians' scrutiny and examination. If enough specific actions were combined with enough revelatory minutiae, then it might be so adduced that the subject had, in some manner, cut through the barriers of time and reported upon a scene and upon its actors with a degree of accuracy which would lie far beyond chance.

Professor Hapgood, an historian of considerable repute, feels that a good number of convincing time travel experiments were conducted by the psychical research group at Keene.

"Our success with time travel into the past inspired me to see whether we might not be able to project our subjects into the future," Professor Hapgood recalls. "I reasoned that time travel, if it exists, should work both ways."

To Professor Hapgood's utter amazement, the psychical research group at Keene State College was quite successful in projecting subjects into the future. In several instances they managed to project the subjects two or three days ahead. This had the advantage that it was easy to check what the subjects had said about the future under hypnosis.

One of their subjects was a boy named Jay. On a Sunday evening he was put into trance and received the suggestion that, at the hypnotist's count of six, it would be the following Wednesday.

The hypnotist counted to six and asked the subject to name the day of the week. Jay replied, "Wednesday." They asked Jay to give them the headlines of the Wednesday newspaper, but he could not. (On the following Wednesday, Professor Hapgood reported, they established the fact that Jay did not see a newspaper or listen to radio or television news on that day.)

Jay told them that he was at the Keene Airport and that he was picking up a very interesting story which had to do with an airplane accident that had occurred at Montpelier a year before. There had never been a satisfactory explanation of the accident, and Jay had been especially interested in learning more about the incident. Now, in trance, reporting the experiences of three days ahead in the future, Jay said that he was at the airport listening to a complete account of the disaster as it was being related to him by a pilot who happened to be between flights.

Professor Hapgood asked the students in the circle to watch Jay closely during the following Wednesday to see whether the events throughout the day (such as class assignments, tests, luncheon menu, etc.) would correspond to those details given to them by Jay in trance on Sunday. In a post-hypnotic suggestion, Jay was asked to come visit Professor Hapgood on Wednesday evening.

"When Jay came," Professor Hapgood said, "I asked him where he had been. He said he had been to the Keene Airport. I asked him when he had decided to go down there, and he said it had been about the middle of the afternoon and he had asked his girlfriend to accompany him. I asked him whether he went down there often, and he said, no, he went about once a month. Then I asked him whether anything interesting had happened, and he told me exactly the same story he had given us Sunday—he had met this flier who was just passing through, purely by accident, and had learned the cause of the Montpelier crash."

Later, when the students who had attended the hypnotic session reported back to Professor Hapgood, they found that ". . .a comparison of the details of the entire day showed a nearly complete agreement between the events of the day and the trance precognition. Incredible as it seemed, it was clear that Jay had lived through an entire day three days before it happened!"

Professor Hapgood feels that an even more dramatic case is that of a subject named Henry. This young man was entranced on a Sunday evening and "progressed" to the following Thursday.

Under trance and ahead four days in the future, Henry told the experimenters that he was going to Brattleboro that evening to have a good time, *i.e.*, to get drunk. They asked him how he was going to get there, and he said he was going to borrow his friend's car.

The hypnotist progressed Henry along a few hours, and he told them that he was in a diner drinking beer with two women, who were making improper advances to him and saying very uncomplimentary things about their husbands. When pressed under hypnosis to relay these remarks, Henry refused to do so, as it would conflict with his ethical standards.

However, he did tell the experimenters that he returned to Keene about 2:00 A.M. and had some trouble with the dogs at home, because they barked and awakened the family. Henry had hoped that he might get to bed without his condition being noticed by his family.

The following Friday, Professor Hapgood saw Henry in the Student Union.

"Henry," he hailed him. "I know where you were last night!"

Henry smiled, decided to call the professor's bluff. "I'll bet you don't!"

"You went to Brattleboro," Professor Hapgood said, enjoying the look of surprise on Henry's face. "You took Jim's car and went to the ——— diner and had a lot of beer."

Henry looked absolutely amazed, then said: "But I bet you don't know what else happened!"

"Yes, I do, Henry," Professor Hapgood assured him. "You met two women there and talked with them."

At this point Henry began to show real alarm. "But you don't know what they said, do you?"

Professor Hapgood calmed him. "No, Henry. You refused to tell us that last Sunday when you told us the future under hypnotic trance."

"To those who flatly deny the possibility of this, I say simply to try it with any good hypnotist and any good hypnotic subject," Professor Hapgood told me. "No amount of second-hand evidence can be convincing, but it is within the power of anyone to see the direct evidence for himself if he will take the trouble."

There are those who would choose to explain away our haughty lady from old Scotland, "Fiona," and all cases suggestive of reincarnation, even those with enormous confirmatory evidence, as being examples of psychic "time travel." Such a theory would suppose that it is possible to travel back in time and to identify with someone from the past period, thereby coming into possession of the memory of that person's lifetime. There might even be a process of psychological attraction involved by which one would naturally pick out past lives that would complement and complete one's own present life, making up for its deficiencies or explaining them.

It seems to me, however, that the principal difference between the past-life memory and time travel is that when the subject has been moved back into another time period independently of reincarnation memories, he becomes merely an observer, never a participant.

For example, when we sent "Rita" back to observe the Spanish invasion of Mexico in the fifteenth century, she described the streets of the cities and the bloody slaughters with equal dispassion. It was as if she were telling us about a particularly graphic movie which she was watching. Earlier, when we had regressed Rita to what seemed to be an authentic past life memory, she was living, feeling, reacting, suffering. She was the central protagonist, rather than a mere reporter.

On the eve of a solid week of controlled mind travel experiments (June 22, 1969), the beloved singer-actress Judy Garland passed away. A good number of those witnesses and vounteer subjects who arrived at my offices for the sessions brought up nostalgic references to the tragic, diminutive figure, who had so vainly sought for her right to a "somewhere over the rainbow." Those who had virtually grown up with Judy Garland had their own memories of sodas, malts, jukebox Saturday nights, and they commisserated with one another over the passing of an era.

It was perhaps on the third night of the experiments that someone suggested placing a subject in trance and asking the subject to attempt to travel backward in time to trace the evolution of Judy Garland through her various past lives.

Now, to entertain such a suggestion, one has to accept, first of all, the possibility of reincarnation. To further fulfill such a suggestion, one next has to recognize the possibility of controlled retrocognition, or hypnotically directed out-of-body projection into the past. If occultists are correct in their esoteric pronouncements about the Akashic Records, those etheric impressions of each individual's past lives, then it would be possible for an entranced subject to read these spiritual file cards in the manner of the "sleeping prophet" Edgar Cayce.

Absolutely no claims are made for the following transcript. No amount of objective proof could possibly be made available which would confirm any of the data revealed by our entranced subject. For those individuals to whom such an experiment is utter nonsense, no amount of empirical evidence could possibly convince them of the experiment's validity. For those individuals who are predisposed toward such concepts as reincarnation, Karma and the Akashic Records, the transcript may seem to provide certain significant insights into the tormented entertainer's life.

The subject was directed to go back in time until he first contacted the entity who was known in this existence as Frances Gumm, Judy Garland. Once contact had been established, the subject was told to observe the entity and report what activily the entity might be pursuing.

Interviewer: Go back, farther and farther back in time, until the first time that the entity whom we know as Frances Gumm, Judy Garland, inhabited a fleshly body on the earth plane. At the count of three... Do you see her now?

Subject: Yes, she is in a temple in Egypt. Her name is something that she does not know, but they call her in honor of the goddess, because she sings and brings the messages. No one knows her name. She is a temple priestess, so she has given up her name.

Interviewer: Go into her thoughts and tell us what she is thinking.

Subject: She is thinking that she will serve whomever she encounters. She has learned how a soul can raise another soul to spiritual elevation.

Interviewer: How did she learn this?

Subject: She was taught in her sleep by a spiritual master. The master taught her how to sing so that her voice might prove a blessing to her fellowman. As a child she was singled apart from the others for special instruction.

Interviewer: Listen to her sing and sing along with her. Perhaps the words will be unfamiliar, but at least hum along with her.

[Since the subject possessed a good voice and musical training, he was soon humming a pleasant melody, completely unknown to all who witnessed the experiment].

Interviewer: Move ahead to a later time now. The entity will be an older woman. At the count of three, tell us what she is doing. . . .

Subject: She teaches. She looks at the children to see which ones were born to be priests and priestesses, which ones were born to be healers, which ones were born with other gifts. She uses her spiritual gifts very well.

Interviewer: Now let us leave this life as a temple priestess and move on to another earthly existence of the entity whom we know as Frances Gumm, Judy Garland. One. . .two. . .three. . .

Subject: I see sand. . .a marketplace. I hear shouting. . .raucous laughter.

Interviewer: Do you see the entity?

Subject: Yes. This time the entity is a man.

Interviewer: What is his name?

Subject: [phonetically] Ali Hasa.

Interviewer: How old is he? What does he do for a living?

Subject: He is forty-seven. He is a trader in a marketplace.

Interviewer: Where is this? And when?

Subject: It is a desert-like country. They do not mark years as we do. [laughing] Ali Hasa is a great cheat.

Interviewer: Why does he cheat people?

Subject: To make money. It is expected of one in the marketplace. He does not feel as though he is doing wrong.

Interviewer: Does he deal in slaves?

Subject: Yes. And in intoxicants. . .and opium.

Interviewer: Does he himself use opium?

Subject: Yes, he feels it makes the world easier to live in. He believes that it clears his mind and helps him see things more correctly. He sees the world as a great marketplace.

Interviewer: Does he have a family?

Subject: Yes, a wife and child. No mistresses, though. When he wants a woman other than his wife, he takes a prostitute or a slave. They are always accessible.

Interviewer: Move ahead another ten years.... What is Ali Hasa doing now?

Subject: His place at the market is empty. He is no longer there.

Interviewer: Go back until you see him. One...two...three...

Subject: He has been stabbed in the back by other traders who have grown tired of his cheating them. He screams and throws up his hands. Now he is dead. He walks about in confusion and darkness. Now his real self is beginning to float...to float...

Interviewer: At the count of three, time will progress and you will continue to follow the entity to another birth. One...two...three... Where are you now?

Subject: Opera. Singing opera. On stage.

Interviewer: What is the entity's name?

Subject: Something that begins with an "R." Rudmilla. Something like Rudmilla.

Interviewer: What is she doing? is she an opera singer?

Subject: No. Now I see more clearly. She is entertaining at court. She is singing for them.

Interviewer: Can you sing along with her?

[The subject once again hummed along with the observed entity. The song, although unidentifiable to any of those present at the experiment, did have a definite eighteenth-century mid-European flavor.]

Interviewer: Where is this court for whom she is singing?

Subject: Austria. Yes, Austria. But she travels about from court to court with her music. She is a court musician...and a courtesan.

Interviewer: How old is she now?

Subject: She is twenty-nine.

Interviewer: At the count of three, you will move ahead another ten years in Rudmilla's life....

Subject: She is singing. She sings; she dances; she laughs.

Interviewer: Move ahead another ten years at the count of three.

Subject: She is still a court musician. She is popular because of her ever-youthful voice. And she is still a very good lover. She does not feel she is immoral. She feels that to make love is a necessary part of her work.

Interviewer: Another ten years at the count of three....

Subject: She is still active in court life, but now she teaches more than performs. Yes, she still has lovers. Young men are attracted to her.

Interviewer: Another ten years...

Subject: She is nearly seventy. She doesn't go out much anymore. She cannot sing anymore. But the young still admire her for what she once was.

Interviewer: At the count of three you will go to her last moments as Rudmilla....

Subject: She has been hurt. It was an accident. She is dying of injuries. She is leaving the body. She realizes that she has been happy, but that she has been very vain. She has not thought much about heaven or an after-life.

Interviewer: Follow the entity now through time and space until it experiences another rebirth. You will not lose sight of the entity. At the count of three, you will see the entity in a new life. One...two...three...

Subject: Her blonde hair is in braids. Her skin is white. She is a Swiss girl who sits tending goats. She has mountains and grass and rocky pasture all around her. The year? It is 1836.

Interviewer: Move ahead five years...

Subject: She is sitting in the sun in front of her stone cottage. She is watching her child.

Interviewer: At the count of three, you will be inside the mind of this entity and you will be able to tell us what she is thinking....

Subject: She is thinking about her son. She is wishing that they could live in the city where there is more excitement. It is gayer there. She is young and she wants excitement and good times.

Interviewer: At the count of three, go on three more years....

Subject: She is in a village, but it is not a city. It is better than her pasture, but she still yearns for the city. She no longer watches the goats. She works in a small shop.

Interviewer: Another five years...

Subject: She is in an old shack. She is brooding about her wasted life. She is about thirty years old. Her name? I am still not certain about the last name, but now I hear that her name is Gisella.

Interviewer: Move ahead ten more years and once again be inside her thoughts....

Subject: She remains bitter that she must still live in a small village while the excitement of the large city still eludes her. She is now nearly forty. She has long ago left her husband with the goats in the pasture. She does not care to see him. She has had another child, but it is illegitimate. She hoped to make enough money in her shop to travel to the city, but business was never that good.

Interviewer: Ten more years...

Subject: She now thinks of her husband and wishes that she had not abused him so. Her son has gone away. The other one died. She ekes out a sparse living selling bread. She thinks now of the mountains which she forsook...the husband which she deserted...the son who scorned her. She never did get to go to the city. She misses her son. She wishes she knew where her husband was.

Interviewer: Move ahead to the entity's last day as Gisella. Tell us her last thoughts....

Subject: She thinks of how sad it is when one must stay all the time in one place, yet yearn always for another. She thinks of how sad it is to spend one's entire life being dissatisfied and to come to one's last moments and realize that one has not lived at all, that she has never really been able to do anything about her life.

Interviewer: Observe the death experience. Remember that you are only watching. You will feel no suffering or pain.

Subject: She dies in her sleep. Heart attack. Paralysis comes in the night and she passes on.

Interviewer: You will be able to see her clearly and distinctly after death.

Subject: She is happy now. She knows now that dreams are good, but that one must have substance in order to live happily on the physical plane. An hour after she dies she does not care about her own body.

Interviewer: Enter the entity's essence. What is the entity thinking?

Subject: She is a young girl again. She thinks of herself as a young girl. She does not think of the future.

Interviewer: Move ahead in time. Maybe fifty years, seventy years. Drift with the entity until it once again assumes a physical form of the earth plane. One...two...three...

Subject: I see a baby.

Interviewer: What is its name?

Subject: Frances...Frances Gumm....

If you would like to try an experiment of your own in reading the Akashic Records, here is an exercise which my wife Francie and I have used with exciting results. Once again, utilize one of the relaxation techniques provided in chapters 7 and 9, following the same instructions. After the induction process has taken place, proceed with the following suggestions:

You are peaceful, beautifully relaxed. You can feel the real you, your inner self, your spiritual self within becoming stronger, becoming more alive, as you become aware of another reality existing near you.

You feel that your true eyes—your inner eyes—can now see much farther than you've ever seen before. Your true ears can hear the sounds of beautiful, celestial music that you've never heard before. You sense that your true body—your spirit body—can move more freely than ever before. And you know with firm conviction that your spirit body...the real you...can slip out of its physical shell and soar free of time and space in order to read the Akashic Records of a past life about which you need to know for your good and your gaining.

See before you a staircase consisting of nine steps. It is as though a veil has been lifted, and you can see a place in space that was not previously visible. You may always have sensed its existence, but now you see it quite clearly.

The steps appear as solid as white marble, yet there is a slight translucent quality to them. You want so to climb those magnificent stairs, and you find you have but to wish it...and you have slipped out of your body...as an egg from a shell...as a letter from the envelope...as a hand from a glove. You slip from your body and feel the freedom of weightlessness. You are free from the physical laws of gravity.

You move toward the staircase feeling exhilarated, totally free, and you place your spirit foot on the first stair. You know that you will rise in awareness with each step upward that you take. You know that you will rise higher in awareness than you ever thought possible.

You move to Step Number Two...and you feel your awareness increasing. Your eyes envision a most perfect, small rose bush covered with tiny buds. Touch the shiny leaves. Feel them. Smell the fragrance of the bush. It is so wonderful, so elevating, so beautifully perfect.

You ascend to Step Three...to Step Four...feeling yourself increasing in awareness, becoming more and more aware of the true reality that exists before you.

You move up to Step Number Five, and your eyes perceive a beautiful patch of flowers that are wide, full, velvety. The petals caress you...seem to brush softly and warmly against you.

You ascend to Step Number Six and even greater awareness fills your being...your spiritual being. From this step you can see before you a huge, magnificent building made of the same material as the stairs. It is sparkling in the sunlight, and you see clearly that it consists of a large, central dome amidst a square foundation.

You know that this building, this temple, is the one that houses the Akashic Records. You know that you will receive knowledge within that will raise your spiritual awareness. You sense that you have become more aware simply by approaching it. You perceive that merely ascending the stairway has increased your awareness of all things.

You step to Number Seven, and something magical seems to be swelling within you...a greater, more powerful spiritual love vibrates through your essence.

You rise to Step Number Eight, and you feel the awareness of eternity. Timelessness exists here. On this step there is no beginning and no end. Eternity reigns supreme.

With joyous anticipation, you rise to Step Number Nine. You can clearly see the magnificent temple, the domain where the Akashic Records await you. You walk through a beautiful garden that surrounds the majectic building, then you enter the large, arched doorway and proceed through a winding hallway.

Within moments you find yourself in the main, central chamber, where throngs of beautiful beings in white, shining garments greet you. They are the recorders of the spiritual records. You see others such as yourself there—some you now know...others you will one day meet...all seeking knowledge of their Akashic Records.

All in this chamber are assembled around a platform in the center of the room. A bright light shines down from the domed crystal peak and bursts forth on the platform. Within this bright beam of light is the figure of a High Being, and you can see this being first vaguely, then more clearly, as the image wavers in the brilliant, almost blinding, light.

The High Being speaks, and the words are felt as much as they are heard. Mental images and thought forms are entering your mind, for the awarenesses which you receive are beyond words. You listen...you feel... you receive permission from the High Being to read the Akashic Records of your past lives in the great book which is materializing before you now.

You are now reading the records of your first physical expression on Earth. In what country—as you would understand it today—did you live? In what period of time did you live?

What sex were you? What was your physical appearance?

How many brothers and sisters did you have? What kind of relationship did you have with them and with your parents?

What kind of work did you do?

Did you ever marry? Did you ever have children?

Were your life situations basically happy or unhappy?

What were your greatest conflicts, your greatest sorrows?

What was the most important lesson that you were to learn from that lifetime? What lesson or work did you leave unfinished that you must complete in your present life experience?

Who came with you from that lifetime to your present life experience?

You are now reading the Akashic Records and understanding about a lifetime in which you lived as someone of a sex opposite your present one. Feel that body and become fully and completely aware of it. Concentrate on those parts of it which feel totally different from your present body.

How did you feel about your body in that life? How did you feel about your sexual role?

Understand completely how being that sex made your life different from what it is now.

How did your father or your mother react to you because of your sex? If you had brothers or sisters, how did they react to you because of your sex?

If you married, understand your sex role with your spouse in that lifetime. If you had children, take a moment to explore your relationship with them.

Reflect upon whether you were basically happy or unhappy in that lifetime. Understand how much your happiness depended upon your sex role.

See clearly, but without emotion, how you died in that lifetime.

What was the most important lesson that you were to receive from that lifetime? Who came with you from that life to your present existence?

You are now reading the Akashic Records of a past life that is very closely connected to your present life experience. Many seeds which were sown then are bearing fruit today. Some of these fruits are positive, some, negative. This past life is so closely connected to your present life experience that it may be called your Karmic Counterpart.

See now if you were a man or a woman in that past life. See totally your physical appearance, your mode of dress.

Understand your relationship with your father...your mother... with any other close members of your family.

Know and understand what kind of work you did...what goals you set for yourself.

See clearly the faces of those who supported you in your efforts and your striving toward your goals. See clearly the faces of any who might have opposed you in your achievements. Now know and understand if any of those men or women have come with you in your present life experience...to complete a lesson left unlearned.

See now the face of the one you loved most in that lifetime. See the eyes, the mouth, the hair, the physical form. This is the one who was always there at your side. This is the one who was always there to calm you, to soothe you, to love you. Understand completely your relationship. Know totally how this beloved one supported and sustained you in times of crisis. And now, look into the eyes of this beloved one and see if the one who loved you most has come with you in your present life experience...to complete a lesson left unlearned...to complete work left undone.

If you had children in that lifetime, see their faces now before you. Understand completely your relationship with them. Now look into their eyes and see if they have come with you in your present life experience. They may not have come this time as your children, but as your friends, your parents, even as your spouse. But look closely, and you will know if they have come with you again...to complete a lesson left unlearned...to complete work left undone.

See clearly now what lesson you were to have learned most completely in that life experience. Understand if you succeeded in your gaining, or if you left the task incomplete.

Know and fully understand why this particular past life is so closely bound to your present life experience. See what Karmic threads wrap the two lifetimes so tightly together. Know and fully understand what steps you may best take to make your present life a more complete and spiritually elevating existence. See clearly how you may best complete your mission here on Earth.

When you awaken, you will remember all that you need to recall for your good and your gaining. You will awaken feeling completely refreshed and filled with unconditional love for all living things.

For additional input to this volume, I asked my wife Francie if she would offer some comments and techniques on out-of-body experience from her unique perspective as a mystic and as a channel for other-worldly intelligences. As one who has been taken out of her body in order to receive vision teachings since she was a child of five, Francie is an accomplished mind traveller. Herewith are her comments:

"There exist many ways by which one might achieve out-of-body experiences, yet most exercises rest on the sole accomplishment of mind control. The ability to disassociate ourselves from the physical body and to detach ourselves from earthly things permits us to become immersed and involved in spiritual matters and to soar free of the material world. It is our thoughts, passions, desires and attachments to both animate and inanimate things that hold us firmly to Earth.

"Obviously, attachments to inanimate objects, those things which do not possess inner spirits, are ties of a lesser sort; but such ties still lessen our perspective, lower our awareness, and bind us to earthly treasures. It thereby behooves us to develop the ability and the resultant awareness to eliminate passionate attachments to nonliving things by such mental techniques as controlled concentration or by such physical means as the actual removal of the object.

"In our consuming love for animate, living things we should practice recognition and respect for the existing spirit within, but we should rise above obsessive concern for the physical manifestation that houses the spirit.

"Such detachment becomes simpler if you understand that you have three aspects to your existence—spiritual, mental and physical. It is important that you achieve control of the mental aspect of yourself so that you may choose the things of the spirit, thereby permitting your energy to direct the spirit within so that it might soar into the spiritual realm. On the other hand, if your mental plane chooses those things of the physical world, your energy will direct your spirit within to remain immersed in the fleshly attachments to be found in the material realm.

"Make a list of all the things which you hold dear, dividing your list into animate and inanimate objects. Concentrate on nonliving things and begin to consider your true feelings about those objects, while, at the same time, you are assessing your system of values. What is more important to you? The spiritual life, which exists beyond the death of physical matter, or the obtaining of material objects and clinging to them? Know and decide your beliefs, your values, then set aside those things which stand in your path. Release your attachment to them and proceed forward to the Source, God.

"In the matter of animate, living things, recognize the spirit within you as a part of the spirit of God. Center your energy on this facet of your being, loving it unconditionally. Conditional love ties you to the physical matter that the spirit inhabits, transforming that matter into a god that will control you.

"Know and remember the full meaning of a universal truth: We were advised to place no other God before the One God.

"We were admonished to permit nothing to gain the power of controlling our energy. Instead, we are to use the free will of our mental plane of existence and choose those things in the spirit that have the god essence.

"When we grant the control of our energy to anything physical, we make it our idol. Dedicate yourself anew to God's energy before you begin your experiments in out-of-body travel.

"When your dedication is vowed, you may take the first steps in soaring free through time and space. Learn to relax your body fully. You might try rapidly tightening, then releasing, the muscles of your body, beginning with your feet and continuing upward to your scalp and face.

"As you perform the tightening and releasing sequences, be certain to feel love, faith and trust flowing into every cell of your body, thereby causing it to relax completely and to fall gently asleep.

"Next, imagine circles emanating before you. They may be vague at first, then they will become clearer, moving toward you, growing gradually larger, until they can pass easily over your body and completely encircle you.

"Continue this mental exercise until countless circles have passed over and around you and the electrical emanations of those circles have permeated your being, causing you to vibrate and to quicken your own energy, raising your spirit out of the physical world into the spiritual realm. Once you are free of the fleshly world, rise higher by thinking of those things of the spirit and of God.

"There are many props which may aid you in relaxation, such as background music, flickering or revolving lights, incense and luminous stars on your ceiling.

"For those who experience an inability to "think" their muscles into relaxing, perhaps the method of diverting attention from the physical and concentrating on the spiritual will work better.

"If you possess an art object that depicts that which you spiritually love, place it before you and concentrate fully on nothing else but that object and what it represents to you. Eliminate all other thoughts from your mind. Place your mental energy into that beloved expression of art. Soon your body will relax and sleep, but your mind will ascend up the energy of your belief and transcend the physical world to the spiritual realm.

"Here is a technique that is a favorite of mine and which involves the use of easy imagery.

"Imagine that you are walking upon a wide path that goes straight through a magnificent forest. In the beginning, your path and the surrounding trees may seem a bit vague, but as you continue on you will note that your imagery becomes clearer.

"After approximately eight to ten minutes from the time that the images become clearer you should start to run along the path. You should look straight ahead and permit yourself to see the trees along the sides of your forest whiz by from the perspective of your peripheral vision.

"Continue to run as fast as you wish, and you will soon notice that your feet are barely touching the ground. You are almost flying.

"Then imagine that you *are* flying...flying while remaining in an upright, standing position. Once this "flying" has been achieved, you may direct your consciousness to take you wherever you wish.

"After repeated use of any one of the above exercises, you will find yourself travelling through the vastness of space to the spiritual realm beyond. From this vantage point, you will thereby gain the unearthly perspective of the total picture of all things. You will have achieved Star Consciousness."

18

Hypnosis, Mind Control and ESP

In February, 1948, a concert being given in the Dutch resort city of Scheveningen went disastrously awry under most peculiar conditions.

The solo violinist was rendering a fine performance of a Bach concerto when suddenly he lapsed into a screeching cachophony of sound. After murderously scrubbing his bow against the strings for a few moments, he abruptly stopped and stared at his instrument, confounded, as though he did not know what it was.

The equally puzzled audience watched with sympathy as the violinist's face registered shock and profound embarrassment. Then, with obvious effort, he regained control of himself, resuming playing and eventually finished in as fine a style as he had begun.

But the concert was not yet over. Next on the program was a difficult piano concerto, to be played by an accomplished French *artiste*. She plunged into the piece with great skill, as had the violinist before her.

About halfway through the concerto she was struck with a malady similar to that of the violinist. Her fingers started to trip over themselves, producing a harsh discord to the orchestra's accompaniment. Then she came to a dead halt.

For nearly forty bars the orchestra played without her, then, by visible effort of will, she shook herself out of her seeming "trance" and finished the piece.

In the ensuing days the city talked about the bumbling musicians. Two excellent, trained professionals making such mistakes in a concert hall! No one knew quite how to explain it.

The entire affair was recorded in the March 1, 1948, issue of *Time* magazine. The Dutch critics had at first placed the blame at the feet of the conductor for not having rehearsed the orchestra properly, until it was pointed out that the soloists had been the ones who had mangled the music. *Time* continued with the narrative, following the pianist back to Paris.

On reaching home soil the pianist, still seething with anger, told reporters this story:

"There is a dutch building contractor whose hobby is hypnotizing by telepathy. This man made a bet that he could ruin the concert with telehypnosis. I had gotten to the middle of the last movement. There were no more difficult places ahead and nothing to provoke any confusion. Then, suddenly, my memory went blank.

"...One of the musicians in the orchestra went out to the casino terrace after the concert. At the table next to him he heard four men exchanging congratulations for having successfully upset the performance by telehypnosis. Three of the men handed a fifty florin bill to the fourth one."

This story, incredible as it may sound, did happen, and was carried by one of our nation's foremost news magazines. Entitled "Svengali in Scheveningen," it is a rather startling example of hypnosis, achieved not through audio means or visual fixation, but solely through the strength of the hypnotist's thought.

Not all experiments in telehypnosis are carried out in the same fashion as that of the Dutch contractor, however. Many other successful attempts have been made that do not publicly humiliate a hapless victim.

Wade T. Hampton, Ph.D., has done extensive work in hypnosis, some of which he reported in the November, 1956, issue of *Fate*. One aspect he has worked on is telehypnosis.

Dr. Hampton related an incident in which he was sitting in a doctor's waiting room with a friend. Across from them sat a young woman, deeply engrossed in a magazine. The friend, having heard Hampton speak often of hypnotizing a person without his or her knowledge, suggested that Hampton put the young woman to sleep—by telepathy.

"You are becoming very tired," Dr. Hampton intoned mentally. "Your eyes are becoming very weary...you are too tired to read any longer...you feel so relaxed and comfortable that you find yourself getting sleepier and sleepier...your eyelids are so heavy...they are beginning to close...your eyes are closing and you're falling fast asleep...your eyes are closed now and you are in a deep sleep...deep sleep...deep sleep."

Dr. Hampton's first attempts were unsuccessful, but after he had repeated these suggestions for about ten minutes they began to take effect. First the woman's head began to nod. As her head fell further forward, her eyes began to close, her chin fell on her chest, her eyes completely closed and she appeared to be in a sound sleep.

The doctor's companion was convinced. "Now let's see if you can wake her up."

Just as Dr. Hampton was about to comply with a mental command, however, the magazine the woman had been reading slipped from her fingers. The sound of the magazine hitting the floor immediately caused her head to jerk up and her eyes to spring open. She bent to pick up the magazine and resumed reading.

Dr. Hampton explained that if he had had time to give the suggestion that she would awaken only at his command, she would not have been disturbed by the falling magazine. He was also quick to point out that the young woman in question must have been sensitive to begin with, or it would have been impossible to hypnotize her so rapidly in that manner. Telepathic induction of hypnosis is normally very difficult.

Nevertheless, experiments such as these are being conducted by interested parties around the world. Most of them are performed in the spirit of scientific progress and understanding, although a few, like those of the Dutch building contractor, are uneasily suggestive of mind control. The more nefarious uses of telephynosis will be discussed later in the chapter.

It would have been impossible for the exponents of hypnosis and the paranormal to avoid each other for very long. Both areas of investigation deal with the unknown and, as yet, unexplainable levels of the mind, and both occupy the extreme fringes of scientific respectability. The boundaries of the two fields continually overlap.

When Franz Anton Mesmer reintroduced hypnotism to the modern world, paranormal activities and occult dealings were asociated with his works. Even before Mesmer's time "occult explanations were given to hypnotic phenomena," according to Dr. Stanley Krippner, author of a study entitled *The Hypnotic Trance, the Psychedelic Experience, and Psi Induction: A Review of the Clinical and Experimental Literature.*

"From the beginnings of recorded history, paranormal occurrences were so closely associated with hypnotic suggestion that they were taken to be the products of hypnosis," Dr. Krippner writes. "The celebrated Ebers papyrus, over 3,000 years old, described the use of hypnotic procedures of Egyptian soothsayers."

Krippner goes on to point out that tribal medicine men, witch doctors and religious leaders throughout the ages have used hypnosis to heal the sick and to foretell the future. Then, in the fifteenth century, Swiss physician Philippus Aureolus Paracelsus released his theory of what he called magnetic healing. Paracelsus used magnets to treat disease, believing that magnets, as well as the magnetic influence of heavenly bodies, had therapeutic effects.

Magnetic treatment theories went through several stages of evolution and were examined by numerous scientists. It was during the latter part of the eighteenth century that Mesmer, acting on the hypotheses of these men, developed his own theory of "animal magnetism" and hypnosis.

Hypnosis entails, according to Mesmer, the specific action of one organism on another. This action is produced by a "magnetic force" which radiates from bodily organs and has therapeutic uses. Hypnotism therefore makes use of this force, or the vibrations, issuing from the hypnotist's eyes and fingers.

As the popularlity of hypnotism spread throughout Europe, those working with it began to discover some rather peculiar things. One subject suddenly was able to locate a missing pet dog clairvoyantly. Another was able to diagnose bodily disorders. Commissions were organized to investigate this aspect of hypnosis. Some researchers uncovered ample evidence to support the manifestation of ESP under hypnosis, while others reached completely negative results.

In the latter part of the nineteenth century the British Society for Psychical Research appointed a commission for the study of pain transference from hypnotist to hypnotized subject. At the same time, psychologist Edmund Gurney and his assistant Frank Podmore experimented with a similar area of research.

In the Gurney–Podmore experiments the hypnotist stood behind the blindfolded subject. The hypnotist was then pinched, and the subject told that he would be able to feel the pain in the corresponding area of his own body. Gurney and Podmore reported substantial success, although none of their experiments were carried out with the hypnotist and researcher at any great distance from the subject.

Research continued into the extrasensory aspects of hypnosis, despite hostility from the established sciences. In 1876 Sir William Barrett, an English physicist, presented the results of his experiments in clairvoyant card reading to the British Association for the Advancement of Science. A number of Barrett's colleagues rewarded the physicist's extensive endeavor by walking out during his presentation.

Hypnosis and ESP arrived on the threshold of the twentieth century under much the same cloud that they had carried with them from Mesmer's day. A more enlightened outlook was beginning to be sustained by some members of the scientific establishment, but the two ogres of the Scientific Method—predictability and repeatability—refused to be satisfied.

Just what is the relationship between hypnosis and ESP? Researchers have recognized for some time now that the hypnotic state closely resembles the state of consciousness in which manifestations of ESP occur. Although a description of this state is difficult to achieve, it appears to be very much like that somnambulistic state between sleeping and waking. Somewhere within this nebulous "between," conscious mental activity ceases and deprives the mind of its usual sensory impressions, thereby directing all attention to one, expectant, area. It is from this area that psychic impressions presumably come.

There seems scant difference between the trance of a psychic and the hypnotic state. The only immediately discernible difference is that one is self-induced, while the other is induced by, and subject to, the control of the hypnotist. The argument therefore reads: If ESP can be manifested under trance, then why cannot a hypnotist so manipulate the hypnotic state as to achieve the proper state of consciousness and thereby, literally, induce ESP?

And that is exactly what several hypnotists have done.

At the Duke University Parapsychology Laboratory, Dr. J.B. Rhine and his associates experimented with hypnotic induction in an attempt to achieve better scoring on ESP and psychokinesis (PK) tests. Experiments involving the use of hypnosis were run during the early years in the parapsychology lab.

In order to test for psychokinetic ability a subject was hypnotized, then told that he would try very hard to influence the fall of ninety-six dice at a time. He was told that through his directed mental effort he would be able to make more of the ninety-six target faces turn up at his randomly selected number than the laws of chance would indicate.

There were six subjects involved in this experiment. All scored well before hypnotic induction. While in the hypnotic state, however, four subjects dropped below chance, while the other two continued to score above chance.

In an attempt to understand these results, considerable attention was directed at the procedure. It was then noted that the two consistently above-chance scorers had both asked for a break in the middle of the testing period. In light of this information, two of the other subjects were re-hypnotized. All references to "concentrated effort" were absent this time. Instead, a "spirit of fun and relaxation" was encouraged, with the result being that the two subjects returned to their usual high level of scoring.

In the 1946 *Journal of Parapsychology,* Volume 10, Dr. Rhine speculated on the rather significant difference between these two conditions. He decided that the subjects had subconsciously resisted the more forceful commands of the hypnotist, a condition which had resulted in four subjects scoring below chance and the other two requesting a break in order to achieve a better frame of mind for high scoring.

Hypnosis was also used at Duke to inaugurate the ESP cards, a deck of twenty-five cards containing five types of symbols—a circle, a cross, a square, a star and three wavy lines. Shortly after the introduction of this deck, Dr. Rhine discontinued use of hypnosis, declaring that "there does not seem to be sufficient advantage to warrant the greater expenditure of time and effort which hypnotic induction demands."

Dr. Rhine admitted that suggestions of encouragement and increased confidence aided the subjects, but he really did not know what to tell the hypnotized subject to do in order to raise his or her score. He concluded that ". . .it is not a fair test of hypnosis to tell a subject in blanket fashion that he will be able to score high, that he will be able to see the concealed subject or anything else of that kind."

At that time Dr. Rhine viewed telepathy, clairvoyance and precognition as unconscious processes, occurring separately from the subject's conscious awareness. Conversely, he believed hypnosis to be "not so much a phenomenon of unconscious nature as of limited consciousness." Hypnosis, according to Dr. Rhine was "a state of highly restricted consciousness to the point where attention is focused in a highly controlled fashion on a small area designated by the hypnotist." Within this focal point of highly concentrated and limited attention, Dr. Rhine believed that there existed full conscious awareness, which would therefore not be in accord with his hypothesis of the separation of "psi" from conscious awareness.

Work done by Stanley V. Mitchell has uncovered some fascinating side aspects of ESP and hypnosis. In the February 1963 issue of *Fate* magazine ("Can Hypnosis Break the Language Barrier?") Mitchell reported a strange incident which happened to him while visiting a clinic in Russia.

On this same trip Mitchell spent some time in Poland, where he worked with a young American who spoke Polish fluently. As Mitchell began to hypnotize this young man, he noticed an older woman, a relative of the man, watching closely. As Mitchell proceeded, he was astounded to see that the Polish woman was also carrying out every suggestion he made.

Mitchell's curiosity was piqued. He brought the subjects out of hypnosis and questioned the woman. She had difficulty speaking and understanding English, but eventually said: "When you hypnotize I understand what you say, but when you do not hypnotize all you say is 'cha-cha-cha.' "

Until Dr. J.B. Rhine gave telepathy a more respectable name, men of science were loath to admit that such a faculty of mind existed. When it was suggested that it might be possible to hypnotize via telepathy, such a coupling of two of science's bastard offspring was met with official disdain. How could one mind act upon another without the media of the senses? Scientists have been prone to suggest duplicity on the part of the subject or the researcher, or to lay the cause for all effects on the unleashed power of suggestion. Undeniably, the hypnotic state is an extremely suggestible one.

Edmund Shaftesbury, in his book *Operations of the Other Mind*, offers an example in which hypnosis was achieved by a strong expectation of the same.

Professor Christianson of Edinburgh once hypnotized a woman and, when he brought her out of the hypnotic state, informed her that he would place her in trance again on noon the following day. He would perform this operation, however, from a distance. The next day the professor was in the midst of a lecture and completely forgot what he had told the woman. She, on the other hand, was so convinced she would be hypnotized that at noon she fell into a deep hypnotic trance, which she slept off naturally.

Obviously this is not a genuine example of telehypnosis. The trance the woman fell into was self-induced, achieved by auto-suggestion. And it would be unfair to judge all instances of telehypnosis on the basis of this case. The story of the Dutch contractor who hypnotized the musicians and disrupted the concert is ample evidence against the auto-suggestion theory. No professional musician would endanger his or her reputation by ruining a solo in the midst of a concert performance through auto-suggestion.

Certainly one of the strongest objections to telehypnosis is the fear that it might enable one person to gain control over another. This fear strikes at the delicate theological root of free will. To surrender control over one's will, either consciously or unconsciously, may place entirely too much power in the hands of someone else who may not be equipped to handle it. However, hypnotists have staunchly insisted that no individual can be hypnotized unless he or she wishes it. Dr. Wade T. Hampton, who has done extensive work with telehypnosis, believes this to be true in successful telepathic induction as well. He states:

"In the telepathically-induced trance the subject goes to sleep without being aware of any reason for doing so. Such subjects are not influenced against their will—only without their knowledge. If they knew that an attempt was being made to influence them they could bring their conscious 'will' into play and successfully resist the most powerful efforts made by the hypnotist.... If a person has an unconscious fear of being influenced, he cannot be telepathically hypnotized, even without his conscious knowledge. In such instances the subject is protected by a constantly active, although unconscious, resistance to 'control' suggestions."

Despite the reassurance, it cannot be denied that hypnosis operates in the area of the unconscious where most of our mental mischief takes place. Some psychiatrists are seriously questioning whether or not some delicate cerebral balance can be upset by indiscriminate hypnotic probing. They are seeking to determine at what point such experimentation could become dangerous, even destructive.

Just as users of psychedelic drugs cannot be certain when the drug is going to turn on them, producing a "bad trip," perhaps hypnotists may be equally ignorant of what their questions may trigger in the unknown areas of their subject's psyche.

Equally disturbing are the moral questions, whether or not a hypnotic subject could be persuaded to rob, rape, murder or commit suicide. The classic example has the hypnotist placing a gun in the subject's hands and saying: "See, you are holding a camera in your hand. If you just press this part of it, you will be able to take a picture. Now, take a picture of that man standing over there."

Would the subject do it? Some hypnotists say yes. Others emphatically insist "Never." Those in the latter category state that even an apparently pliable subject would never do something against his or her moral code. The ego still serves as watchdog.

Instances have been reported of individuals complying with a hypnotist's commands if they have already demonstrated latent desires in those areas, but the largest body of research indicates that no person can be hypnotized without his or her consent, nor can anyone be made to perform tasks alien to his or her moral character.

Telepathy is not the only "psi" ability manifested in hypnotic sessions. In an attempt to determine the amount of clairvoyance the hypnotic state might produce, extensive laboratory tests have been deliberately designed to achieve a hypnotic state amenable to manifestations of ESP.

In one experiment Dr. Jarl Fahler, a Finnish psychologist, had four subjects go through 360 runs of an ESP deck, performing half of them in a waking state and the other half in an hypnotic state. Previously, 190 runs had been recorded, and the other half appeared in random order. Therefore, the latter half of the experiment tested precognition, the former, clairvoyance.

The results of this experiment showed scoring at chance level in the waking state, with significantly higher scoring in the hypnotic state. The subjects did much better on the part of the experiment that tested clairvoyance than on the precognition portion.

Dr. Fahler further investigated precognition faculties with Dr. Karlis Osis, this time using two subjects who were chosen because they believed that they had been aware of their correct guesses in previous extrasensory experiments. The subjects were instructed to call out "Mark!" when they felt that the numbers they stated would be identical to the ones to be randomly chosen the next day.

In the *Journal* of the American Society for Psychical Research, 1966, Volume 60, Dr. Osis and Dr. Fahler reported that the trials on which the subjects had called "Mark" were "significantly better than the other trials . . . the odds were one in fifty million that coincidence alone could have been responsible for the results."

The usual procedure with the trance state of hypnosis is to suggest that the subject will do as the controller wishes. New York investigator J.J. Grela considered the variable that hypnotic subjects were told they would perform well, while waking subjects were not thus motivated. Grela, therefore, designed an experiment similar to others, but with additional controls.

Grela told a group of hypnotized subjects that they would score well on the ESP deck, and gave similar encouragement to a group of subjects performing in the waking state. This method produced positive results in both groups, although the scoring done by the hypnotic group was significantly higher than by those in the waking state.

On two other occasions Grela first avoided giving any encouragement at all and then implanted a negative suggestion. The scores obtained under these conditions were lower than previous testing, with the lowest scores occurring at the suggestion that the subject would do poorly.

Lawrence Casler, another New Yorker, took the results of these tests one step further. His experiment was designed to test whether hypnosis alone, without the aid of positive suggestions, would increase the level of telepathic scoring. He placed an agent in a room with a deck of ESP cards. As the agent concentrated on the cards, the subject, in another room, attempted to identify them. Fifteen subjects were used, each completing four runs in the hypnotic state and an additional four in the waking state. In accordance with the growing body of substantiated research, scoring was significantly higher under the influence of hypnosis.

In an experiment designed to test the effect of the subject's attitude on his or her scoring, parapsychologist Charles Honorton issued a questionnaire to separate potentially high scorers from potentially low scorers. Six subjects were selected, their potential for scoring determined by their attitude toward ESP. The two subjects chosen for low scoring performed at chance level in the waking state, and, interestingly, performed significantly below chance during hypnosis—additional evidence that a subject cannot be forced to do something against his or her beliefs while under the influence of hypnosis.

Stanley V. Mitchell reported a rather startling example involving both telepathy and clairvoyance by two of his students of hypnosis, a Spanish professor and a pathology student at Northwestern University in Chicago. The pathology student happened to be a particularly good hypnotic subject, who Mitchell decided would afford good practice for the Spanish professor.

The induction proceeded fairly well until the professor attempted to do something he had not been taught by Mitchell: he suggested to the subject that he, the professor, was writing the numbers from one to ten on the blackboard, and would erase the number five. Of course he did not actually do so. After he informed the subject that he was "erasing the number five," the pathology student was to count from one to ten. The professor decided the subject had not reached a good state of hypnosis when he counted "one, two, three, four, *five*, six, seven. . . ."

Mitchell explained to the professor that the reason for his failure was that he had forgotten to tell the subject that he was erasing the number five from the subject's memory, as well as from the blackboard. Had he done so, the student would have counted to ten, omitting the five. Or, if the professor had told the subject he was erasing the five from the blackboard, then asked him to read off the numbers *from the blackboard*, the subject would have also skipped the five.

The experiment would have ended there had not the subject, when brought out of hypnosis, remarked to the professor, "Joe, you sure do make a funny seven."

Mitchell sensed that something unusual had transpired and sent the subject out of the room with another man, giving the other man instructions to have the subject write a seven as he had "seen" the professor do it on the blackboard. When the subject left the room, Mitchell turned to the professor and had him write a seven the way he generally did on a slip of paper. He produced a European seven, sporting little curls at the top and bottom, and a small European cross through the stem.

When the subject returned to the room the two seven's were compared. "They were found to be not only identical in size and curvature, but they looked like carbon copies of each other," reported Mitchell.

In some way, the hypnotic trance had enabled the pathology student to "see" the seven as the professor had drawn it. Furthermore, his memory was so complete he could make an exact copy once out of trance.

Several cases have been presented which demonstrate a spontaneous or encouraged manifestation of extrasensory perception through hypnosis. By this time one might seriously ponder the following: If hypnosis can be used to manifest latent ESP, can it also be used to build extrasensory ability in an individual until the crutch of hypnotic trance is no longer required? This was the question that so intrigued Dr. Milan Ryzl.

Dr. Ryzl, a Czechoslovakian chemist and physicist, became interested in the field of parapsychology sixteen years ago. In 1967 he came to this country, settling in San Jose, California. He was a frequent teacher and lecturer for the California Parapsychology Foundation while he continued his extensive research.

Ryzl's working hypothesis stated that, if the hypnotic trance could produce the proper level of consciousness for manifestation of ESP, then not only could these extrasensory abilities be induced hypnotically, but they could also eventually be brought forth spontaneously by the subject without the aid of hypnosis.

Ryzl's experiment involved three major phases: (1) achievement of the proper level of consciousness through hypnosis, (2) perfection of the manifested ESP by a long and intense training period, and (3) self-induction by the subject for the state of consciousness receptive to "psi" manifestation, with encouragement for the subject to use ESP faculties independently of the experimenter by whom he or she was trained.

As can be deduced from even such a brief outline of Ryzl's experiment, the entire process was quite demanding. A great deal of time and patience was required from both the experimenter and the subject. Dr. Ryzl originated his experiment with 463 subjects, mostly university student volunteers between the ages of sixteen and thirty. Out of this large group only three individuals had sufficient patience and diligence to complete the extensive training period with any degree of proficiency.

The parapsychologist's most talented subject was Pavel Stepanek, a man who came to Dr. Ryzl's laboratory at the age of thirty. When he began the experiment, Stepanek demonstrated no extrasensory abilities and was adjudged psychologically normal. Stepanek's case is most frequently used to exemplify Dr. Ryzl's work because his unusual tenacity made it possible for him to be studied over a period of three years.

Dr. Ryzl has trained others with more dramatic records—including a woman who now reports daily paranormal experiences—but Stepanek's record is more interesting from the standpoint of quantitative analysis. His consistent performances, for both Dr. Ryzl and visiting parapsychologists, seem to invalidate those two previously unsatisfied scientific ogres of predictability and repeatability.

Stepanek was given a standard test throughout the experiment. He was asked to tell whether the green or the white side of a two-color card was facing up. Under these conditions a chance score would have been 50 percent.

To test the repeatability of Stepanek's above-chance scoring, and to confirm to visiting researchers that the subject was free from any dependency on Ryzl, the testing procedure involved three phases. In the first, or control, phase of the experiment, Dr. Ryzl handled the proceedings with the visitors observing. In the second phase, Dr. Ryzl was present to stimulate the subject but with the procedure in the hands of the guests. The third phase was conducted entirely by the visitors, with Dr. Ryzl in no way present or participating.

In the actual procedure of the experiment, Pavel Stepanek was to ascertain the color of the face-up card from a series of ten two-color cards completely enclosed in opaque covers. As the experiment progressed, even more precautions were taken. The cards were shut up in packs of opaque cardboard and wrapped in layers of blue wrapping paper. Enclosed in the pack was a strip of sensitive photographic film, which was examined after each test for further assurance that the deck had not been opened.

In an adjoining room Mrs. Ryzl prepared the cards, determining their order by astronomical data available for the day of the experiment. She handed the cards to Dr. Ryzl, then sat in a corner of the room. Ryzl and Stepanek were separated by an opaque screen through which no one could possibly see the cards or the envelopes.

The first test of two hundred sets was run, giving a total of 2,000 individual cards. For this test Stepanek performed under hypnosis, not having achieved a high enough degree of proficiency to function without it. He scored 1,144 hits and 856 misses. In all successive tests the subject brought himself to the proper level of consciousness.

Several parapsychologists began accepting Dr. Ryzl's invitation to come to Prague to take part in the experiments. Among those who came were British psychologist John Beloff, American parapsychologist John Freeman, Indian parapsychologist B.K. Kanthamni and noted American parapsychologist J.G. Pratt. Each of these men suggested variations of the test; and from these variations, additional observations were devised for the steadily growing body of research. Stepanek consistently scored above chance.

At one point, however, his abilities did begin to deteriorate. To help him regain his ability, Ryzl gave Stepanek a deck and told him to go home and try to rebuild his psychic powers himself. Dr. Ryzl suggested that he return when he once more felt confidence in his abilities.

This Stepanek did. Eventually he did return to the lab, stating that he once more felt assured of successful high scoring. The tests were resumed and Stepanek immediately regained his former high level of accuracy. Dr. Ryzl interpreted Stepanek's ability to retrain his ESP powers by himself, without any outside help, as indicative of the fact that the subject exerted at least some conscious control over his extrasensory process.

In his review of the total experiment, Dr. Ryzl concluded that there had been a number of obstacles to overcome. The first occurred during the initial phase of the experiment, when the subject was first brought to a hypnotic trance corresponding to the proper level of consciousness in which ESP manifests.

At this stage the subject was in an extremely suggestible state. Unfortunately, the maintenance of such a state requires the suspension of critical thinking. Without this discriminatory aid the subject makes mistakes, as he is unable to determine the difference between true impressions and other sensory impressions.

To overcome this difficulty, Dr. Ryzl juggled the different levels of hypnosis. Thus, while the subject was in deep sleep, he was more receptive to extrasensory impressions, and while in the lighter stages, he could use his critical faculties and memory. In this way the subject was able to progress by correcting his own mistakes and by learning to rely upon, and trust, his own judgment.

An interesting problem arose concerning the recalcitrant aspect of psychic impressions. "Psi" impressions do not seem to occur in the same set patterns and symbology as do sensory impressions. Extrasensory perceptions are usually perceived subjectively and manifest most frequently through the physical senses as hallucinatory experiences. This means that a color may manifest itself as a texture, sound or temperature.

"The interpretation of such an impression is dependent upon the particular orientation of the subject's psyche," wrote Dr. Ryzl.

"Therefore the difficulty in testing for ESP lies in the fact that psychically received impressions, manifesting as false sensory hallucinations, are frequently indistinguishable from conventional hypnotic hallucinations. An ESP subject must double his energy for he must constantly be assessing his impressions against what he knows to be reality."

A third problem is immediately understandable. As the subject was increasingly encouraged to use his ESP consciously, he developed a dependency on his initial trainer and on hypnosis itself. This was perhaps the most difficult obstacle to overcome.

The final frustration to Ryzl's experiment was both psychological and sociological, and it rightly belongs in these pages.

Frequently the attitudes held by society toward psychics inhibit the growth of the subject's extrasensory abilities. Too many people still believe that the psychic or sensitive is in some crucial way "different" from other members of the community.

Such an attitude may cause the developing psychic to fear that he or she is becoming a human anomaly and may also fear an invasion of private life or ridicule from neighbors. These are the apprehensions that plague both natural and artificially developed psychics. Sometimes adults consciously suppress "psi" ability in children, but more often it is the unconscious reactions of adults that cause the psychically gifted child to suppress these abilities.

It is these bogeymen of hypnosis and the paranormal that have kept the two fields of study so long in the dark and have encouraged inept amateurs and fraudulent practitioners to continue plying their vulturous trade on human emotions. It is time for the average person to stop associating genuine paranormal gifts with the few sentences of commercially prepared psychic pap he or she reads daily in syndicated astrology columns. It is time for the orthodox scientist to do likewise.

"In our experiments we trained the ESP ability in our subjects by means of an exact method," reads Milan Ryzl's report. "We continued to investigate ESP in the experiments wherein the subject had to ascertain freely chosen scenes and objects with the aid of ESP. We then appraised the qualitative agreements in the subject's statements with the reality. These qualitative experiments afforded us a great many opportunities to study the psychological dynamics of manifestations of ESP and their dependence on the subject's psyche."

There, certainly, is an authoritative statement made by a man who knows what he is about and who has the research to prove it. Dr. Ryzl further points out that the hypothesis of the so-called "psi field" as the carrier of ESP information, which may be interpreted as similar to other physical fields like gravitational and electromagnetic, indicates that, in the long run, parapsychological research may also have consequences significant in the field of theoretical physics. A far cry from the abracadabra and hocus-pocus some believe the field of parapsychology to be.

19

Medical Diagnosis and Therapy through Mind Travel

On June 16, 1969, at Philadelphia's St. Joseph's Hospital, Mary Dunphy had her uterus removed in a forty-five minute operation without anesthetics. She later told physicians and reporters that she had felt absolutely no pain, because she had placed herself in a self-induced hypnotic state before the operation.

Miss Dunphy had always been interested in hypnosis, so when a tumor was discovered in her uterus the year before she had asked her physician, Dr. Columbus Gengemi, if he would coach her in hypnoanesthesiology. Miss Dunphy claimed she learned to master self-induction of the hypnotic state in seven sessions spread over a few months.

Dr. Salvatore Cucinetta, clinical director of obstetrics and gynecology at St. Joseph's Hospital, expressed his hope that more people might come to know of surgery under hypnosis.

Many people dread the thought of having a splinter removed without anesthetics, to say nothing of the removal of a uterus or an appendix. Many reading a news item like the one above describing major surgery with hypnosis as the only anesthetic, tend to doubt whether such stories are really true. If hypnosis is so beneficial during surgery (less bleeding, less shock to the body's nervous system), they argue, why don't all doctors employ it?

Doctors, like most people, tend to follow the path of least resistance. Any intelligent person with the proper training can anesthetize a surgical patient, and conventional anesthetics can work quickly for all patients.

Hypnosis requires a great deal of training. Furthermore, not all people can be hypnotized deeply enough, or rapidly enough, for all surgical purposes.

My intention in this chapter, however, is not to discuss the potential of hypnosis as a surgical anesthetic. Most informed physicians and lay readers are well aware of the benefits and the validity of the hypnotic trance state used under satisfactory surgical conditions. What this chapter presents is a facet of hypnosis that is much more controversial. It examines the possibility that a hypnotized subject may be able to diagnose the state of health of people both nearby and at great distances via controlled out-of-body projection.

Loring Williams had several years experience with the more conventional applications of hypnotherapy, the treatment of disease with the aid of hypnosis. Because the origin of many of our human afflictions are conceded to be psychosomatic, as Williams theorized some years ago, it seems to follow that, since hypnosis deals directly with the subconscious, hypnotherapy might also effectively control many of our ailments.

Subsequent experience convinced Williams that such was the case. For many years he successfully relieved the symptoms of, and apparently in some cases eliminated the cause of, many physical disorders. In the majority of cases, results were extremely rapid and remained permanent.

One of Williams' early experimental subjects was the always intellectually active Dr. Charles Hapgood. The following is Hapgood's report of that experiment:

"I confess I was startled when Williams first told me of his experiments in diagnosis. This possible use of hypnosis had not occurred to me. A great advantage of this kind of research was, however, that experiments could be immediately confirmed, by a doctor if necessary.

On two or three occasions Williams ran medical checkups on me. One such experiment was made while Williams and his hypnotic subject were in Hinsdale, New Hampshire, and I was in South Newport, about sixty miles away. At the conclusion of the experiment, Williams wrote me the following report, which was completely accurate."

"Dear Charlie,

In our phone conversation, you asked for a complete physical which you have been given. Understand that I gave the subject no details of your condition whatsoever, so that all this is only what he saw.

"This was a thorough physical. We started from the feet and went to the top of your head.

"First off, probably of no consequence, you have weak arches. You have one vein bothering you in your right leg. The prostate gland is swollen. Stomach is good; heart and lungs, etc., are good.
really little organically wrong with you, but you are very nervous. I cannot overemphasize the extent of this nervousness. Your nervous condition is affecting your eyes to some extent. You should have them checked. You are worrying about your stomach and your heart and this is aggravating your condition. You have nothing to worry about on this score; but if you continue to do so, you will develop an ulcer.

"Doctors cannot do much to help you in this case. You will have to help yourself. You must completely relax. I say again: Completely *relax* and continue to do so for some time. You probably know enough about self-hypnosis to relax yourself to some extent.

"If you wish, when you get to your camp or before, I will get together with you and help induce this relaxation.

"Once again, the important thing is not to worry and lose weight.

Yours,
Bill"

"When I say that this report was accurate, I did not realize its accuracy at the time.

"With some points of it I disagreed. There was no indication of a swollen prostate. I was not aware of any vein bothering me, and I did not believe I had weak arches. On the contrary, I have always prided myself on the fact that because they were so very high they could never fall.

"However, the right foot and leg were bothering me a great deal and my other leg was bothering some. I would have to get up at night and walk or soak the feet in hot water. I considered my trouble to be rheumatism and not worth mentioning. Consequently, I had not mentioned it to Bill.

"It was not until a year and a half later that I discovered that my high arches were the cause of the trouble, which was cured by buying arch supporters. A year after this hypnotic examination, doctors operated to remove the prostate gland. The eye trouble was indeed relieved by rest and relaxation. Only one thing remained the same: my weight."

"My experiments in psychical research with hypnosis seem to suggest that more than just psychosomatic illnesses can be relieved, and perhaps cured, with hypnotherapy." Williams observed. "Or could it be that most, or all, disease is of mental origin? Perhaps it is time for a complete investigation and reevaluation of the cause of disease.

"Why is it that when we have many people living in similar environments, with similar diets, that some live to a healthy old age, while others are disease-riddled from their youth?" Williams went on. "We were all born with similar body chemistry, and we all breathe the same germs. Why do we all not suffer the same effects? The answer could well be in the mind, and in each individual's basic outlook and attitudes."

In his own experience as a hypnotherapist, Williams saw chronic persistent allergies and severe skin conditions, such as psoriasis, completely and permanently disappear after hypnotic treatment. Many people came to him regularly with a wide assortment of aches and pains.

Williams always cautioned them, however, that hypnotic treatment is *not* a substitute for medical aid. "But," he added, "it can be a great supplement."

It was Williams' conviction that hypnosis is neither a plaything nor a toy to be used in mental parlor games. "Anyone who learns how to hypnotize should do so only for the purpose of using it for the constructive advancement of mankind," Williams believed.

It was certainly nothing less than a desire to aid a fellow human in pain that inspired Williams to fashion the healing beam of a "mental flashlight." In numerous experiments the hypnotist instructed entranced mind travellers to "see" individuals in x-ray form and to diagnose their ailments and diseases.

In every case these diagnoses were passed along to orthodox medical doctors who could use the information as they chose. Some acknowledged that the diagnosis acquired through mind travel complemented their own evaluation of the patient's malady; others did not respond in any manner, negatively or positively.

In these various tests, Williams noticed that the mind travellers seemed always to see the illness, bone damage or nervous condition as a "black spot" within the target individual's body. While Rita was serving as subject and we were "looking in" on a friend of mine in England, Bill suggested that Rita train a bright "flashlight beam" on the dark areas and dissolve them with light.

Rita's reaction was to squint her closed eyes, furrow her forehead and visibly apply great concentration on areas that remained unseen to our eyes. A sigh, and then: "Okay. They're gone."

Had the illness really been erased? My friend was in England, too far away to respond quickly. But there were others with ailments nearby.

A close friend of mind was extremely skeptical about spontaneous healing. With a broad grin on his face, he asked Rita if she might "burn away" a small cyst on his ankle.

He had mentioned it to me before the session began that evening, and explained that, although it had been adjudged benign by his family physician, it had appeared virtually overnight. His doctor recommended that it be removed by simple surgery.

But then that night: "I actually felt the heat in my ankle," he told me later. "And when I lifted the leg of my trousers, the lump had disappeared."

In order to test the most unusual "mental flashlight" a bit further, I put in a call to Dr. J., our family doctor, the next day and asked him to select, at random, a number of cases from his files and bring them to my office that afternoon.

I explained briefly what we were attempting to achieve, and although he was dubious of any results we might attain, he was not skeptical about hypnosis. One of his instructors in medical school had accomplished a difficult leg amputation while the patient rested peacefully in a state of hypnoanesthesia.

Dr. J. generously devoted a portion of his golfing afternoon that day to assist us with a number of experiments in out-of-body diagnosis. Our *modus operandi* was quite simple. Bill would place Rita in trance and instruct her to travel mentally to a patient whose name and address was supplied by Dr. J. When she felt she was in the presence of the target personality, Rita would describe the patient's physical appearance for verification by Dr. J.

Once Dr. J. acknowledged that the mental travel was accurate, Rita would "see" the patient in x-ray form and describe the particular physical malfunctions as she perceived them in the hypnotic state.

Dr. J. was favorably impressed by Rita's ability to describe accurately the target patient's physical appearance, but he was dismayed by the vague general manner in which Rita described the various ailments. In fact, such terms as "abdominal area" can mean something quite different to a layperson than they do to a trained anatomist and physician. Although Dr. J. conceded that Rita did hit on some of the ailments with a degree of accuracy, some of the other descriptions were obscured by her lack of knowledge of basic anatomy and her meager medical vocabulary.

"But wouldn't this all be interesting if you hypnotized a trained medical student to do this sort of thing?" Dr. J. speculated. This is precisely the sort of thing I think should be done. Rita could apparently "see" blighted areas within the patient's body, but her ability to describe them and to diagnose them would be considered most rudimentary to a highly trained diagnostician such as Dr. J.

On the other side of the coin, Rita's inability to name the affected portions of the body does nothing to negate her incredible ability to "shine the light" on them and to implement their healing.

As I see it, such out-of-body diagnosis should only be used as an aid, or complement, to orthodox medical practice. Healing is very much more an art than it is a science. One and one may always make two, but the same pill certainly does not work for every patient.

There are so many variables and subtle mental factors involved in healing. The delicate relationship between doctor and patient, the patient's will to recover, the doctor's own confidence in his or her ability to heal—all remain intangibles forever out of the reach of test tube and mortar and pestle.

That out-of-body diagnosis and out-of-body therapy should supplant the physician is the last thing I would suggest. Rather I would challenge them to investigate hypnotically controlled out-of-body diagnosis without bias.

Consider the case of G.W.'s feet.

G.W. and his wife drove several miles to sit in on our experiments solely as observers and witnesses. On the particular night they attended, Rita was going about the circle of witnesses "reading" their past and present health conditions. When she got to G.W., she at once picked up an old high school football injury and a more recent injury to his feet.

Some individuals requested that Rita "shine her light" on them that night, so they might assess the results for themselves. After Rita had described the damage done to G.W.'s feet, his wife suggested that she attempt to "erase" the great areas of darkness which she perceived in that area.

I shook my head before Bill reinforced Rita's hypnotic suggestion. "Don't bother," I whispered to Williams.

"Why not?" Williams frowned.

"There's no use," I told him. "G.W. is scheduled for amputation in three months."

I had known G.W. for about a year and had become familiar with the painful history of his terribly damaged feet. G.W. fell out of a helicopter when he was in the military service and both feet had been thoroughly smashed.

Physicians tried every form of therapy and temporary repair throughout the course of ten years; the last resort, amputation, was now all that remained for G.W. He had already resigned himself to six months in a wheelchair and the awkward process of learning to walk all over again. Our toes may look rather inconsequential down there sticking out from our lower extremeties, but if we tried to walk without them, we would find we lacked the necessary balance.

Williams merely shrugged. "Never too late," he said.

"It is in this case," I insisted. "The medics are going to shave off his toes in October. It has gone past the treatment stage. They've already set a date for the amputation."

"Then he has nothing to lose, has he?" Williams pointed out. I could hardly argue with his yankee logic, and I stepped back so that Williams might again direct Rita to shine her extraordinary mental light over the dark spots on G.W.'s feet.

There is no need to prolong the story just to build suspense. A month later an excited G.W. telephoned me to say that his scheduled amputation had been called off. Pleased, but puzzled, doctors were talking in hushed tones about a "medical miracle." They were at a loss to explain how the alleged miracle had come to pass.

Some time later G.W. called with two exciting developments in his case: (1) A medical journal arrived to take pictures of his feet for an article on the strange and sudden healing process which had taken place; (2) While walking in Chicago, his long insensate feet had developed blisters. He was rejoicing in the fact that he could once again actually feel his feet.

Again I emphasize that I am not trying to hassle the American Medical Association. I only wish that physicians would become as excited as I am about this tremendous power of healing. It is a power that apparently the mind can plug into and direct to benefit its own body and the bodies of others. I also wish that some unbiased medical researchers would become as interested as I am in determining the sources from which such healing may originate.

Rita, in her hypnotic trance, must surely lead a number of readers to draw an obvious comparison between her and the "sleeping prophet" and medical diagnostician, Edgar Cayce.

Cayce, as is well known, contracted a throat ailment and was told that he would never again be able to speak above a whisper. In 1901 a hypnotic practitioner helped Cayce into trance, and then stood by while the afflicted dry goods clerk began to describe his medical condition in minute detail. By the time the trance had ended, Cayce not only had uttered a prescription for his inoperative throat muscles and nerves, but also had accomplished a self-healing that left his voice fully restored.

Cayce obligingly went to "sleep" for thousands of other people for the next forty-five years. In each trance, he visualized the patient's body and prescribed remediation. In many instances his prescriptions involved drug products which, awaiting delivery in company warehouses had not yet been made available to the public. In other cases, Cayce prescribed herbs with rich natural sources of drugs. Ironically, orthodox doctors would one day write prescriptions for their synthetic counterparts.

Cayce's much chronicled talents may have been the result of intuitive knowledge, extrasensory perception or an ability to draw on some great universal psychic reservoir of wisdom. Whatever the source for Cayce's abilities, orthodox science continues to ignore him in death as it did in life. Serious researchers have lamented the fact that an impartial medical study and follow-up of the numerous cases in the files of Edgar Cayce's documented readings have never been made.

I sincerely hope that the potential which mind travel may offer humankind will not be ignored as completely by orthodoxy as was the work of Edgar Cayce. And most of all, I pray that controlled out-of-body experience will not be relegated to the shadow world of the occult and swept under the enormous rug which science keeps always ready to smother uncomfortable theories, facts and anomalies.

In 1953 Luby Pollack wrote in her book, *Your Normal Mind: Its Tricks and Quirks*, that over a century ago the Scottish surgeon Dr. Escaile filled dozens of hospital wards with successful surgical cases, all accomplished under hypnosis. Today, Mrs. Pollack writes, most surgeons won't touch hypnosis because they maintain they can never be certain the sleep is deep enough, or the results can ever be as predictable as those given by anesthetics. She quotes James Ward, who once said: "Many miracles of healing...become credible...when explained by 'suggestion,' but to explain the explanation is a task for our future."

Mrs. Pollack concludes: "When that ultimate explanation is in our hands, however, this amazing trick of the mind could some day turn out to be one of the most precious instruments in medical science for the cure of human ills."

Dr. A. Silva Mello, a member of the Brazilian Academy of Medicine, deals much more skeptically with hypnosis in his book, *Mysteries and Realities of This World and the Next*. Dr. Silva Mello is especially cynical toward claims of diagnosis through entranced hypnotic subjects. He muses that the field of medicine has always been a propitious one for all manner of occultism, and that from the most primitive times magic and medicine have always marched hand in hand. Hypnotism, Dr. Mello reminds his readers, has always played an important role in the sorcerer-doctor-priest's regimen of cures and healings.

"When the individual [under hypnosis] predicts his own or other people's illnesses and these develop along the lines of his predictions, this is merely due to the fact that the patients are dominated by the prophecy, and succeeding events adapt themselves to that pre-vision," Dr. Silva Mello writes. "This is all a part of the familiar mechanism of suggestion, corresponding also to the obedience given in cases of post-hypnotic orders carried out blindly for no apparent reason."

This may well be true, but in none of our hypnotically controlled out-of-body diagnoses or therapies did the subject ever make predictions about an individual's future condition, so we cannot plead guilty of dominating the development of any of our witnesses' illnesses. One cannot deny, however, that for a witness susceptible to such suggestion, a strong belief in Rita's ability to "shine" away an ailment might have aided and abetted the removal of the malady.

"Can the somnambulist diagnose illness and find the correct remedy without reference to the physician in cases which are beyond his capabilities?" Dr. Silva Mello asks. "No, such a thing is not possible and all the evidence in favor of this contingency arises from faulty and erroneous interpretations."

"Impossible." "Faulty and erroneous interpretations." How often have we heard those official pronouncements. "Impossible." But then there are those glorious blisters on G.W.'s feet.

20

Science Looks at Consciousness and Out-of-Body Experience

"If Western science is to understand and utilize the phenomena associated with ESP, PK [psychokinesis], creativity, hypnosis and psychedelic substances, it must recognize the value of studying consciousness.... Furthermore, science must face up to the fact that consciousness is not unitary; it comes in many forms and within the course of a single day an individual may flicker in and out of several states of consciousness. Finally, science must abandon the notion that waking, rational consciousness is the only form of any value and that all other kinds are pathological. Research may well reveal that man's most important discoveries, his highest peaks of ecstasy, and his greatest moments of inspiration occur in reverie, in dreams, in drug states, in hypnotically induced states and in other states presently 215ared by the professional world and the general public."

The above quotation was taken from a paper presented by Dr. Stanley Krippner, Director of the William C. Menninger Dream Laboratory, Maimonides Medical Center, Brooklyn, N.Y., at a conference on "Hypnosis, Drugs and Psi Induction," sponsored by the Parapsychology Foundation and held at Le Piol, St. Paul de Vence, France, on June 9 to 12, 1967. Dr. Krippner's paper, "The Hypnotic Trance, the Psychedelic Experience and Psi Induction: A Review of the Clinical and Experimental Literature," argued strongly for science to resume the study of consciousness that has been all but ignored since William James. I think it would be of great value to list the twenty states of consciousness which psychologist Krippner categorized in his paper and which he feels may be described with some degree of preciseness.

First there are the six states of "Nonreflective consciousness" which are characterized by the absence of self-consciousness.

1. *Bodily feelings* are induced by normal bodily functioning, and characterized by nonreflective awareness in the organs and tissues of the digestive, glandular, respiratory and other bodily systems. This awareness does not become self-conscious unless such stimuli as pain, hunger and drug ingestion intensifies a bodily feeling.

2. *Stored memories* do not become self-conscious until the individual reactivates them. At this time, the "... 'laws' of learning, imprinting and conditioning determine which memories will enter self-consciousness."

3. *Coma*, induced by illness, epileptic seizures and physical injuries to the brain, is characterized by prolonged nonreflective consciousness of the entire organism.

4. *Stupor*, induced by psychosis, narcotics and over-indulgence in alcohol, is characterized by greatly reduced ability to perceive incoming sensations.

5. *Nonrapid-eye-movement sleep* is a normal part of the sleep cycle at night or during daytime naps, and is characterized by a minimal amount of mental activity, which may sometimes be recalled upon awakening.

6. *Rapid-eye-movement sleep* is a normal part of the nighttime sleep cycle, and is characterized by the mental activity known as dreams.

The reflective, or self-conscious, states of consciousness constitute fourteen categories.

7. *Pragmatic consciousness* is induced by normal bodily functioning and cultural conditioning. It is the everyday, waking conscious state, sometimes called the "spotlight mind" because it focuses attention on one thing at a time. It is characterized by alertness, logic and rationality, cause-and-effect thinking, goal-directedness, the feeling that one is in control, thinking by means of language symbols, division between subject and object and the ability to move at will from perceptual activity to conceptual thinking to idea formation to motor activity.

8. *Lethargic consciousness* is characterized by sluggish mental activity induced by fatigue, sleep deprivation, feelings of depression or certain drugs.

9. *Hyperalert consciousness* can be brought about by heightened vigilance, such as sentry duty, or by certain drugs, such as amphetamines (pep pills). This state is characterized by prolonged and increased alertness.

10. *Rapturous consciousness* is characterized by intense feeling and overpowering emotion. It may be induced by sexual stimulation, sexual intercourse and sexual orgasm; frenzied dances; orgiastic rituals, such as those performed during witchcraft and voodoo ceremonies; primitive puberty rites; the fervor of "revival" meetings; the emotion of religious

conversion; speaking-in-tongues (*glossolalia*); and the ingestion of certain drugs.

11. *Hysterical consciousness* is induced by rage, jealousy, fear, neurotic anxiety, violent mob activity and certain drugs. As opposed to rapturous consciousness, which is generally evaluated as pleasant and positive, hysterical consciousness is considered negative and destructive.

12. *Fragmented consciousness,* a lack of integration among important segments of the total personality, generally results in psychosis, severe neurosis, amnesia, multiple personality or dissociation. Such a state of consciousness is induced by severe psychological stress over a period of time. It may also be induced temporarily by accidents and the psychedelic drugs.

13. *Retarded consciousness* produces a behavior that is inappropriate in terms of the individual's chronological age and general appearance. Such a state is brought about by genetic factors or by brain injury.

14. *Regressed consciousness,* induced by hypnotic age regression, drugs and accidents, also leads to behavior that is clearly inappropriate in terms of the individual's chronological age; but whereas retarded consciousness is permanent, regressed consciousness affects one's mental functioning only temporarily.

15. *Sociopathic consciousness* is brought about by a lack of attention and affection in infancy and produces a mental state apparently devoid of any capacity for empathy, compassion or love. The internalized standards of behavior are absent; and shame, guilt and personal commitment do not exist.

16. *Feral consciousness* is characterized by a mental state that produces behavior resembling that of lower level mammals. This state of consciousness can be brought about through hypnosis and certain drugs; and, of course, there are cases of infants being reared in the wild by animals.

17. *Relaxed consciousness* is a state of minimal mental activity, passivity and an absence of motor activity. This state of consciousness may be brought about by lack of external stimulation, such as sunbathing, floating in water and certain drugs.

18. *Daydreaming* is characterized by rapidly occurring thoughts which bear no correspondence to the individual's external environment. Common to everyone's experience, the daydream is induced by boredom, social isolation or sensory deprivation.

19. *Trance consciousness* may be induced by rapt attentiveness to a single stimulus; the voice of a hypnotist; one's own heartbeat; a chant; certain drugs; prolonged watching of a revolving object; trance-inducing rituals associated with mediumistic rites and primitive dances; "brainwashing" and repetitive "grilling"; lullabys and soothing music; becoming caught up in dramatic presentations; performing a task which requires attentiveness but involves little variation in response, such as

watching a radar screen or staring at the white line in the middle of the highway while driving. The trance state is characterized by hypersuggestiblility and the concentrated attention on one stimulus to the exclusion of all other stimuli.

20. *Expanded consciousness,* or the "floodlight mind," was originally described by the psychedelic researchers R.E.L. Masters and Jean Houston as being comprised of four levels: the sensory level, the recollective-analytic level, the symbolic level and the integrative level. Each of these four levels is induced by psychedelic drugs, hypnosis, meditation, prayer or free association during psychoanalysis.

The sensory level is characterized by subjective reports of space, time, the body image or sense impressions having been altered. The recollective-analytic level summons up memories of one's past, providing insight concerning oneself, one's work and personal relationships. The symbolic level brings about an identification of the individual with historical or legendary persons and is often characterized by vivid visual imagery of mythical, religious and historic symbols, people and events. The integrative level is one of intense religious experience in which the percipient experiences a dissolution of self, an "ego death," and finds her or himself confronted with God.

Dr. Krippner calls for renewed scientific interest in the states of consciousness. We need to know, for example, which states can coexist with each other and which cannot. We need to know more about each of the various states of consciousness and to learn the particular significance of each state on the totality of humankind. We need to plumb the full implication of the trance state, which seems to grant men and women access to a realm that exists beyond unseen boundaries. Psychiatrist Arnold Ludwig once remarked that one's capacity to enter the trance state must serve a more profound purpose than that of being able to "go under" at the command of a stage hypnotist.

And, during their new and intensified examination of the states of human consciousness, will the scientists receive the kind of absolute proof they cherish concerning the "most extraordinary achievement of the human will...the power to cause a semblance of oneself to appear at a distance?"

Will they discover that, not only has consciousness many states and many levels within individual states, but that sometimes, under certain conditions of emotional stress, illness, pain, childbirth and the time of death, the very essence of one's *true* consciousness can leave the physical body and travel free of time, space and physical barriers?

And will they be able to determine just where it is that the adepts have located the "trap door in the brain" that allows them to project their minds from their bodies whenever they choose?

Just how would science go about providing out-of-body experiences in the time-honored terms the profession demands? Can an astral, or soul, body be weighed and measured? Can it be seen as it rises from the host body of a laboratory volunteer? Certainly it cannot be followed to determine the validity of the experience, nor can it disturb carefully arranged flour dusted on the floor.

Several scientists are convinced of the reality of out-of-body travel, and their dilemma is even more real. It is almost impossible to satisfy their colleagues' demand for controlled laboratory proof. Science is the art of definition; therefore, the intangible must somehow be made tangible.

A small but dedicated group of scientists, both here and abroad, are determined to achieve such a goal: to provide convincing laboratory proof that the soul can separate itself from the body, that some people do this involuntarily while others achieve it at will. To substantiate this claim, a number of ingenious experiments have been devised, usually involving some task an individual in a normal physical state could not perform, but which a mind disengaged from its body might.

Growing up around these experiments is a significant body of research which delves into such questions as: When is an out-of-body projection most likely to occur? Can an OBE be induced by artificial means? Is there any validity to the drug culture's claim that one bite from the sacred mushroom will "flip you out?"

There is a wealth of literature from all ages reporting excursions into the nether world of drugs—ranging all the way from the religious ingestion of peyote by Mexican and American Indians to the hallucinogenic underworld of many hippie communities. Many spontaneous OBEs have been reported under these conditions, as well as other forms of extrasensory perception. The difficulty in assessing the drug experience, however, is in its intensely subjective nature and in the tendency of the percipient to view the experience as a cosmic whole, immune to laboratory scrutiny.

To make the drug experience more amenable to scientific investigation, qualitative experiments have been employed from which statistical evidence has been obtained. These experiments were subjected to the same rigid control as would be expected from any scientific endeavor.

The chemical compound lysergic acid diethylamide-25, more commonly known as LSD, is relatively new to the psychedelic scene. Its properties were first recognized in 1943 when Swiss chemist Albert Hoffman accidently ingested some of the drug and reported "a not unpleasant delerium which was marked by an extreme degree of fantasy," along with a marked alteration in consciousness.

Lysergic acid occurs naturally in the ergot fungus (*Claviceps purpurea*), from which Hoffman isolated the compound in 1938. In the Middle Ages the fungus sometimes infested wheat, producing frightening hallucinations in uncomprehending peasants who feared they were losing their minds. Some species of morning glory seeds also belong to the LSD family.

In 1960, John Whittlesey, a data-processing agent, conducted an experiment with psychiatric out-patients receiving psychotherapy. He used the Carl Zener ESP deck and had twenty-seven subjects make two runs of twenty-five guesses each. The first run was made before ingestion of LSD; the second was made while under its influence. On both runs the subjects scored at chance level.

On the basis of this data, Whittlesey was able to make a few stabs at the myth that psychism and insanity are interrelated. He felt that the results he obtained backed up statements made by Gertrude Schmeidler and Robert McConnell, who believe psychic manifestations spring from well-functioning, emotionally balanced individuals, rather than from emotionally unstable persons.

A more conclusive experiment was conducted in 1966 by R.E.L. Masters, a sexologist, and Jean Houston, a philosopher. Masters and Houston were originally running LSD, mescaline and psilocybin experiments at the Foundation for Mind Research. During this study a number of subjects reported instances of telepathy and clairvoyance. These consistent reports were responsible for Houston and Master's inauguration of a specific ESP experiment. Their goal was to elicit extrasensory impressions during the psychedelic sessions.

One of the incidents reported to the researchers before the official ESP experiment involved a housewife, and particularly concerns us in this chapter. This woman, during a session with LSD, reported seeing her daughter searching through the kitchen cabinets in the absence of her mother. In the course of her rummaging, the daughter knocked a sugar bowl off the shelf. At the conclusion of the session, the woman returned to her home where she was informed by her husband that their daughter had knocked a sugar bowl to the floor while searching for cookies. Houston and Masters recognized that some form of "psi" phenomena must have been in operation.

The original setup of the experiment required twenty-seven subjects to run through an ESP deck ten times. The cards were reshuffled after each run of twenty-five.

This procedure proved boring to the subjects, who were more interested in following the subjective impressions being triggered in their minds by the drug. The majority of the subjects, twenty-three, scored consistently at chance or below-chance levels. They averaged a score of 3.5, which is below chance. The other four subjects averaged a score of 8.5—considerably above chance—and were personal friends of the guide. They were very cooperative throughout the test, indicating how attitude influences "psi" performances.

Masters and Houston learned from this experience to make their tests more compatible to the psychedelic state. The testing further revealed that a subject was more likely to manifest ESP during the leveling off segment of his or her "trip," rather than during the core of the experience. The attention span was much greater and more easily motivated toward taking part in the experiment.

On the basis of these developments, Masters and Houston designed a test using ten emotionally charged images of historic or esthetic content in place of the ESP cards. These pictures attempted to trigger the subjective visual impressions a subject would receive while in the drug state.

The agent opened the envelopes containing the target images in an adjoining room. In the room where the subjects were, an assistant attempted to elicit verbal responses from the sixty-two individuals who had volunteered for the test. Of the sixty-two, forty-eight described approximate images at least two times out of ten. Of the sixty-two, only fourteen were unable to give descriptions corresponding to at least two of the images, and these poor performers were unknown to the experimenter, anxiety-ridden or "primarily interested in eliciting personal psychological material."

To illustrate how the subjects' images tallied with the target pictures, the statements of a subject who scored seven out of ten are recorded below:

Subject's Statement	Target Image
Snake with arched head swimming in tossed seas.	Viking ship tossed in a storm.
Lush vegetation, exotic flowers, startling trees—all seen through a watery mist.	A rain forest in the Amazon.
Hercules tossing a ball up and down in his hand.	Atlas holding up the world.

A circus.	Greek island with small white houses built on terraced hills.
Sailboat sailing around a cliff.	A sailboat off a rocky coast.
Geisha girl in full Oriental regalia.	New York City traffic scene.
A Negro picking cotton in a field.	A plantation in the Old South.
A camel passing through the inside of a vast labyrinthian tomb.	An Arab on a camel passing a pyramid.
A climbing expedition in the Alps.	The Himalayas—snow-capped peaks.
A forest fire.	Ski slope in New England.

In regard to the final image, it is interesting to note that the agent in the next room was unable to visualize a ski slope and, unaccountably, thought of a forest fire. The subject was unable to describe a ski slope, but correctly duplicated the agent's image. The full results of this experiment were published in 1966 by Masters and Houston in *The Varieties of Psychedelic Experience.*

The chief ingredient in peyote is mescaline. It is unrelated to tryptamine derivatives (such as psilocybin) and ergot derivatives (such as LSD). Peyote is the bud of *Lophophora williamsii,* a cactus found in Mexico and in the southwestern United States.

The records left by the Spanish conquistadores detail the vision and effects of this "diabolical plant." The Spaniards had good cause to regard peyote with fear, as it was used by the natives to predict attacks from their enemies and to reveal the hiding places of lost or stolen articles. These abilities threatened the foreign marauders, who typically attributed the plant's powers to Satan.

Peyote was rediscovered in modern times by an explorer who visited some of the more remote sections of Mexico. In 1892 he sent samples back to the United States where it was experimented with by Weir Mitchell, Havelock Ellis and William James. Mitchell and Ellis were pleasantly transported under the drug's influence, but James reported being violently ill for twenty-four hours after the ingestion of one peyote button. Their experiments generated some interest in the innocuous little cactus bud, but it was the celebrated accounts of Aldous Huxley's mescaline-inspired mysticism that motivated chemical investigation.

Laboratory investigation of mescaline and telepathy was begun at the Pasteur Institute of Paris by Spanish pharmacologist Bascompto Lakanal in the 1920s. An observer at the experiments, Felix Marti-Ibanez, a psychiatrist, claimed that subjects under the influence of mescaline could communicate telepathically with the agent in the next room. The subjects could correctly reproduce words, drawings and musical notes projected by the agent.

In 1965 L.L. Vasiliev, a professor of physiology at Leningrad State University in the Soviet Union, reported from his tests that telepathy functioned under the influence of mescaline "...incomparably more quickly and more accurately than in the usual state." Unfortunately, Vasiliev did not validate his claims with a description of his laboratory procedure, nor did he publish his statistical results.

Perhaps at this juncture note should be made of the ambiguous nature of drug-induced extrasensory perception.

Students of astral projection—bilocation, soul travel, OBE—have frequently commented on the phenomenon of dual consciousness; i.e., they still have complete awareness of their body, its functions and the room it's lying in while they are traveling astrally to visit a faraway person or place. It seems obvious that the lines between out-of-body travel and other "psi" phenomena are extremely nebulous and may overlap a great deal.

The more one studies paranormal phenomena the more he or she is apt to view the entire field as closely interrelated, possibly just the same mannequin in different sets of clothing. When is a medium telepathically reading the mind of the deceased's widow, and when is he or she actually establishing contact with the deceased? When is precognition a telepathic reading of plans already formulated, and when is it actual knowledge of an unpremeditated future? When is astral projection the exercise of a purely clairvoyant faculty, and when is ostensible clairvoyance actually an out-of-body experience?

The previously related case of the woman who, while under the influence of LSD, "saw" her daughter knock a sugar bowl off a shelf is an excellent example of the difficulty of clearly distinguishing and defining "psi" phenomena. The clairvoyant camp could point out that the woman herself did not believe that she had transcended her body, although she did feel "something" paranormal had occurred. The OBE specialists could call upon the phenomenon of dual consciousness, stating that the woman need not have known she was "travelling" in order to have done so.

Clearly, the argument hinges on the all-important and little understood focus for all theosophical, philosophical, psychological and parapsychological debates: *consciousness.*

Altered states of consciousness are generally considered abnormal in Western society. Yet it is from these virtually unmapped, uncharted regions that all our major material and spiritual breakthroughs have come. And, despite the advances such breakthroughs have provided, not only are these altered states of consciousness shunned and scorned, but resistance to the beneficial changes they produce has been the norm for centuries.

Such neglect has fostered a lack of vocabulary when in the altered state of consciousness. People involved in the drug scene are unable to discuss their experiences with anyone who has not "tripped" also. Descriptions of mystical revelations become almost florid as these "instant seers" try to translate their experiences to the language of a technically oriented society.

Frequently, creative geniuses in Western culture compare their moods of inspiration to insanity. Tchaikovsky once described his behavior during creative periods as being "like a madman." The comparison is regrettable, for there are many stages of altered consciousness; and it is unfortunate that our culture can offer no other model than madness for innovators in the throes of creative seizure.

Dr. Charles T. Tart, assistant professor of psychology at the University of California at Davis, has done some excellent pioneer work in bringing the soul out of the body and into the laboratory. His first experiments were conducted in the electroencephalography laboratory at the University of Virginia Hospital. Dr. Tart was primarily concerned with spontaneous OBEs during the sleep state, since this appears to be the most common state in which such projection occurs.

Dr. Tart's two subjects, a man and a woman, were individuals who claimed knowledge of leaving their bodies in sleep. To test the validity of the out-of-body experience, the two subjects were asked to read a five-digit number placed on the shelf of the equipment room in the laboratory. The number was placed so the subject would be unable to see it under normal conditions, but in a state of conscious disengagement from the body the subject supposedly could read it with ease.

The two subjects were tested individually. The first experiment used the male volunteer. In the experiment electrodes were attached to his head for electroencephalograph (EEG) readings. (The EEG records brainwaves.)

Additional equipment was used to measure his rapid eye movements (REMs). A great deal of study in recent years has disclosed that REMs accompany dreams and early sleep stages, but are absent in later stages. Finally, an electrocardiogram was made, recording heart action.

Dr. Tart hoped, with the above equipment, to provide psychophysiological substantiation for the subject's successful—it was hoped—out-of-body projection. He also wished to learn, from bodily responses, more of the nature of an OBE.

The male subject was tested on nine different nights. Although he claimed he could project himself at will, he was unable to do so, by his own account, until the next to last night of the experiment. On that evening he reported leaving his body twice within a few minutes.

The room in which the subject slept was separated by a window and a doorway from the equipment room where a technician controlled the experiment. In the subject's first OBE, he found himself in the presence of two men and one woman, all unknown to him. He tried to arouse their awareness of him by pinching and touching, but was unsuccessful. The validity of this experience could not be verified.

During his second OBE, he reported walking through the doorway into the equipment room. Not finding the technician on duty, he continued on his way to the office. There he found the technician, talking with a man he did not know. Again, he tried to attract their attention. Once more unsuccessful, he returned to his body, awakened and called out to the technician. She confirmed that she had been in the office talking with her husband. The subject's description of her husband was exact.

It was determined by the EEG record within the few minutes before he awakened—which was the time the subject indicated he had been out of his body—that he had been in a state of "stage one" dreaming. It is in this stage that sleep is lighter and dreams are accompanied by rapid eye movements. His heart rate was normal.

Since the subject's experience occurred not in the later or deeper stages of sleep and not in a state of drowsiness, but totally during the dream stage, Dr. Tart labeled the experiment "inconclusive." Even though objective evidence indicated that the tecnhician was not at the controls when the subject said she was not, and that she had been in the office with her husband, whom the subject was able to describe, Tart did not feel he could offer irrefutable evidence that an actual OBE had occurred.

The female subject was tested for four nonsuccessive nights over a period of two months. This woman was subjected to even stricter laboratory controls and physiological response measuring devices. In addition to the REM indicator, the EKG and the EEG, she was also outfitted with a machine to measure her basal skin resistance (BSR) and galvanic skin responses (GSR). A finger photoplethysmograph recorded her heart rate.

According to Elizabeth Read's summary of the experiment in *Fate* magazine, the leads from the electrodes "were bound into a common cable running off the top of her head and terminating in an electrode box at the head of the bed. Although this arrangement caused her [the subject] no discomfort, it prevented her from raising her shoulders more than two feet without disconnecting the wires, which would have shown up on the recording equipment. Thus her movements were well controlled, and she was generally under observation through the window separating the sleep room from the equipment room of the laboratory."

This young woman had reported numerous out-of-body experiences during her lifetime. The majority were of the common sort—she suddenly discovered herself floating, then saw her inert body still resting on her bed. Occasionally she reported finding herself in distant locations, and she appeared to have the peculiarly grim ability to be attracted to scenes of trauma or violence.

In one incident, the subject related to Dr. Tart that she dreamed she was wearing a checked shirt, which she did not own, and felt like she was walking through a deserted section of town in another girl's body. While in this girl's body, she became increasingly terrified as she realized that someone was following her. As the footsteps caught up with her, she dreamed with startling reality that she was being raped and stabbed. She awakened in fear and confusion.

The next morning the subject picked up a newspaper and learned that a girl wearing a checked shirt had been raped and stabbed in the same section of town in which the subject had dreamed she had been in. This subject's efforts in the laboratory were considerably less dramatic, concerned mainly with attempts to read the test numeral Dr. Tart had placed on the shelf.

"Sunday night, vague nightmare, recalled previous experience?" she wrote in her lab report of the dream. "Blocking of much memory—young girl (13 to 16?)—outdoors—stabbing, but not knife, more slender—head hurt (slapped?)—not stabbed surely. Expanse of white, car white? Knew fellow (She knew, not I!) also youngish. Horrible experience but no report in papers this morning. So far, so good."

The subject kept this dream experience to herself until two days later when a young girl was murdered in Marin County, north of San Francisco.

In accord with the subject's "dream," the victim had been a young girl. She had been found outdoors, had been stabbed with an instrument more like an ice pick than a knife—sharper and thinner—and the suspected killer had been seen driving a large white car. The subject reported that the victim's "head hurt," though she did not believe it had been stabbed. When the victim was found, however, her head had been stabbed and her skull crushed. The suspect police were seeking turned out to be the girl's boyfriend.

This example only further immerses us in the giant vat of psychic ambiguity. The subject definitely reported a precognitive dream, for it appears she did foresee an event before its actual occurrence. Was it that specific event, however? And how had she foreseen it? Was it a case of precognition, clairvoyance or out-of-body travel? Certainly, too, there will be those readers who will raise the weary banner, "she just had a bad dream, and *by coincidence* an actual event approximated some of the details of that dream."

Scientists conducting laboratory investigations have little choice other than to leave such colorful incidents behind them as they don their white coats. Only where chance and circumstance can be subjected to some control will results be obtained that will at least induce the skeptic to look carefully at such data. And the skeptic does have a right to be shown something more concrete than "I thought," "I dreamed," "I had a hunch," and "I knew that would happen!"

Dr. Tart was careful to remove any such doubts from his experiment. With the aid of the already described electrode apparatus, Dr. Tart determined that the subject's EEG pattern sequences were "unusual" in comparison with normal EEG patterns. Furthermore, on the first night, it was learned that the subject recorded REMs during "stage one" drowsiness, or at the beginning of sleep. It is extremely uncommon to find rapid eye movements in drowsiness, according to Dr. Tart. The phenomenon is usually reserved exclusively for the mental mechanics of dreaming.

On the second night of the experiment the subject awakened at approximately 3:15 A.M., following an unusual EEG sequence.

"Write down 3:13 A.M.," she called. She later reported that she had, at that time, managed to rise from her body, but not high enough to enable her to read the number from the shelf.

On the third night the subject claimed she had visited her sister in another city, and, although this astral flight could not be verified, her EEG pattern sequence was more "unusual."

On the fourth and final night of the experiment, all of the controls recorded normal processes until 6:00 A.M. With the repeated "unusual" pattern, the subject correctly identified the number on the shelf as 25132. In her subsequent report the subject stated that she had experienced difficulty in floating high enough to read the number, but she had eventually been successful.

Dr. Tart is a man to delight the scientific community, and he hopes to be an eventual scourge to the skeptics. He conceded that this experiment was a "conditional success," but refused to call it conclusive. Jumping ahead of the skeptics' disclaimers, the psychologist decreed that the subject possibly could have seen the number reflected in the black plastic case of a clock. Although Dr. Tart did not believe this, he deemed it necessary to make due note of it.

Dr. Tart's research has led him to believe that OBEs are associated with the borderline areas of sleep. He has stated that, to him, the most significant aspect of his experimentation was not the tentative findings they unearthed, but the fact that such traditionally "occult" manifestations as OBEs can be subjected to scientific study. Whatever lurid Svengali-type case histories may surround these unusual psychic abilities, it is possible to bring them into the laboratory for controlled investigation.

Others in the scientific community join Dr. Tart in their optimistic belief that psychic phenomena can be subjected to the skeptical scrutiny of scientific inquiry.

Dr. Eugene E. Bernard, professor of psychology at North Carolina State University, who studied astral projection extensively, has stated: "It is improbable that so many people who are apparently psychologically healthy are having hallucinations. There is still much we don't know about the mind and its abilities. I don't know how long it will take, but I believe the astral projection theory can be proved and controlled."

"Once we rid ourselves of the stubborn and conventional notions that man is separate from his universe," writes Dr. Stanley Krippner, "that external reality is separate from internal reality, and that the study of consciousness is a waste of time, the taboos against imaginative investigation in creativity, parapsychology, hypnosis and the psychedelics will diminish. The data emerging from the research already suggests that all phenomena are of one piece and that the intensive study of consciousness has been postponed too long.

"To perceive and understand reality in its totality, we will want to utilize the insights obtained in altered states of consciousness, as well as those available to us in the everyday, waking state. We will return from our trips to the deeper conscious levels ready to put the new insights to work, realizing that a permanent state of transcendence is neither desirable nor practical. Nevertheless, a revolution is in order concerning our notions about consciousness. A further revolution is critically needed in consciousness itself if mankind is to fulfill its vast potential—indeed, if mankind is to survive at all."

Index

5/22